Get Out and *Thrive!*

Critical insight for Veterans separating from the Military

Updated for 2020

Olan Prentice

Edited by Olivia R. Dees and Catherine S. Nolan
Cover art by Jackson Branton

Bekah Publishing

Get Out and Thrive! Copyright ©2017, 2018, 2019, 2020 by Olan Prentice. All rights reserved. Printed in the United States of America. No part of this book may be reproduced in any manner whatsoever without written permission except in the case of reprints in the context of reviews. For more information write Bekah Publishing P.O. Box 2517 McDonough GA 30252.

Library of Congress Control Number: 2017953970

ISBN 978-0-692-92256-9

This publication is designed to provide accurate and authoritative information in regard to the subject matter covered. It is sold with the understanding that neither the publisher nor the author is engaged in rendering legal, investment, accounting, or other professional services. If legal advice or other expert assistance is required, the services of a competent professional person should be sought and secured.

Acknowledgments

For Tracie and Olivia. This book was only possible because of the unwavering support from my wife and daughter.

For my mother, who taught me to read and fostered my love of reading so many years ago.

To the many friends who contributed, especially my editors who invested so much time and effort, I am humbled by your friendship and support.

Many thanks to my friend and author William Walsh III for his insight, support, and encouragement.

Get out and Thrive!

Table of Contents

Intro 12

Chapter 1 – Committing to Change 14

Chapter 2 – Core Concepts 16

    Core One – You are NOT like the others 17

    Core Two - You have been forged in fires your peers can't understand 19

    Core Three – There are less of us than you may realize 22

    Core Four - You are uniquely prepared to manage your own future 25

    Core Five - You have skills and capabilities that are marketable 28

    Core Six – You have gaps in your skills and capabilities that you need to close 33

    Core Seven – You now have more responsibility for your life, and much more opportunity to screw it up 38

    Core Eight - Life is still hard 41

    Core Nine – The Republic is powered by the engine of Capitalism 45

Chapter 3 – The rate of change is accelerating 50

Chapter 4 – It's not always about what you know 58

Chapter 5 – Family First 63

Chapter 6 – Goal Setting 68

Chapter 7 – What's next (travel or settle) 78

Chapter 8 – Your next job 82

Chapter 9 – Getting Hired 98

Chapter 10 – Owning your own business 120

Chapter 11 – Succeeding in your new Career 128

Chapter 12 – Do THIS instead of THAT 152

Chapter 13 – Technology and You 158

Chapter 14 – Faith and Religion 172

Chapter 15 – Money Management 176

Chapter 16 - Education 216

Chapter 17 – Insurance 228

Chapter 18 – Hiring Advantages 244

Chapter 19 – Veterans Affairs 254

Chapter 20 – Aging and staying healthy 264

Chapter 21 – The potential downside of your military service 274

Chapter 22 – Simple timelines and Checklists 280

Chapter 23 - Books to Read 308

Chapter 24 – Retirement financials 312

Chapter 25 – Plan Now for Later 324

Chapter 26 – Being Thankful 332

Chapter 27 – RaNdOm thoUghtS 334

References and Links 336

    Military Oaths 336

    Military Holidays and other important dates 339

    Military demographics 345

    Veterans Unemployment Compensation by State 346

    Veteran Preference – Federal Regulations 348

    Veteran Assistance and/or Benefits Programs by state; 352

    List of trusted Veterans organizations that you should be aware of; 355

    US Military Reserve websites 356

    Miscellaneous Military Discounts 356

    Discounted dining for Military & Veterans 357

    Fun Discounts for Military & Veterans 358

    Retail Discounts for Military & Veterans 359

    Travel Discounts for Military & Veterans 362

    Banking Discounts for Military & Veterans 363

    Wireless Discounts for Military & Veterans 363

    Misc. links 364

Dedication

This book is dedicated to the men and women of the Military. Your past, present, and future sacrifices make possible the greatest civilization in the history of the world.

Preface

I left the service full of confidence and conviction, sure that I would quickly conquer the next phase of my life as a Veteran. I was well-educated, experienced diligently checked every box in the military's transition program. I researched and planned. With a tremendous resume, I just knew I would find immediate success, as it was inevitable.

There was just one big problem; *I didn't know what I didn't know*. Because of that I couldn't plan for the steps I needed to take to ensure success. Transitioning was far more difficult than I had anticipated. Every decision exposed multiple factors I wasn't sure about. I needed some type of advantage like a how to reference, a comparative frame of reference, a cheat sheet, a list of lessons learned...anything.

I know now what I really needed was a mentor and a coach. Back then, I wasn't experienced enough to understand the importance of those two roles. I fully subscribed to the school of thought that said if I could just work harder and it would all work out. It did work out eventually, but along the way it was confusing, expensive, and exhausting. I ran headlong into a lot of dead ends and wasted a significant amount of time and effort. On the positive side, along the way I completed my degree, worked as a teacher, programmer, computer operator, owner of several successful small businesses, public speaker, published author, successful consultant and as a Senior Vice President of one of the largest banks in the world.

This book was conceptually born in those early days of my own transition. Along the way, I took notes, made friends and allies, and even alienated some persons by mistake. The idea grew over the years as I befriended, mentored, coached and in some cases hired and fired freshly separated Veterans. It matured into print only with the help and input of many of these same Veterans who've shared their experiences. So many lessons learned, so many avoidable mistakes made and even more successes experienced. I, and by extension all the brave contributors, (it takes courage to talk about your mistakes), want to share these insights with you. The sole purpose of this book is to help you avoid the mistakes we made and give you a competitive advantage in what comes next.

Intro

Welcome to a brave new world. If you are reading this book, Bravo Zulu! You are thinking ahead. Whether you get out tomorrow or at some time in the future, you have a lot of work to do, many things to consider and a lot of tough decisions that only *YOU* can and should make.

You are likely in turmoil at the prospect of leaving the military. It's a tough decision, but at some point, whether it's after our first hitch or our sunset tour, we ALL get out. The driving force for each of us to exit is different and sometimes beyond our control. What is important is that you prepare for the transition. Separation may seem similar to other challenges you've faced and overcome in recent years, but it is not.

For a proper frame of reference, you should compare your exit from the military to your (usually disorienting) entry into military life. Think back. No matter how well you thought you were prepared, the reality of being in uniform and on duty, was like stepping into a new world. Leaving the military will be even more difficult because when you re-enter the civilian environment, you won't be speaking their language, you won't understand their perspective and they won't understand you.

However, these things only become an issue if you don't map out the territory and intelligently approach the challenge. The truth is that you have extremely high potential but are dramatically less prepared than you think. This book is designed to help you, but it won't be worth your time if you don't keep an open mind. You need to have or develop a flexible perspective. It's important to realize that you have huge gaps in those life skills not directly aligned to your core expertise. Closing these gaps will be crucial for you to become recognized as an expert rather than a skilled novice or amateur. You must leverage your strengths plus understand and compensate for your weaknesses to become competitive and thrive.

You need to make some changes, and frameworks are important when attempting change. This book has an intentional framework of core concepts which will provide a contextual, running frame of reference for the data and insights in each chapter. Here's the first one:

You are NOT like the others.

Pause here and take a few minutes to think about this core concept. You may not feel different, but fundamentally you are completely different from your civilian counterparts.

You are a unique combination of hard-won skills, experience and maturity that goes beyond your physical age and those in your civilian educated peer group. This is particularly true for those of you who are ages twenty-two to thirty and for everyone regardless of age when considering the direct application of military knowledge and training.

You will also see the term "sliding scale" several times in this book. That is because younger Americans are often silly, frivolous creatures, but as they age many acquire wisdom and respect for our country, the armed forces and the men and women who have sacrificed and served. You must factor in age and experience into consideration when dealing with civilians.

At the end of each chapter, we have provided select "personal perspective" insights. The majority of these are not from the author, but from the Veterans interviewed over the years this book was developed.

You will notice that many of the ideas and issues addressed can be complex and as well as intertwined and may crop up in unexpected chapters and topics. The method of presentation and review will sometimes mesh tightly but at other times be loosely coupled. Hopefully you will find the information that follows helpful and useful as you prepare for your separation from your military organization. Please know that I wish you the absolute best luck in your life as a Veteran. You will never be a civilian, no matter how much time and space separates you from your last official day. You will always be on watch and your service will always be appreciated. Now, let's get to it.

Chapter 1 – Committing to Change

Some of you will leave after a full ride, but the majority of service members will leave long before that point. This will be one of the toughest decisions of your life. When and how you leave the military will literally shape the rest of your life. The earlier you make the decision, commit and plan for it, the more successful your transition will be. There are so many variables and factors which are unique to your situation that there is no way for anyone to provide you an exact roadmap on how and when to separate. For the purposes of this book, we will cover both sides of the issue and provide insight into what to consider for those of you contemplating the decision to get out, as well as for those of you who have reached the point of retirement and are committed to your exit.

Assuming you have committed to change, let me be one of the first to congratulate you and thank you for your service. As a Veteran, I understand the precious years of our lives spent in protecting our country and way of life comes at a steep price and level of sacrifice. You deserve to be successful in all your endeavors as a Veteran. No slight intended for those who made the larger commitment and stayed for the full ride to retirement (thank you), but for the sake of simplicity I will use the universal term of Veteran throughout this book.

Our society expects so much from its heroes then, in many ways, turns its back on them after their sacrifice. Every person who has served has made sacrifices, great and small. Thank you for your service.

What happens next in your life will be primarily determined by the decisions you make from this point on.

Unless you are an adrenaline junky or one of those rare persons who is a pure warrior from head to toe, the less time you've spent in the military, the less difficult your transition will be. For those of you who fit into one of those previous categories, we'll talk about some options for you a little later in the book but, spoiler alert, you will find that an occupation closely aligned to your MOS will be critical if you want to feel fulfilled and complete in your post military life. Start planning now, even if you have years to go. Don't worry, we will cover both long and short game strategies and preparation for each.

When I was trying to get a firm grip on the pro's and con's for separating or staying in, I had an interesting experience. I struck up a conversation with a reservist on active duty who was successful both in service and as a civilian. After I opened with the topic of getting out and options, he invested a good bit of time in asking what I thought at the time was a superset of lightly related questions. He didn't rush. Over the course of a few days on deployment he would occasionally revisit my responses and ask for clarification. It was more attention and focus than I expected. Finally, he told me I wasn't ready to thrive in the civilian world. I did not care for that response, and not having much of a poker face in those days made my reaction easy to read. He literally patted me on the shoulder and said, "take your time and chew through what I've said, I wish you the best in all that you do." My internal dialogue immediately went on the defensive and I started mentally reciting all the things I had done, excelled at, and experienced during my service. Don't do that! Don't try to rationalize why you should be considered a top candidate "as is." My defensive perspective delayed both my transition and my critical preparations. Keep your mind open, seek mentors and take the time to think about the ideas, concepts, and recommendations they provide. Before you start declaring your level of expertise, think about the very first day of your service and the difference between that person compared to the person you are today. You are entering the same type of scenario here. Realize that you are back to the novice level of experience with your new environment. Be as smart as you can, assess your gaps and pick your battles.

Although commitment is required to be successful in any effort, that alone, as you know, is not sufficient. You must prepare, train, sharpen old skills, learn new ones, and create a social and professional network to increase your chances for success.

As part of committing to change, make a point to read the entire book. Each one of you has different experiences which form a unique baseline at this new starting point in your life. Some things may not be applicable, but even one small insight from this material can have a huge positive impact on what comes next in your life.

Chapter 2 – Core Concepts

There are some universal truths (pardon the dramatic language) about you and those with whom you've served. The following core concepts are important. They will help you understand your advantages and disadvantages as you transition and that they apply whether you are retiring straight to the beach or joining the civilian workforce.

Consider these nine concepts as an essential a frame of reference for your future actions. It really matters how well you understand the difference between where you are coming from and the world you are stepping into. If you have already mastered and integrated these concepts into your world view, so much the better. With that said, we're betting you have some gaps and that's why you bought this book.

1. You are NOT like the others
2. You have been forged in fires that your peers can't understand
3. There are less of us than you may realize
4. You are uniquely prepared to manage your own future
5. You have skills and capabilities that are marketable
6. You have gaps in your skills and capabilities that you need to close
7. You now have more responsibility for your life, and much more opportunity to screw it up
8. Life is still hard
9. The Republic is powered by the engine of Capitalism

Core One – You are NOT like the others

Let's get this out in the open because if you don't get this concept then you will simply miss out on leveraging a lot of your potential.

Think back to that person who first entered the military. For some, it was ROTC in high school or college. For others, it was boot camp or OCS, and some came in via a service academy.

You will never be that civilian again.

Think about the first day at your first duty station. Can you remember that person? Take a moment to reflect on that poor soul who thought he or she had the world by the tail, but had no idea what he or she was getting into.

You will never be that inexperienced again.

Only a small fraction of those who join the military have the slightest clue about what they are signing up for. Playing the statistical odds here, you probably enjoyed a steep learning curve from almost the second the process started. When you signed on the dotted line, a process was set into motion that was designed to get you in and as quickly as possible make you an effective cog in the military machine. During the induction process, you were intentionally torn down and rebuilt to a higher standard.

You will never be that immature again.

Some individuals reading this work will have weathered some of the most extreme situations a person can live through, and some will have had a less intense experience while serving. Regardless, you've done your part, filled your role, and undergone a fundamental shift from your time in uniform.

You will never be that unprepared again, unless you choose to be.

Regardless, of your Rank, MOS, experience, time of service and world events that occurred during your time in the service; you are a different person that the one who raised a hand and swore to "defend the Constitution against all enemies, foreign and domestic."

The shift from who you were to who you are is like being subjected to some futuristic gene therapy that altered your core DNA. You see everything with a sharper perspective. Regardless of your religious beliefs, your politics, city, country, ethnicity, or other lens you belong to a small family of people who think differently.

You are a unique combination of hard-won skills, experience and maturity that goes beyond your physical age and those in your civilian educated peer group. This is particularly true for those of you who are age twenty-two to thirty and for everyone regardless of age when considering the direct application of military knowledge and training.

You are a problem solver: you want to cut to the chase and dispense with the endless verbal trappings that civilians wrap around any issue, problem, or challenge. You will constantly find yourself asking how these people have survived in their existing world. Most would not survive in your old world, and it's important to recognize why. The people around you now have been isolated and protected because of the sacrifice and hardships endured by. Civilians have been allowed to live their American life of safety and luxury because of you.

Even more important is the fact you know the US (or any functional democracy like the UK or Australia) is the very best place to live in this crazy world. Your fellow citizens who haven't served, aren't as convinced about this as you are.

Until the end of your days you will always be that soldier, sailor, airman, or marine forged in the fires of your experience.

Don't give that away or let someone diminish you. You are different and your experience sets you apart.

Personal perspective:

I was fresh out of the service in the early 90s and stumbled into a chance encounter with legendary Marine Corps General Ray Davis in my home town at the local grocery store. He was politely remonstrating a clean-cut young man with a high and tight haircut. The gist of the polite but clear correction was the military Medal of Honor winner stating there are no "ex-Marines" and it was clear that he certainly did not consider himself as such. That concept was something I hadn't given much thought to and while I was listening to the conversation the thought came to me that he was spot on. Since that day I have never addressed anyone as "ex-military," only as a Veteran. You can't shed your time in the service, it stays with you, always.

Core Two - You have been forged in fires your peers can't understand

Reality vs. Actuality. Most of the non-military contacts you will make simply don't have any context to understand why you think the way you do. They can't imagine you weren't based in some college dorm-like setting with maid service throughout your military career, nor can they imagine the intensity of the training you experienced. Most of your peers have seen people die from common causes but expect these deaths to occur after a long life or illness. The military trains hard and puts its personnel into danger on a daily basis. You've likely seen more than your fair share of those who've lost their lives from training exercises, unexpected illnesses, combat operations or just plain bad luck.

Dick Cheney once said, "You go to war with the army you have," meaning you saddle up and move out when necessary, not when the stars align or that next generation weapon system gets out of R&D and into field use.

You don't get through military service without hearing the sound of weapons. A small fraction will have learned the immediate and shocking difference between a weapon being fired nearby and a weapon being fired at them., however that's not the point. Whether you served during peace or war make no mistake, you were crucial to the safety of our nation. You bore the brunt of the effects of a large imperfect organization trying to be always ready with too little time, personnel, funding, and training. At *ANY POINT IN TIME* you needed to be as prepared as possible to climb into transport for a ride across the world or across the base to perform your job and engage the enemy or possibly something more mundane but just as dangerous. You trained with weapons for a reason.

Ask yourself, never mind how they see you – how in the world do I connect to these people who don't get it; particularly the youngest segments of the population. They think they supported you by buying the latest patriotic sounding song and listening to it on their phone while exercising. That's probably not fair, but let's go with it for now as an analogy of how far they are separated from you in both actuality and reality.

They can't imagine not having enough blankets, desperately needing a _cold_ drink of water without some chemical aftertaste, being unable to bathe for days on end, being stationed at the ass-end of the world surrounded by people who will steal you blind and could care less if you got killed or injured. No matter where you looked there were far too few trustworthy individuals, far too many who just wanted your money. Never knowing if the man, woman, or child you've seen every day just outside the gate might one day be a danger to life and limb. If you think I'm talking only about overseas deployments, think again. The toxic subcultures that spring up outside many stateside military bases have their own dangers. How would the average civilian like to see those types of predatory establishments show up in their communities?

How about that time you worked for a week with less than 8 hours of sleep, none of it in a bed? The endless drills and the hostile weather you worked in to complete the mission. While these may not apply directly to you, I'm sure you have your own "what have I gotten myself into" experiences that civilians have a tough time relating to. The amount of stress and responsibility you had to step up to, at every stage of your military career is mind-boggling.

Here's an example that most of us have experienced and can relate to. How many times have you told an earnest and true tale of your experiences from the service which was met with surprising levels of skepticism (at best) and utter disbelief (at worst)? This happens all the time, to the point that most Veterans will stop trying to tell the whole story, eliminating, or de-emphasizing the more incredible bits, and telling only the humorous, moral, or tragic parts.

The older you are and the more mature the persons with whom you interact, the less this rule applies. In my experience and the experience of those whom I've had the honor to serve with or interview for this book agree that the majority of non-service persons will never really understand why you see the world differently. A lot of folks will be sympathetic, respectful, and appreciative, but still never fully connect the dots to who you are and how the military transformed you to a stronger person.

There's a phenomenon that sometimes occurs in Veteran-to-civilian interactions you should be aware of, as it can be very disturbing. Though rare, it will absolutely happen to you unless you choose to become a recluse. For some reason there is a small and vocal subset of the population who simply won't like you because of your military service. It's a complicated psychological perspective that has a lot to do with politics, controlling personalities and the fear that you are immune to influence and intimidation (true!). Not something to lose sleep over, but don't forget that these clowns are lurking in corners and just waiting to open-up an attack vector.

Personal perspective:

I had been out of the service for less than a year, and was at an early dinner one evening with some coworkers. After a couple of drinks, everyone had shared some type of background story. Everyone but me that is. When they noticed that I hadn't shared anything, they pressed me to tell a tale from my active duty experiences. I knew this was going to happen and had been trying to come up with a believable, G rated story. It went like this; I was Air Force, and my job required us to fly around the world sampling air particulates to monitor the fall-out from Russian Nuclear testing. The timeframe for the story was late 1980s. As a point of reference, I threw in the fact that the Russians had conducted 178 nuclear weapons tests between 1980 and 1989. We had landed in at an airfield in Alaska and it was cold. It was January and though the average temp was normally around -17 degrees it was in the -20s that week with a brutal wind chill. I shared with them that we had entertained ourselves for hours early one morning by stepping outside with a fresh, near-boiling cup of coffee tossed up into the air before it could cool. The coffee instantly exploded into a fine, frozen powder from the brutal cold. Some of the faces were entranced, some skeptical, a couple down right disbelieving and challenging. I was confused. What would they think if I told them a "real" story of the military?

Core Three – There are less of us than you may realize

If you had to guess, what percentage of Americans would you say have served in the military?

Most will guess between 30% and 40%.

Unfortunately, the numbers are significantly lower, and you are privileged to be part of this unique minority.

We know the current military personnel count (including reserves) is about 2,200,000 out of a US population of approximately 300,000,000. That is a footprint of *less than 1%* of the population. This number is in decline as a percentage of the overall population and could be cut in half over the next 20 years.

Based on the 2012 US Census, here's the Veteran population broken out by state and territory and percentage of the population. Overall, Veterans make up about 8.6% of the population of the US.

State	%	State	%	State	%	State	%
Alabama	10.4	Illinois	7.5	Montana	12.7	Puerto Rico	3.8
Alaska	13.6	Indiana	9.2	Nebraska	10.4	Rhode Island	8.5
Arizona	10.7	Iowa	9.7	Nevada	11	South Carolina	10.9
Arkansas	10.4	Kansa	10	New Hampshire	10.6	South Dakota	11
California	6.5	Kentucky	9.4	New Jersey	6.4	Tennessee	9.6
Colorado	10.4	Louisiana	8.9	New Mexico	11.4	Texas	8.5
Connecticut	7.7	Maine	11.6	New York	5.8	Utah	7.4
Delaware	10.8	Maryland	9.7	North Carolina	9.8	Vermont	9.6
District of Columbia	6.0	Massachusetts	7.3	North Dakota	10.5	Virginia	11.7
Florida	10.2	Michigan	8.7	Ohio	9.6	Washington	11.2
Georgia	9.5	Minnesota	9.0	Oklahoma	11.2	West Virginia	11.1
Hawaii	11.1	Mississippi	9.1	Oregon	10.7	Wisconsin	9.2
Idaho	10.6	Missouri	10.4	Pennsylvania	9.3	Wyoming	11.1

From http://factfinder2.census.gov which is the US Department of Commerce US Census website

If we were to add up all the active duty, reserve personnel and all living Veterans the result would be *less than 10% of the US population*. In real world terms, that means there are about five Veterans per twenty US citizens you encounter.

Taking both Veteran and active duty numbers into consideration, let's drill down into even more rarefied percentages. Of the total active duty and Veteran population, less than twenty-five percent were combat troops. Most service members never actually see combat, even with a career that can span thirty years. The remaining serve in equally important roles and support functions such as medical, supply, transportation, electronics, maintenance, quartermaster, communications, data, food service, accounting, ordinance, fire direction, intelligence, JAG, and air traffic control to mention a few. While some of the service members in these positions may see combat, they are not technically Combat Arms, but let's not get into that debate. Combat Arms are justifiably proud of their heritage and mission, but I can and will argue that it takes one hell of a support organization to get one combatant into the position with the right kit to be effective.

All Veterans deserve the highest respect, but there is a real difference between being in theatre and being exposed to incoming fire. Keep in mind that only about 3% of our citizen soldiers were part of boots on the ground operations. If you run into one of these persons in your travels, take note. If your service did not involve hands-on, line of sight to the enemy type ground operations, you might learn a thing or two from a friend who was there.

The National Center for Veterans Analysis and Statistics study from 2014 indicates that all WWII and Korean War Veterans will no longer be alive by 2033, and our Vietnam Veterans will constitute less than 8% of our Veteran population by 2043. The Gulf War Veterans and War on Terror Veterans will be with us for quite a bit longer.

Demographics within the population of Veterans are changing: our female Veteran population stands about 9% today and will increase to about 16% by 2043. Black Veteran numbers will see an increase from the current 12% to about 17% higher than the overall population of about 13%. Hispanic will double from 6% to 12%, lower than the 17% of the general population. All other races move from about 3% to 6% in the 2014 to 2043 timeframe.

In the end, Veterans are a small percentage of the overall US population. Even with the Moms, Dads, and other supporters, it is likely that you will always be the minority in any general group of people. Sometimes this means paying attention to what you say. Sometimes it means standing in church or at a gathering when all Veterans asked to stand for recognition for Veterans Day or the Fourth of July. Stand proudly and make eye contact. You are not like the others.

These statistics should help illustrate why you might have difficulty in relating to your fellow citizens. Your politics (whatever they may be) will be influenced by your experiences. You may find your opinion under attack just because those around you know you are a Veteran.

But it's not *all* dire and foreboding, you will have allies. Most of your fellow citizens appreciate those who've served and show it in many different ways. We are a minority and we have all points of view, widely varying political beliefs, and every variation of religious orientation. Given our experiences abroad, often with the underbelly of the world, it is likely that you and your fellow Veterans believe more fiercely our country is the best place in the world. And you are right; flawed and imperfect, but still the best place now and in the known history of the world. Your charge is simple, continue to protect it from itself, even when you take off the uniform.

Personal perspective:

Rude awakening. My first job out of the military was with a company in a rapidly expanding industry. It was incredibly fast paced and much of the rigor of my military job was MIA. The company had to turn away business. New people being hired all the time, building out jury rigged infrastructure, hacked solutions with little to no documentation. While unnerving, it was energizing and invigorating to experience this explosion of invention to *"get it working now, we'll make it permanent later"* approach. Unfortunately, any time that I offered a suggestion or idea and that particular person was in the room I was shot down with some version of "that's dumb idea, you aren't in the military anymore." It was more than frustrating. Truthfully, some of the criticism was fair, but it was completely over the top. At one point, I had had enough and cornered this person where we could speak privately. I didn't get a lot of satisfaction from that talk, much less a resolution. This person, after glancing around to check for anyone in earshot, admitted that they did not care for anyone who had served in the military. The reason hinted at was that I hadn't "earned" my position by doing it right and getting a college degree (I did complete my degree later, but not because of this idiot). I wasn't some kid at this point' I had put in in my 20 years and retired, which was another "unearned" benefit apparently. I was angry and still embarrassed from the slam in the meeting earlier in the day. I wish I had been prepared for that encounter as I probably didn't get three words out after the initial question. I was just too stunned by the hostility. That is the last time that I put up with that in public or private conversation. Going forward, I didn't walk away or let a person intimidate me. I challenged back when my perspective or input was unprofessionally challenged. I never won over this person and when I started pushing back, they just switched to more subtle tactics that I had to deal with.

Core Four - You are uniquely prepared to manage your own future

Take a moment and think about all you've done, experienced and observed. Basically, you have been training for success your entire military career. Unless you ran into some bad actors, everyone along the line has done their best to help you succeed. Sometimes it was done because it was the right thing to do or maybe it was more mercenary, because if you didn't succeed it would cost everyone.

Remember the Core One concept? *"You are not like the others."* You have been immersed in a culture focused on success. How many times did your unit FAIL a readiness check or other military exercise? All the way back to the military academy, ROTC, Officer Basic, Boot Camp or any other entry point, ask yourself how many times were you even allowed to fail?

This may sound trite, but you were doing the "wax on" and "wax off" thing your entire military career. (Not up on obscure film references? Go look it up, you'll enjoy what you find.) You were also immersed in a culture of continuous learning. You don't get a promotion in the modern military unless you can learn something, demonstrate what you learned, and apply it under stress. This will be one of your more valuable skills when you hit the civilian job market. Keep learning, make it something you do better than the others.

Why do we use the word immersed? It's a good, descriptive word that is applicable. It describes the fact you were surrounded by leadership examples, heroic and sometimes moronic behaviors. Your military service was a force fed, rapid fire, concentrated, never-ending crash course of humans at their best and worst. No matter the length of your service, it is likely that you were exposed to, participated in, or had to make more meaningful decisions and live with the results than your civilian counterparts will experience until much later in their lives. Let's get ahead of this quickly and say you may not be so far ahead of Law Enforcement and First Responders or certain Medical Professionals as their professional experiences have many similarities to yours.

You don't have all the answers and at this point in your life you don't really have a clue (assuming you are still in the military or have very recently separated) of how to navigate the civilian world. What you DO have is an incredible work ethic, self-confidence, and a proven ability to absorb knowledge like a sponge.

Your experience gives you a tremendous advantage should you choose to use it. There are a ridiculous number of companies who will want to hire you, though it's not a blank check. You still must present well, demonstrate your abilities and mesh with the culture of your prospective employer. You absolutely should go back to school and get your degree (Bachelors, Masters, or PH. D). We will cover this topic in greater detail in the Education chapter later in the book.

You need a crash course to learn about finances.

You need to start constantly monitoring and managing your fiscal health.

You need goals.

You need to read and study continuously, for the rest of your life.

All said, you are well positioned to manage your own future. Take the framework of leadership, success and learning and apply it to your next career. If you apply yourself your advantage is almost unfair. But to be successful, you need a plan for your life. Figure out what you REALLY want and take steps every day towards achieving that goal. At a minimum, don't allow yourself to lose ground working toward your goals. Plan and execute, it's something you've been doing for years if not decades.

You really are uniquely prepared to manage your future and your biggest advantage is the fact that you are accustomed to success. Don't lose that confidence and drive: you know that hard work, continuous improvement and being a life-long learner are critical components for the recipe of success.

Personal perspective:

I was in the service with a fellow who was, frankly, overweight. He was a father of three beautiful children who loved their Dad. However, he couldn't pass the minimum PT and he couldn't get past the current weight-height standards. After much frustration with his lack of progress, his command was forced to either separate him or do something drastic. He was a fantastic NCO and great guy, so no one wanted to boot him out. He also wasn't the only senior NCO with this problem. To that end, the command created a program that offered these folks a completely voluntary option to literally either shape up or ship out. All these senior staff NCOs opted to move into a bare-bones barracks, do PT twice a day, stand for daily weigh ins and subject themselves to all the other micromanagement you would expect. They could not leave the base, which was a blow to their families. They had daily inspections to prevent snacking, they were not allowed into the PX unsupervised, their meals were closely monitored, and they had a curfew. Again, this was completely voluntary, and they knew they had put themselves in a position that was about to end their careers, so they decided to do something about it.

Almost all the NCOs got it together. The lost weight dramatically improved their level of physical fitness and some became real hard assess as they regained their self-confidence. It was inspiring, and some of them probably went on to create their own fitness videos as a result of getting that particular type of religion.

There's a moral to this story: the military will try mightily to help its people. Do you really think the companies in the civilian world have the patience and extra money lying around to do something like this? Most do not; survival and success are very much up to you.

Core Five - You have skills and capabilities that are marketable

Let's translate. You are good at lots of things, more than you probably realize.

If you really paid attention to the fourth Core principle "You are uniquely prepared to manage your own future," then you should be starting to get your head around the overall concept that you are well positioned to take on the world.

Even better, employers are willing to pay you for the experience you've garnered during your service. The real trick is to figure out how to tell the civilian world about your military experience in terms that relate to their jobs and the skills they are looking for.

What do you have to offer? Even generically speaking, your skills are likely to be far above your competition, and the younger you are the more dramatic the gap. Let's take the extreme example of a civilian college graduate vs. an E-5 from any service ready to enter the workforce. We use an E-5 for comparison because the time in service and time in grade requirements take an average of four years to achieve, which is good enough for this example.

If you've been in the service for four years and haven't made E-5, then you need to work harder and make better choices. There are no excuses for failure to achieve a minimal level of success.

For the record, a college degree is absolutely required in these times. Everyone should fully recognize the advantages, economic and social, gained from the college experience. We should also demonstrate the utmost respect for those persons who commit huge parts of their lives as educators from K4 through PH. D levels.

Let's get back to the comparison.

The college graduate has proven he or she can stick with a four-year curriculum and has learned to navigate a complex system of financial aid, professors, timelines and deliverables, administrators, and bureaucrats. The graduate has chosen a path and gained not only knowledge but permanent recognition for that effort. Along the way, this graduate has very possibly created lifelong connections to other motivated and likely-to-be successful persons which will be of great benefit as life progresses. While having a degree is important, having the right type of degree is critical. Being a huge fan of college education does not mean that every degree is useful. Be smart about picking your degree.

Education is important but education plus experience is even better. In the short run, experience, even without a degree can be a competitive advantage.

How does our trusty enlisted compare? Our E-5 initially looks to be at a serious disadvantage when compared to our college graduate holding any reasonable undergraduate degree. Our poor schmuck has slogged through boot camp, had every day pre-programmed for months at a time and has been at the complete mercy of senior NCOs and a seemingly uncaring, bureaucratic administration. This E-5 has likely been assigned to every low level, low skill task in the unit as while progressing through the ranks. Things look bleak from this point of view. But the good news is that's not all our E-5 has done because at least one primary training and certification course is required for each focus specialty. This E-5 has demonstrated systems, specialist, and service proficiencies and has been promoted four times. As a result, all services consider an E-5 rank as a Non-Commissioned Officer (hereafter known as an "NCO" for purposes of streamlining the text), meaning an E-5 is firmly entrenched in the management and leadership role of their branch and unit.

Both individuals want to hit the job market hard and land the job.

The best and brightest of graduates are heavily recruited out of college into good jobs or graduate programs, but that happens only to the cream of the crop. Our newly minted college graduate likely isn't in that tiny percentage and starts working the recruiting and job boards with a gleam in their eye towards that first decent paying job. School was not a picnic, and someone has burned a lot of late-night hours studying and working on complex projects and assignments. Odds are our college graduate is under financial stress because many college graduates will exit school owing $30K to $100K of student debt. Less than six out of ten (59%) of college students will graduate with a four-year degree after six years of study. The graduation rate for four years study is 10-15% lower. But the future is just around the corner…six-digit salaries and a corner office. College students have been told that all they need to do is get the degree and the dream job will be there for the asking.

For those graduating with Science, Technology, Energy and Math degrees employment options abound. For those with degrees that don't directly translate into market needs, their next job may not be in their chosen field. Even with a degree, you are not guaranteed a job in your field, or at a reasonable pay rate. The job market is tough and there are a lot of under-employed persons in any field who are likely more educated and experienced than a new graduate.

The Bureau of Labor Statistics recently published a chart called "Education Pays." Comparing the income of a college graduate (approx. $1K per week) and those of a high school graduate (approx. $600 per week). That's about $54K per year before taxes. Please fill in the usual caveats about variations such as age, specialty, and number of years out of college, but remember that number.

The Census Bureau says that between 41%, the recent low water mark in 2000 and 59% of college graduates the recent high-water mark in 2012, were under-employed. We'll talk more on this issue later.

So, back to the comparison.

Bright shiny new college graduate vs. our rough around the edges E-5 with little to no formal education. Both of our candidates are working every angle to land a job. Which person has the advantage? If your answer is the college graduate, then you must have slept through your military service.

This is what an E-5 looks like from an overall experience perspective:

- Experienced with a large multinational (equivalent) organization that is culturally diverse and supports multiple goals and mission profiles

- Experienced in at least three different commands (boot camp, initial training, assigned unit)

- Earned four promotions, each requiring the candidate meet performance requirements, pass multiple qualification exams and a service wide exam for their specialty. Individuals must also continuously demonstrate the mastery of their current and next rank requirements before promotion.

- Completed at least one rigorous primary skill (MOS) training course

- Has been immersed in a culture of success, leadership, and continuous learning for four years

- Supervised large and small units and work groups on a daily basis

- Has been part of a deployment work up and actual deployment

- Traveled and lived in a foreign country (most)

- Thrived in an environment where every aspect of professional life is defined

- Adjusted to the fact that a great deal of your private life is governed by military requirements

- Lived a drug-free life and passed multiple drug screenings during this period

- About 50% are married and have learned how to balance military life with family life

- Some will have earned an Associate's degree and in some cases a Bachelor Degree

- Much higher number of training hours as every job, watch and task is on-the-job (OJT) training, supervised and performance continuously reviewed by senior staff (see Core Concept Six for the actual calculations)

- Certified small arms proficient

- Familiar with (if not expert) logistics, transport, training, and computerized systems of various flavors

- Certified security element watch stander proficient

- Significant emergency first aid training (CPR, trauma)

- Completed service-specific leadership training courses to qualify for promotion

- Demonstrated communication skills

- Physically fit and strong

- Demonstrated ability to work well under incredible stress of the real world, not the artificial environment of academia

- Trained in proven leadership concepts, demonstrated ability and practical application of leadership principles

- Has been directly responsible for peer and subordinate coaching

- Experienced with large supply chain management concepts and practical implementations

- Denied "safe spaces" to hide from the world (sorry, couldn't resist)

In general, our E-5 should win easily in this comparison. If you are higher up the leadership chain as an Officer or Enlisted, you need to start cataloging your skills and experience and humbly make note of who you have become. You have a huge competitive advantage.

We'll talk more about this in the next Core Concept and close here by saying that the author of this book obviously would choose a "qualified" prior service candidate wherever possible when we hire. It would be stupid just to hire a Veteran regardless of qualifications and fit. Start thinking specialized training, social networking, and the age-old concept of "it's not what you know, but who you know."

Personal perspective:

I once interviewed for a job I wanted but didn't have specific skill or experience listed on the job posting. I was candid with the HR and hiring managers, and unfortunately the interview with the hiring manager didn't go well. She was impatient and blunt, making it clear that it was a big problem not having the specific skills she needed. She gave me a little lesson economics saying the best outcome of a new hire was to bring someone on board who would take the least amount of time to become productive. Up to that point, I hadn't realized that hiring someone who needed training was a drain on the whole team and to some degree, as all new hires required some type of training. I realized that this manager was responsible for real productivity and bottom line contribution to the company. Driving away from that interview, I felt a bit depressed because I really wanted the job, but it didn't look good. When I received the call a week later and heard that they were willing to take a chance on me, I was ecstatic. The HR manager told me the company had a good track record with Vets and if I was willing to step up to an aggressive training program, they would hire me on an interim basis. Of course, I agreed. I was "hired for attitude and trained for aptitude" because of my military background and experience. What more could you ask for?

Core Six – You have gaps in your skills and capabilities that you need to close

As you rise in rank, Officer and Enlisted, you become more skilled and knowledgeable, and in many cases, you get locked into a specialization. If that is the path you want to pursue after you finish with the military, then you are well-positioned well. However, if you want or need to continue to draw a paycheck and your specialization is not marketable in the civilian space, you must either switch to another skill or find some type of military support contractor to work with.

You may be the absolute top of your field for your military occupation. Regardless of your rank, from E-1 to an O-6, you still have a lot to learn.

We're going to exclude Flag officers from this dialog, as the air is certainly thin up there and one doesn't obtain that rank without mastery of the requisite personal, professional, and social skills. Please note that if you have mastered these skills at any rank, no disparagement is intended. The more senior your rank, it is most likely the farther up the learning curve you are. If you can land a job as a military contractor or with one of the big Defense Department vendor suppliers, you will find a somewhat friendlier culture to prior service members.

To complete this section, we are going to assume that (a) you are not a master politician, (b) you don't have a six-figure job waiting on you in the defense industry and (c) you've been focused on your job and career for the last few years and welcome any insight we can provide.

If we establish a framework for education and training you will see that the "always on" aspect of military service really piles on the hours vs. your civilian-only competition. And yes, the word competition is very specifically used because you will be fighting for every raise and promotion from this point on.

Education framework

- Bachelors requires 120 credit hours = 5,400 hours of study (high side)
    - Lecture courses (3 credits) 45 hours class time + 90 hours prep = 135 hours
    - Lab courses (4 credits) = 45 hours class + 45 hours lab + 90 hours prep = 180 hours

- Enlisted (E-5) with Four years of service = 12,600 hours of service
    - Assume 48 weeks of service per year
    - Assume an average of 12 hours OJT/Training/Watch duty. This includes overnight duty.
    - Assume 5.5 days' work per week (often uses weekend to prep)
    - 4 years X 48 weeks X 5.5 days X 12 hours = 12,600
- Officer (O-3) with Four years of service = 12,600 base + 5,400 degree = 19,000 hours
    - A good argument could be made for even higher numbers (+10%) for the Officer Corps given the greater responsibility and management overhead required

Both our E-5 and our O-3 are overqualified in the areas of leadership, motivation, problem solving, and maturity compared to their civilian competition. Sounds arrogant, doesn't it? Our perspective comes from real life personal and observed experience. But ask yourself, would you want any random 22 to 26-year-old civilian (that is not a First Responder) to back you up in a crisis? Think about it and make your own call.

Unfortunately, outside of certain defense contractor economies, you won't get full credit for the sum of your experience and capabilities. You will find that most companies are military-friendly and appreciate your service while acknowledging you are a generally more capable individual. All of that, however, won't get you a job.

Thriving in a capitalist economy (the best economic framework) is about the bottom line, and you need to lock down that concept. If you are looking for employment, this becomes critical because you want to land the highest paying job possible. To do that, you need to sharpen your focus.

To thrive, you must learn new skills and master some that you already have. You are moving from one super-system to another with a new framework for success. Adapt and overcome.

Likely, your personal skills are subpar and it's not likely anyone around to evaluate you and coach you to where you need to be. You have moved from a world where a collar device, shoulder board or sleeve rank insignia told you almost everything you needed to know about the other person in the conversation.

Some people will like you and some won't. You get to learn all about passive-aggressive behavior, a concept and behavior that is completely frustrating. Someone who says yes to you but quietly and with a subtle and almost undetectable method, works against you when out of sight. You need to develop the skills and mannerisms that let you deal effectively with all types of personalities and agendas.

The ability to disagree with a person's perspective, politics, or agenda and still like that person has been described as the only true indicator of intelligence. Think about that.

I'm sure you ran into petty tyrants, egoists, zealots and manipulating personalities during your time in the service. However, most of the time there was a framework and method where these persons would be held accountable for their performance if not always their behavior. On this new side of the fence, you may find yourself needing the services of a specific person who absolutely doesn't care about your situation or urgency and may even enjoy pointing that out to you. Your recourse is simple, play by their rules or find another way to solve your problem. The least likely successful path is where you try to "force" this person to behave according to societal or moral norms.

Often your specialized military training does NOT exceed the training and experience of your civilian counterparts. You may have mastered the military MOS but are less well trained than a journeyman or apprentice.

Business owners and corporations alike want to hire experts. While they will absolutely hire lower-skilled individuals and pay them at commensurately lower rates, the preference is to hire the most experience they can find/afford.

The yardstick for measuring expertise, or mastery, came from Malcom Gladwell's New York Times bestseller, *Outliers,* published in 2008. The author frequently cites 10,000 hours of practice as "the magic number of greatness." That's certainly not a hard science as other research has shown that it's the average of training, dedication, and experience for those that have achieved remarkable success.

Everywhere you look, someone wants to take your money by selling you their "shortcut" to knowledge, experience, and success. Don't fall for it. You learned in the service it takes dedication, an incredible work ethic, great instructors and practice, practice, practice. Then you must constantly apply what you've learned to master a skill. While the path to mastery will vary and some individuals will have a shorter path than others, there are no shortcuts.

Let's use this as our default measuring stick; 1,000 hours to master a skill and 10,000 hours to become an Expert.

If you were the hiring employer, which would you want? No relevant training or skill, or the 1K hour candidate or the 10K hour experienced candidate? Just for the record, the 10K experience pool of candidates is shallow, fickle, and expensive. Persons in the 10K experience pool don't suffer fools or foolish policies for long.

No matter what, you should continue your education and the younger you are the more important this is. If you don't have a Bachelor's degree, go get one, then go get your Master's degree.

Step one is recognizing right now, this minute, that you have critical gaps in your skills and capabilities which must be closed to allow you to thrive.

Step two is closing those gaps in a specific order that give you a competitive advantage.

The rest of this book is about helping you identify and build the perspective and skills you need to bridge your specific critical gaps.

Personal perspective:

Imagine a young man, fresh out of the Marine Corps with all the vim and vigor you would expect. He is also filled from top to bottom with all the moral fiber the Corps could instill into him. Take this Corporal, running his own construction business and building quality houses for discriminating buyers. On one occasion, he needs to run a vertical vent for the plumbing system in the house. He whips out the county building code book he carries in his back pocket, finds the appropriate section, and makes note that the vent pipe needs to be a minimum of X inches. He checks his truck and doesn't have size X, but has a slightly larger diameter pipe and finishes the job. Fast forward to the county inspector on the site who needs to sign off on the progress so the next draw (needed to pay for materials and contractors) can be obtained from the bank. The inspector notes the slightly larger diameter pipe on the vertical vent and tells our Corporal that he won't sign off on it. Out comes the code book, the young builder pointing out the "minimum size" language in the code. No confrontation intended as our Corporal is sure it's just a misunderstanding. Unperturbed, the inspector leans close and says "I don't care what that damn book says. If you want build houses in this county, you need to do what I tell you, not what some book says…

Our Corporal, always fast on the uptake makes a snap decision. He realized that this wasn't the Corps and he needed to get paid. He understood that he was fighting city hall and couldn't win meaning this is not the time for a smart-ass reply. He quickly asks the inspector if he can wait while he corrects the issue. The guy agrees to come back same day which in itself is pretty much unheard of. The work gets done and the inspector signs off. The lesson here was that the rules are what the guy in control says they are, sometimes. Choose your battles carefully.

Core Seven – You now have more responsibility for your life, and much more opportunity to screw it up

Possibly for the first time in your life, you are now 100% responsible for your own success or failure. We're not talking about the time where you found yourself in a do or die scenario (fill in your best story here) from your service. This is about the day-to-day journey that constitutes the rest of your life.

When you leave the military, you leave behind huge, complex, and very effective social-professional safety networks. These web-like structures came with layers and layers of detection and response mechanisms which safeguarded you, your family, and friends.

During your time in-service these processes, and the people behind them, operated for the most part without your active participation and sometimes even without your knowledge that they existed. The work that was done on your behalf ensured you got paid, had safe water to drink, nutritious food to eat each day, were provided healthcare and a myriad of other things you likely took for granted. Someone else defined what training you would get, the work you needed to do each day and where you needed to be at what time, often down to the minute. You knew exactly was required for your next promotion. All of this was handed to you in varying degrees based on your military specialty and rank.

None of that exists where you are going; at least not wrapped up in one neat package.

Let's say that again but in a slightly differently, because you probably don't get it yet.

You are now performing without a net.

You and I could probably draft another book just on this topic.

Transitioning out after returning from a conflict area can often amplify and exaggerate the feelings of isolation and loneliness that are normal when leaving the service. These Veterans can find themselves stressed and impacted without a clear idea why it is happening. Feelings of vulnerability at innocuous gatherings like church aren't unusual. Feelings of lost comradery and aimlessness without a common and meaningful mission are common. Having a significant injury or any degree of PTSD just makes things more difficult.

While dealing with the echoes of your service banging around in your head or dealing with service-related injuries, you still have to get on with life. Lots of decisions lie ahead along with lots of things you've haven't really had to think about before.

What happens when you get sick and can't work? What medical, vision, dental coverage will you have? What types of life insurance do you need? Where will you live? How much home can you afford on your retiree benefits or your new salary? Are you changing careers? When should you go back to school to get that next degree? What type of lifestyle do you want? These questions are just the tip of the iceberg that is now your life.

Let's take an essential like healthcare for a quick peek to see how far that iceberg extends below the surface. Healthcare can be incredibly complicated and you need to fully understand your options or you may miss out on much needed benefits. Did you know that unless you have a service-related disability, your VA benefits and access will be denied if your income is too high? There is some variability, but for a family of four, the income limit is about $45K, which isn't a lot of money. Your previous year's reported income will be verified with the IRS so if you think there's a way around that limit, think again. For retirees, you will be eligible for Tricare. Have you heard of these assistance programs; Transitional Assistance Management Program (TAMP) or Continued Health Care Benefit Program (CHCBP)?

Suddenly and immediately, with no do-overs or forgiveness, you are wholly and solely responsible for your life. Your job, your pay, where and how you live, where you children go to school, who you choose to associate with - everything is wide open. There are no more deployments, no more base housing, or Basic Allowance for Housing (BAH) to help you afford to live in the local economy. Most of the benefits (at an admittedly low pay rate) you've enjoyed are simply gone. Now, you must make every choice and exercise control over all those restricted aspects of life that you chafed about in the service, and all those choices matter.

You now have all the responsibility, and in some cases less than optimal to absolutely no control over some aspects of your life.

No matter how difficult, you should build your life around this absolute truism: "Your job doesn't love you, but your family does."

Make smart choices. The impact of leaving the services will impact many, many aspects of your life and the more effort you put in ahead of time, the easier the transition will be for you and your family.

Personal perspective:

A friend who retired as a Chief Petty Officer after twenty years, woke up on a Monday, which was the first day of his retirement and had a small (very small, he's a Chief after all!) panic attack. The question on his mind that triggered this mental anomaly? *What the hell was he going to wear on his first day of his retired life?* He also realized that he needed to double, and triple check those things in his life that had been taken care of by the service infrastructure and processes while he was still active. Weeks later he had put all that to rest, but to this day he still struggles to decide what clothes to wear each day.

Core Eight - Life is still hard

Look at this from the perspective of the end of your service +1 second. You have served your country and made a real difference in the world. Those with intelligence and character will always appreciate what you've sacrificed and done for their---our country. There's no walk back on that, you deserve those accolades and more. You should take some time to appreciate the change in the severity and criticality of the stressors in your life. Never forget what you've accomplished, where you came from and most importantly who you are now. Now move on. For you, the world just changed in the blink of an eye. Between one second and the next, you became a Veteran.

Even if you have planned well for this chapter of your life, the transition will still be hard. If you have let the clock run down on your planning and prep time life will be much harder, but you can still win and live your life your way.

No matter how much your service is appreciated or admired, no one is going to hand you success. As we discussed in the previous Core Concept, you have a lot to learn and many decisions to make.

Unless you are already financially independent, you'll need to generate income. For most, that means finding a job and for some, that means owning your own business. For either, you need to be able to do two things simultaneously:

1) Declare and demonstrate marketable skills
2) Constantly and consistently provide valuable services

You need to produce something and more importantly, you must produce something every day.

Competition is fierce and global. You are competing against people who are just as smart, if not smarter, than you and who may have many times your experience. The air can become quite rarified and you could easily find yourself competing against someone with both a better education and better contacts.

To be successful, you are going to have to do all those things discussed in Core Concepts 1-7 simultaneously. The earlier you start building a plan, the better for you and yours.

The term "lifelong learner" describes someone who is a voracious consumer of information; a person who constantly works to turn data, information and experience into knowledge and skills. A "lifelong learner" is also someone who constantly seeks mentors who can help them achieve their goals and is someone who tackles every aspect of their life with energy and focus, doing whatever is needed to succeed. That is who and what you need to become...yesterday. Yes, no matter where you are on your timeline, you are most likely behind the curve. You have years of integration, social networking and career-specific knowledge acquisition and effort ahead of you.

In the service, most of what you needed to know was pushed at you, even down your throat and then your competency was constantly checked. That "push" of information, knowledge and skills likely became invisible to you at some point in your career, just part of your job. The people and processes that provided the "push" oversight are now gone. It's all up to you now, and if you fail to maintain your own discipline and replace that "push" system with a self-managed "pull" process, you will fall short of your potential.

You will be constantly surrounded by mediocrity. There will be those that don't exercise good judgement; those who stop learning; those that hoard their knowledge; those that could help, but just don't want to make the effort and those who got a degree or specialized training but can barely function in that field because they are too lazy to maintain themselves. Other people will drink too much or live at the edge of acceptable professional and societal norms. The bottom line is these people are not your role models, and they will constantly ask you why you work so hard, what are you training for or why do you need to know that? When you find those that have risen above mediocrity, cherish and hold them close.

This isn't just about a job or career because you have to keep the rest of your world together.

You will be joining a new world which is 24 x 7, not just when you are off duty. You need to seek out new friends and acquaintances of all types and you will need to evaluate and choose who you let into your life and that of your family. You also will need to build a new social web. It will be hard to choose where to invest in select individuals the precious time you have.

Hopefully, you are blessed with parenthood which the most important job in the world! As we all know, being a parent doesn't end when the little ones grow up and move out. Plan to be in their lives every second that you can.

After parenthood, the second most important responsibility you will ever have is being a terrific significant other or spouse. Too many people think that a successful relationship is about "feelings," it is not, has never been and never will be. Real love is deliberate and is a choice you make every day. If you aren't particularly good at it, consciously do those things that make you get better because it is incredibly hard under the best circumstances. As you literally change your world and alter the stressors you must deal with, relationships can become overwhelming. Don't be overwhelmed, be the shining example.

Your parents are getting older. Hopefully you have a great relationship with them. They will need your help as time passes, no matter how much money they have. They also want you in their lives. Find the time to be there for your parents if you are lucky enough to still have them with you, be there for them. If you haven't already done so, you should embrace the philosophy that *"you owe your parents a debt you can never repay, but you should never stop trying."* It will be terribly hard to watch them age and support them through that process, but that is your responsibility.

Build habits and discipline to protect yourself from the constant onslaught of mediocrity, stress, and change. It will be hard, but the quality of your life will reward you daily.

Things will break, people will become ill, some will die unexpectedly. Young persons will depart this life far too soon; children will grow up and away; relationships will bend, twist and fracture. You will experience pain, loss, and tragedy.

How you handle these personal challenges will define you.

Personal perspective:

While serving, I arrived at a duty station at about the same time and point in my career as several others. After a couple of years, we all faced a similar question. Any extension of our service would put us over the ten-year mark. Most of us subscribed to the "if you pass the halfway point to retirement, might as well go all the way" philosophy. So, as you can see, the decision to stay or leave was significant. The base was also a long-term military command with the usual bevy of retirees scattered around the community. Over the course of the previous three years, we had all come into contact with the retiree community as friends and seniors retired. Some had planned well but for others the financial circumstances were bleak. Many were fortunate enough to have jobs lined up as contractors performing almost the same job at double or better salary. For those trying to make the "stay for twenty or get out" decision, the dynamic was quite different. They would have no income from their time in the service and needed to secure a decent job with benefits as most had families at that point.

I watched a disturbing phenomenon take place with several service members who were contemplating leaving the service. It was kind of like some slow-motion car crash where various service members would attempt to penetrate the civilian job market with all these grand aspirations. They believed that, surely, they would be immediately snatched up at a premium price. These folks were, top tier in their specialties, and after a few weeks, sometimes months for those that started the job search early, they would regroup and begin espousing the benefit of staying in the service. As we all know, the military pay scale is abysmal, but the extra pay and benefits make things more tolerable.

Watching these bright minds recanting their ambitions and trying to convince themselves vicariously through us as they counted the multiple add-ons provided by the military above base pay was disturbing to say the least. They had made the decision to separate and not stay for the full ride, but they were woefully unprepared. They had no jobs, no contacts, no plan, and worst of all no financial reserve to help tide them over until they could land a decent job. The economy was surging, the job market was wide open and hot. These individuals were top tier, experienced with all the right skills. This should have resulted in multiple job offers the minute they hit the job market.

Unfortunately, they did nothing until the very last minute. They had simply failed to plan. These very capable individuals failed because they expected the military to help them separate and move on to the next phase of their lives. They failed because they had one income, no real savings, and no plan. They failed because they had no contacts or relationships to lean on. They received the equivalent of a false negative test result. As for me, I think watching this process spurred me to exit. There was no war or conflict raging, just the military day in and day out, in other words nothing to keep me. In retrospect, I think that I couldn't stand the thought of staying in the military because I was afraid I would fail on the outside. I was almost as unprepared as the rest of my peers, but simply could not stay out of fear that I wouldn't measure up. I still miss the service but, I made the right decision for me. The lesson here is that you should prepare your life to keep your options open and a huge part of that is being financially stable so you can make a choice.

Core Nine – The Republic is powered by the engine of Capitalism

Let's talk about you. Whether you are already a captain of industry, independently wealthy or, like many of us at separation who aren't either of those things, please read this section carefully. This Core Concept requires you to develop an understanding of how wealth is created and expenses managed. Though creating a budget and sticking to it is a part of having fiscal discipline that is only the tip of the financial knowledge iceberg you should master.

You need to be very data driven and unfortunately the various information sources that influenced you in the past should be carefully re-evaluated. The financial and retail industries want you to ignore your debt and focus on how much of a payment you can "afford." You will have to do much better than that if you want to be successful. As a rule, during your time in service you were overworked and under-paid. Of course, you know that, but what you may not have realized is that this forced paycheck-to-paycheck focus likely severely stunted your acquisition of critical financial skills that are required for success. You need to understand the difference between hype and real data. You need to incorporate into your world view a far deeper understanding of income, revenue, expenses, and net worth. As you grow your competencies around your personal financial management, you can expand to include savings, investments, future value of a dollar, taxes, insurance, life expectancy and sustainable lifestyles at different ages.

Let's return to the concept of being data driven. What follows in this paragraph is one of the most atrocious examples of unabashed lies and falsehoods presented as "facts." There are a couple of studies available from the Congressional Budget Office (CBO) that attempt to inflate the compensation received by service members. Did you know that the CBO claims that the "average" E-4 receives approximately $70K per year in compensation AND that compensation is on par with civilians of the same age who have a four-year college degree? In the math used for this $70K chimera you will find an assumption that 38% of this annual compensation comes in the form of deferred income that will be provided in retirement. Given the fact that less than 20% of the military stay in for the full ride, this is a ludicrous spin that is presented a fact.

When you dig into the data behind the analysis you will find this number also includes both Regular Military Compensation (RMC) and an overly generous allotment of the following noncash compensation including the cost of healthcare for service members and their families, the subsidized groceries available at commissaries, the use of subsidized preschool or after-school child care for the member with children and deferred compensation (mentioned above) including the accrued cost of retirement pay, health care for retirees and Veterans' benefits.

For some reason, both Social Security and Medicare taxes that the DoD pays on behalf of service members and payments to the Unemployment Compensation for Ex-Servicemen program are included in the calculations. Those payments are similar to civilian employers' FICA (Federal Insurance Contributions Act) and unemployment insurance contributions. The information included in this paragraph is puzzling as it was a footnote in the main body of the report and seems to imply that this is somehow an extra non-cash benefit which it is not, by the way, as civilians and their employers pay the equivalent.

The military vs. civilian comparison provided above is referenced from a study called the *"The Eleventh Quadrennial Review of Military Compensation"* published by the Department of Defense in 2011. While the comparison of compensation is deeply flawed, the report is brimming with other important and usable data. The report/study is required by law; under section 1008(b) of title 37, United States Code, every 4 years the President is required to complete a review of the compensation system for the uniformed service members of the Department of Defense, the Coast Guard, and the commissioned corps of the National Oceanic and Atmospheric Administration and Public Health Service. The Fiscal Year 2013 National Defense Authorization Act (Public Law 112-239) established the Military Compensation and Retirement Modernization Commission which is mainly focused on quality of life, healthcare, and retirement for military service members. Unfortunately for us our 44th President (Obama) ignored the United States Code requirement by deciding he no longer needed to provide the Quadrennial review and that the work done by the MCRMC was good enough. The 2015, 302-page report published by the MCRMC is important, but pretty much totally ignores service member actual compensation which should be constantly and critically analyzed. You just can't make this up.

https://www.whitehouse.gov/the-press-office/2015/01/09/presidential-memorandum-twelfth-quadrennial-review-military-compensation

Let's reset our focus. We wandered into the non-data information provided by the US government as an example that you can relate directly to. It's a garbage analysis based on good data with the analysis presented as fact. The lesson here is that the civilian world is just as capable of providing sound bites that businesses want you to use to make long term financial decisions. If you go unarmed into that decision-making process you will literally pay a premium for your naivety.

Money is not a panacea for all the challenges in life. However, money, particularly discretionary funds (what's left over after you pay for the basics) will have a significant impact on the quality of your life. The question is, how much will you have left after you cover the basics? Will it support the lifestyle you desire? This is not a fuzzy math question that can be dealt with by hope. Your personal and business finances are concrete, hard numbers. You will want to maximize your discretionary dollars and be very data driven in this area of your life.

Chances are, you have tremendous energy and potential, but little actual capital or savings

The largest wealth-building decision most Americans ever make is home ownership. Most reading this will not own a home outright or even have a mortgage.

You probably don't have much in the way of savings either. A good rule of thumb is to have a minimum of six months' expenses in cash excluding any retirement savings.

Depending on your age and maturity (as well as other factors) you probably don't have much of a retirement nest egg. For the purposes of this discussion, assume that your retirement pay and benefits are likely insufficient to allow you to maintain the lifestyle you should have.

Let's do a couple of simple financial health checks. If you meet or exceed, you should be congratulated, no kidding around. If you don't meet or exceed, you need to pay close attention.

- Income check baseline: Your Age X $3,000 (rough calculation)

- Net worth check baseline (don't include your home equity): Your income X Your Age / 10

A 30-year-old making $75,000 a year sounds sweet but would;

- Not meet the minimum of $90,000 income

- Needs a net worth of ($75K X 30 years) / 10 = $225,000

When you run that simple financial health check you may come up short. The good news is that you can always do better and the better news is that you are reading this book which shows you are open to the concept of "better." The challenge comes when we start talking about the "how" and "when" after the "what." There are no shortcuts. There is only understanding of options, choices, and execution within your means.

Back to your current income and net worth. Having enough money to cover the rent, a car payment and an occasional splurge is not enough. You need enough money to save and invest above and beyond normal expenses. You probably have room for improvement, so let's press on.

The good news is that you are in the right place, at the right time to succeed, by your own definition. We love our Republic and our concept of democracy. Those guiding principles paired with the economic benefit of capitalism provide the ability to change the world in large and small ways.

You will need multiple streams of income and you need to save much more than you are probably saving now. Burn in these concepts and we'll revisit them in the Money Management chapter.

The other particularly good news is that our capitalism-based economy has room for you and almost any sound money making idea you have. You can choose your lifestyle based on the effort you want to put into it. You can pick an industry, choose your type and level of education and what work you want to do.

Always remember that life is not experienced as a statistic but as an individual with each unique moment unfolding as you live. Be ever vigilant against sound bites and statistics provided by those who want to sell you something. Live your life in our Republic to its fullest and harness the immense power of capitalism to help you achieve your goals.

Personal perspective:

A couple, both with strong work ethics and family values lived a good life, were productive and responsible members of their community. When retirement came, they literally had most of their financial eggs in one basket and that basket broke on the back of a major company's stock price fall to less than 20% of its highest price.

They lost 80% of their savings because they didn't understand or have access to the mechanism of stop-loss, diversification, and risk management.

Chapter 3 – The rate of change is accelerating

No one likes to hear it, but you are definitely behind this power curve. In the 21st century, change vectors are arriving faster than ever. Some older patterns are being adjusted, polished, made more efficient and then re-anchored; some are being shattered and discarded. The emergence of other disruptive patterns is literally forcing changes to local, state, national and global economies, and cultures seemingly almost overnight. The world is more connected now than at any point in history making it appear vast and tiny at the same time. Population pressures are rising, economies must become more global to prosper. It is almost as if the old saying "what does that have to do with the price of tea in China" was prophetic. The answer to what once was a rhetorical question is now "everything."

I'm going to start this chapter about change by talking about data and information and how it relates to you. I am doing this so you understand the concepts of how data relates to information which relates to how the world is changing and how you can react accordingly. So, let's get started with the basics and then expand on them.

The current generation has access to more data more quickly than at any point in history. For little or no cost, you can access a massive amount of information through the internet, in the library plus through local and online bookstores. Warning, access to all of the information can lead to information overload, a term popularized By Alvin Toffler (American author, futurist, and former editor of Forbes magazine) in his bestselling 1970 book Future Shock.

Our economy is already based on data that is created, stored, and manipulated electronically. The amount of data created and managed is staggering. Did you know that the electronic world collects and creates more data in each day than if you digitized and stored every book, poem, song, painting, drawing, newspaper, or other information created from the dawn of civilization until 2004? That's basically an "Exabyte" of data created daily. Note, by the time you read this, the amount of information created daily may far exceed this comparison. For reference, here's a rough scale;

Byte (8 bits)
- byte: A single character
- 10 bytes: A single word

Kilobyte (1,000 bytes)
- 1 Kilobyte: A very short story
- 1 Kilobyte: 1024 bytes
- 2 Kilobytes: A Typewritten page
- 10 Kilobytes: An encyclopedic page
- 50 Kilobytes: A compressed document image page
- 100 Kilobytes: A low-resolution picture

Megabyte (1,000,000 bytes)
- 1 Megabyte: A small novel printed or electronically stored
- 1.44 Megabyte: 3.5-inch floppy disk
- 2 Megabytes: A high resolution picture
- 5 Megabytes: The complete type written works of Shakespeare
- 10 Megabytes: A digital chest X-ray or Very High definition picture
- 100 Megabytes: 1 meter of shelved books OR A two-volume encyclopedic book
- 500 Megabytes: Capacity of a CD-ROM

Gigabyte (1,000,000,000 bytes)
- 1 Gigabyte: A pickup truck filled with paper (level with the top of the cab)
- 2 Gigabytes: 15 yards of shelved books
- 5 Gigabytes: A modern DVD movie
- 20 Gigabytes: The collection of the works of Beethoven
- 100 Gigabytes: A floor of academic journals
- 500 Gigabytes: Typical PC hard drive

Terabyte (1,000,000,000,000 bytes)
- 1 Terabyte: 1,000 copies of the Encyclopedia Britannica
- 2 Terabytes: An academic research library
- 10 Terabytes: The printed collection of the US Library of Congress

Petabyte (1,000, 000,000,000,000 bytes)
- 1 Petabyte: 20 Million, full, 4 drawer filing cabinets
- 2 Petabytes: 10 Billion photos on Facebook
- 20 Petabytes: Production of hard-disk drives in 1995
- 200 Petabytes: All printed material

Exabyte (1,000,000,000,000,000,000 bytes)
- 1 Exabyte: All printed, painted, written works (if digitized) of humanity created until 2004
- 5 Exabytes: All words ever spoken by human beings.

Zettabyte (1,000,000,000,000,000,000,000 bytes)
Yottabyte (1,000,000,000,000,000,000,000,000 bytes)

Xenottabyte (1,000,000,000,000,000,000,000,000,000 bytes)
Shilentnobyte (1,000,000,000,000,000,000,000,000,000,000 bytes)
Domegemegrottebyte (1,000,000,000,000,000,000,000,000,000,000,000 bytes)
…up to a Googleplex which is 10 X 100th power bytes or 10 followed by 100 zeroes!!

Did you know there is an entire industry devoted to the technology of managing and mining the data that is stored? It's called (no joke) "Big Data," and the business of Big Data is expected to generate over $200 Billion in annual revenue by the year 2020. Big Data is all about storing, analyzing, and mining data to identify trends and relationships to any factor, influence, or pattern. Yahoo and Google are basically Big Data companies with incredible marketing and data presentation mechanisms.

In this brave new world, you need to understand that you have access to data, not information. So, while an internet search might yield you hundreds or thousands of results, you will never have time to read, evaluate and choose the most meaningful context from all that data. Access to data is not equivalent to information.

The difference between data and information? For data to be useful (valuable) it must be placed in context. Some data is structured (think databases) and already has some explicit relationships identified and correlated via the structure of the database that in which it resides. However, most of the data that is created has only loose categorization and is considered to be unstructured. When dealing with unstructured data, a search for the word "blue" could generate 11,314 hits. Someone or some data analysis algorithm would have to create context to correlate these data points. What relationships can be identified or inferred (fuzzy math). For example, how many hits were blue sky, blue jeans, blue birds and so on. You have the power to pull data about almost anything from the most trivial detail to the most precise, near real time financial and economic detail, but data is not information. Data becomes useful information only when its relationship to other data is identified. With very large amounts of data, visualization (which requires contextual placement and transformation) is also critical. For example, all the data available about the performance of a company from two years ago will not help you make a good decision about that company today. You need more current data and you must have the ability to put it into context. Who is the current CEO, what is the trend in the market space, how much R&D funding does the company currently have, , is there customer loyalty and what is the product roadmap. These are the questions that can only be answered by information based on the data you find.

We live in the early days of the information age. I say, *early days* because this age started only when access to the internet became ubiquitous by allowing the world's population access via not only desktop and laptop computers, but also smart phones and tablets. Think about those times when you find yourself isolated from the internet, with no ability to get directions, make a phone call, search the web, IM a contact, or check your email. You likely felt isolated and confused, something previous generations could not have imagined. In some countries, the vast majority of the population will live and die having never owned a PC but will consume internet and data services exclusively through their smartphone. Technology permeates all levels of society, regardless of wealth or social status. As we move into the era of the "internet of things," the embedded information in devices all around us will likely propel us into new challenges and advantages.

For those of you who are considering living off the grid, this also applies to you also. Unless you are prepared to make everything, even your tools by hand, pay attention.

How well you understand and leverage technology will have a profound impact on your life. In business, there is a saying that "everyone can buy the same equipment and hire the same smart people," it is how you deploy and utilize those elements that results in the potential to create a competitive advantage. And be advised, competitive advantages are NEVER permanent. You must always keep looking for the next opportunity to create a personal or business advantage, leveraging technology as the great enabler.

You need to get this. When you become aware of an innovative technology trend, work to embrace it as rapidly as you can, or you will be left behind. For example, one of the most polarizing technologies in recent time has been augmented reality, first seen publicly in a product called Google Glass. The ability to wear and seamlessly integrate information into someone's daily life is the holy grail of technology. However, this technology was not well-received by everyone because of its intrusive nature. You can search the internet and find a video of an early adopter wearing Google Glass being assaulted in a fast food restaurant in France. His surgically implanted glass is literally ripped from his head. Why? Because the management didn't want to be recorded. Apparently, many people are phobic about being recorded, but this is one of those head-in-the-sand moments from my perspective. Any individual can buy, for around $50 (much less than Google Glass) a disguised video recorder that can be worn in plain sight. So, why the big deal for Google Glass? Most wearers aren't that interested in recording the activities of the general populace, and if someone is watching, the target will likely never know they are under observation.

Ultimately, wearables providing augmented reality will become common place whether they are visibly apparent like Google Glass, or hidden and stealthy like a projection on the back of a pair of sunglasses or visible on a high-tech contact. This user interface technology will not stay bottled up behind a tiny screen with a relatively clumsy type and swipe interface.

Technology is just one vector for change, but it is pervasive. Don't be the person left behind because you are a reluctant technology adopter. Be aggressive, keep learning and stay competitive, even if you own your own business. We will do a deep dive into this concept in the "Technology and You" chapter.

Another significant truth about the value of data and information is that a tremendous amount of wealth is being generated at this time in history. New, specific technologies are being invented that change every industry on an almost daily basis. Individuals and corporations are becoming fantastically wealthy in ways that create context out of data that simply didn't exist a few years ago.

Individuals also have access to more ways of generating income and wealth that are directly attributable to technology changes. Residuals and micro transactions are becoming increasingly common in daily life. Need an example? Apple iTunes songs for less than a dollar or Kindle books for a fraction of the cost of a printed copy.

So, what else is changing and why should you care? Everything! You should care about and be informed on the global economy, China and India more specifically. No horror stories here, but the statistics aren't in favor of the good old US dominating the world economy in the long run. We do have certain advantages but will have to leverage technology and innovation to stay on top.

This graph, from Google's public database tells an interesting story over the last 50 years or so.

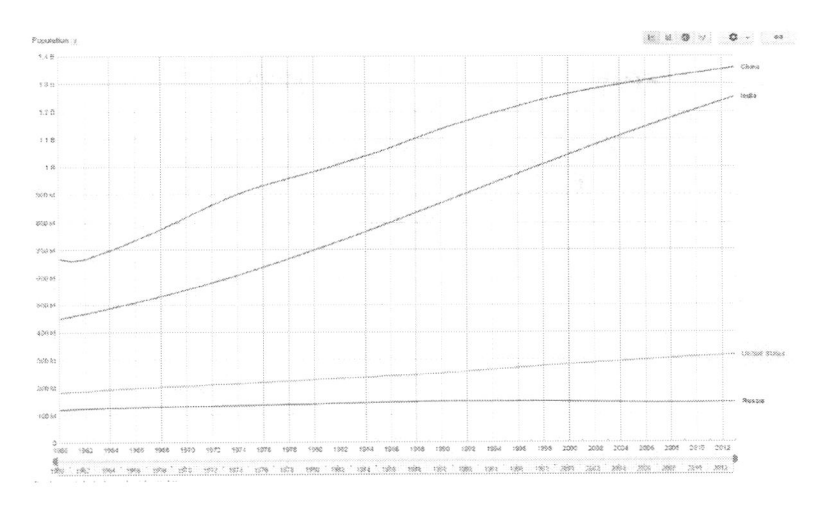

As you can see the current population (as of this writing) of China and India are growing at a rate that the U.S. cannot generate. This should create a bit of concern in your mind. With China, already at six times and India at five times the population of the US, the population gap is only going to get larger in your lifetime. Release your inference and correlation engines to run wild and even then, your imagination may not be up to the task of what's really coming.

A simple internet search will quickly produce some alarming facts including the fact that China has between 4 and 6 times more students in school than the US. The numbers seem overwhelmingly in favor of China until you dig a little deeper and find that the average number of years of education for a Chinese adult is only about six and a half years, but note that is changing as China grows and modernizes. There are many contradictions coming out of these statistics, but the potential of these large populations is incredible. They are also motivated in search of a higher standard of living. No doom and gloom here, but you should pay attention if for nothing else than the potential for doing business with these markets.

Do you speak another language? In the global business community, there's a bit of snide joke. It goes like this;

"What do you call someone who speaks three languages?"

"Trilingual"

"What do you call someone who speaks two languages?"

"Bilingual"

"What do you call someone who speaks one language?"

"American"

Statistically speaking from a US perspective, if you need a second language then that language should be Spanish. From a global perspective, forget about Spanish and learn to speak Chinese and then Hindi. Disclaimer, there are many dialects in both the Chinese and India language pools, do your research. It might be easier to start with Latin or one of the romantic languages, and then move on to learn a second language. If you plan on doing business with other countries, then learn the language, customs, and rules of business. Also, be sure your children learn to speak a second and third language.

The rate of change is accelerating. In almost every aspect of our global, national, and local economies, change is coming faster and faster. For the US to continue to thrive, it will have to become a nation of technology "super users" that are continually inventing and leveraging technologies that shake the foundation of the world.

Again, this is not a "the sky is falling" perspective. It is what it is (a frank acknowledgement and mental shoulder shrug while working on Wall Street). You should understand and stay current on those things that can and will affect your next career. For those of you going straight to retirement, staying current gives you something to argue about at the coffee shop or on the golf course.

Core Concepts mapping

Core One – You are NOT like the others. In the Service, you were exposed to and used systems that were backed by enormous amounts of data. You have practical, hands on experience with systems of varying efficiencies and effectiveness. You are not a naïve user of technology; you have been immersed in a culture that was based on technology and information management.

Core Five – You have skills and capabilities that are marketable. You understand that knowledge is power and that every system is flawed. You've proven that you can learn and use multiple technology systems. Now you just need to decide where you want to focus.

Core Six – You have gaps in your skills and capabilities that you need to close. Some of the systems you used in the service may have been innovative, but many were not. It takes time to harden a system for use and deployment to the degree that it is reliable enough to support the needs of the military. Don't waste your time rationalizing the fact you already understand technology and don't need to invest your time in learning more because technology changes so quickly you will at times be behind this power curve. Depending on your lifestyle choices, you will need to master some commercial, personal technology elements at a minimum.

Core Seven– You now have more responsibility for your life and much more opportunity to screw it up. Ignore the rate of change of various technologies at your peril. Don't be one of those who fall behind and can't use critical to quality of life and business technologies.

Core Eight – Life is still hard. Acquiring working expertise of new systems is hard. Becoming an expert user and understanding the limits and benefits of a new system is even harder. As you age, it will become even more difficult, but don't quit. Work to stay on top of these changes and your life will be better for it.

Core Nine – The Republic is powered by the engine of Capitalism. All this change will continually create new ways to generate wealth and prosperity. Find ways to take advantage of it to give you a competitive edge. It's out there and the opportunities are not limited to closed groups.

Personal perspective:

My brother is a Marine. One of his favorite sayings is that if you aren't busy living then you are busy dying. Unpack that a bit and you'll understand that it simply means you need to change with the times. Not morally or ethically, but you need to keep up and stay connected. Be a life-long learner. This is vital in business and in your personal life. If you don't, then you are choosing to align yourself with a shrinking population that is just sitting around waiting for "something" to happen. To hell with that. Get out there and make "something" happen.

Chapter 4 – It's not always about what you know

There are lots of quaint sayings that are applicable but old and tired. Here's the most recent. It should resonate powerfully with you. If it doesn't, wash, rinse, repeat until it does. Getting this is important.

Blood and access trump talent and hard work…EVERY TIME.

Do we need the disclaimer? Yes, probably. You still need the talent and the ability to work hard and effectively. Your skills, experience and maturity do count, but they don't offset the power of relationships and access. You can't get a job that requires specific training, experience, qualifications, or certifications without them, but what happens after you get that job? How do you thrive? Read on…

There is a concept called the "center of power," and the farther you are from it, the less influential you are. As an example, if you are working for a large bank, you will most likely need to live and work in either New York or Charlotte (depending on the bank) if you want to be a major factor. Don't get me wrong, you can still be influential, but I can't tell you how many times I've seen someone get a job or promotion for which they were not qualified simply because they were close to that company's power structure. Another example, if you want to be part of Wal-Mart's leadership, then you should be prepared to live in Arkansas.

This paradigm holds true for other companies as well, and while some companies are so large they have internal divisions that are Fortune 500 or Fortune 1000 companies all on their own, the same rules apply, but the internal Line of Business may not have its power hub in the same location as the power center for the company's headquarters. Pick your company, determine the center of power (this includes the powerful, influential people as well as the geographical central hub) and decide if that's where you want to live. If that's not where you want to be located, walk away because if you join the company and don't relocate to a power hub don't complain about the promotion you didn't get.

For small and medium sized businesses (SMBs) the concept of "blood and access" is even more true. Many business owners want to pass the company to their children when they retire, sometimes, in spite of the fact that their adult child is a huge ignoramus. In so many cases the blood factor has blinders; and owners and leaders are human and do the most for those that they know.

The second huge concept that you must include in your worldview is:

People do things for people.

This concept probably should be modified to state that "People do things for people that they know and care about." This concept falls under the "access" consideration. You need to be visible, trusted and favorably considered by the decision makers above you in the business. This doesn't mean you get instant credibility by data dumping your life story on someone the first time you have direct access. It means that you must manage your brand and what people think about you. You must be approachable, capable, and responsible in their eyes.

Don't forget about the harsh corollary that includes "Ruthless people do things for people that can advance their agenda." This almost never ends well for the person who has been "helped," particularly when their perceived effectiveness has been exploited. Should you find yourself in this position, the Chinese proverb *'Ch'i 'hu nan hsia pei'* comes into play. Roughly interpreted, it means that once you begin a dangerous course, the safest path may be to see it to the end. You can find all of that and more about the proverb with a quick internet search. Here's the takeaway: always go in with a plan for your end game and have more than one exit strategy, particularly if you are dealing with someone who is using you for their own needs.

Unless you are bullet-proof (and here's a clue...you aren't) you need to make friends and allies in your post-military life. You can forge ahead and ignore those around you, but your success will be limited. Note that no one is telling you to compromise your values or morals, just realize that you do need allies and you must build those over time.

Think about the template for life that includes college sororities and fraternities. What is the main purpose of these organizations? While they may seem wrapped in social activity calendars, the real purpose is to create bonds and relationships that can be leveraged throughout life. These relationships often have an exclusionary aspect. Have you ever heard the term "ring knocker"? If not, you should Google it.

If you are still in service when you are reading this, immediately start working on your network. Create a list of names, numbers, emails, Facebook contacts and any other social networking data structure you can put in place.

You need a mentor (see the Goal Setting chapter for more) who can help you grow and succeed avoiding the painful method of personal trial and error. Did I mention pain? The trial and error method of self-discovery is often expensive in terms of both time and money. You will likely need several mentors throughout your life and hopefully you can create deep and respectful friendships with your mentors.

Consider developing a presence in your Veteran community as you should be active in your local community. All activities should be welcome including anything that gets you out of the job or off the couch and into motion with others. The salient point here is "with others." You can find some type of help, coaching, insight, partnership for Veterans in almost any direction you turn, but to accomplish that you must get engaged and do your homework. Do not count on the Veteran's Administration (VA) to take care of you. Take care of yourself; be informed and be proactive. Here's a list of Veteran's organizations you might want to investigate just to get you warmed up to the fact that you have a lot of support (more links are provided in the Reference section at the back of the book):

Air Force Association - http://www.afa.org/home

Association of the US Navy - http://www.ausn.org/

Marine Corp Association: - https://www.mcafdn.org/

Army Association - http://www.ausa.org/

Coast Guard Foundation - http://www.coastguardfoundation.org/

Disabled American Veterans - http://www.dav.org/

Disabled Veterans National Association - http://www.dvnf.org/

US Department of Veterans affairs - http://www.va.gov/

The list provided is not comprehensive and should not be considered an endorsement of any particular organization. Another short internet search found an interesting website called the VSO-Directory which is supported by the Department of Veterans Affairs. The current link is provided below but if it doesn't work, a quick search should locate the latest version.

http://www.va.gov/vso/

It is very unlikely that any group, individual or organization will provide you with all the support or services you need, plan to have multiple source approach to solving your post service challenges.

You need a presence in your local community. Remember that "people do things for people" and that those most likely to help you are those geographically close to you. Your best friend in Texas or uncle in Maine can't help you on a weekend project. Cultivate friendships and relationships with locals (wherever you happen to be). If you are a religious person, churches are wonderful places to start. Consider other volunteer organizations. There are so many opportunities available, you can find one or more that fit you and your lifestyle. No matter what or how, get involved locally!

Lastly, you need to cast a shadow in your profession. You have already proven yourself with the military, but in your new profession you're just the "new guy/girl." Become an expert in your field; read, research, take a class or get a degree. Make friends, find mentors, write something in your field, blog, invent something and apply for a patent. Do something that helps you excel and stand out from the crowd.

Maintaining the relationships takes time and energy. It is very tempting to think that we can go it alone. Well, go it alone with our cell phones, instant messaging, and internet. Hey, who needs to deal with people face to face in the age of instant, always on, constant communications? That's a path to a lonely and colorless professional and personal life which none of us want What we do want is the ability to live a rich life, surrounded by friends and family and having the means to live comfortably.

Core Concepts mapping

Core One – You are NOT like the others. You already know the value of building personal and professional relationships. You were literally torn down and rebuilt in the service to function as part of team.

Core Two – You have been forged in fires your peers can't understand. You've seen the disastrous results of favoritism. You understand that you can only tolerate a certain deviation from the needs of the team (now business or personal relationships) before just one teammate brings everything down. You've likely watched brilliant, compassionate individuals and leaders become totally blocked and reduced to irrelevance by organizations and individuals who valued their power over doing the right thing.

Core Five – You have skills and capabilities that are marketable. You bring a wealth of experience, relevant skills, and professionalism to the workplace, organization, or circle of friends.

Core Six – You have gaps in your skills and capabilities that you need to close. You understand that it's not enough to be good. You need to build your social and professional networks and tend them constantly.

Core Eight – Life is still hard. No matter what you do, favoritism is found in every job, organization and circle of friends and it is not going away. Be careful not to become part of a toxic relationship. It might serve you well for a brief period, but the long-term damage to your reputation could be devastating.

Personal Perspective:

You may not know it, but the Wall Street financial powerhouses are directly enabled by technology. There is a constant battle for innovation and competitive advantage in all aspects of that business, specifically in Information Technology. Competition for top talent, particularly high end, multi-language coders (writers of computer code) is brutal. Salaries and bonuses for top talent can soar into the hundreds of thousands of dollars. We once had a guy who was the best of the best. He could write more and better code in a day that most top tier coders could complete in two weeks. There was no doubt that he followed his own path, sleeve tats and all, but it didn't matter because he was a maestro when it came to coding. He might have been the best in the business, but we fired him anyway because he was a disruptive, unmitigated ass who alienated every person who tried to support him. He let his need to act out interfere with his talent and career. Buyer beware.

Chapter 5 – Family First

You dedicated a portion of your life to the service and defense of our great country. You are, by definition, a better American than most of the people with whom you will come into contact, and this will hold true for the rest of your life. I'm not saying this sarcastically or facetiously as these are truths, regardless of personal politics, that we hold self-evident.

However, your family has suffered from your absence and missed you when you could not be there with them. If you are still in the service, you may have limited ability to affect your time and presence, keep doing your best. If you are out, or on the way out, put your family first! Don't assume you are on the same page with your family because of your stellar military career, accomplishments, or leadership style. In many cases, your decisions have overwhelmed what your family wants and needs because they understood your limited options while serving. It's time to start paying back your family's sacrifices. You need to work as a unit and you, sir or madam, may have a hole to dig out of.

You've likely never had enough time with your family while serving. You know that something must change to get that time with loved ones and now is the time to correct that deficiency. Make this a priority now and hold to it.

A very senior military mentor once advised that it would be good to keep a running record of your experiences in the military. Many career officers keep a diary and if you kept a record of the good things about the military and the things you didn't like, I wonder how many of the negatives in your journal would have been about the missed family moments.

Your family needs you present and in the moment. They need as much of you as they can get, and they need you there for the everyday grind. They need you to help make memories; they need you to listen when they are hurting or confused. They need you, with all your flaws and shortcomings.

Quality time is a silly concept; what you really need is quantity and quality. Find the time to let them talk to you and take the time to become a better listener. Can you recite ten favorites each family member has? How about five? Can you name their closest friends? What about silly mundane things in their everyday life? You can't get there by a little Q&A or memorizing lists, you need to listen, and you need to think about what you are hearing. Depending on the amount of time you served and how much your family had to put up with, you may have more than a little resentment pent up. It's your job to release the pressure and normalize the family.

You probably think you are a good to great communicator. After all, the military demands you always communicate clearly and effectively , particularly when under tremendous stress. But here we are not talking about the same communication skills because those skills you used in your military life can be a huge derailing factor when dealing with your family and civilians. Non-service members don't have the communications discipline to get past the brunt and direct modes. In the Intro, the point was made that you don't speak their language and, no matter how much you've influenced your own family, it is highly likely that they don't want to talk to you in a military mode either. Right now, you're probably thinking the banter and the sharing in your unit counts for something and you're right. If you think about the time you spent with your unit, you will realize that you spent more time with them than you did with your family. You need to learn to listen to your family like you listened to those in your unit. You need to slow down and you need to start shedding the hyper-focused communication styles indoctrinated into you by the service.

There is an enormous difference between the ways that males and females communicate. A favorite analogy is that males like one "concept" box open in their heads at a time, while females have multiple "concept" boxes going at all times. The same females can comfortably transition across these disparate boxes in a relatively short conversation. This usually leaves a male in the conversation playing confused catch-up, like a pilot who gets "behind the aircraft" while flying. There is an informative video series by Mark Gungor on YouTube who is the Lead Pastor of Celebration Church which I highly recommend you take the time to watch.

Men, the women in your life generally need to exchange more words with you than the men and boys in your life. Women are often unfairly stereotyped as talkers and in many cases, this is because they get so little time with their spouses that they try to fit in as much of their world as they can in the limited time they have with you. You need to listen first and then do the things that are critically important to them. There's a huge gold mine buried in that listening because the women in our lives generally aren't asking you to "fix" everything they talk to you about; they are simply sharing. If you are not sure, simply ask them if they want help, don't assume. The males in our lives are usually more direct, they want to go straight to the doing and will talk during that time and open up to you.

Ladies, you may have just the opposite issue with the men in your life because they may not open up to you when they really need to. Take the time to let them talk to you *and listen*.

Listening is a critical skill. How else will you know what drives your spouses, children, and other family members? Listen as much as you can, do it with intent and focus. Don't pick apart the story or narrative. Listen with your heart and with your soul. Don't assume that your filter or perspective is the same as theirs, particularly with children. This is deadly serious. If they don't belong at home, they will find a place to belong. Too many of our young ones stray from the family into destructive behavior and in the more extreme cases, suicide.

It's hard to rebuild and maintain intimacy and trust. These things only happen over time and with constant reinforcement. If you have room for improvement in these areas, do those things that make a difference.

Find the time for your family. Find it every day and treat every moment like a precious jewel that will shatter if you don't hold it tight. Make memories to last you to the end of your days, and those of your children and grandchildren. Take your family to places and events that celebrate life. Live an epic life and share it with your family.

Core Concepts mapping

Core One – You are NOT like the others. Military families understand sacrifice. They understand unpredictable hours and long deployments. You have missed more than your fair share of time with your children and/or your spouse. That is time that most civilian families have together, and it is time you can't get back.

Core Four – You are uniquely prepared to manage your own future. You've been trained to be goal oriented. You've grown up in a culture that expects success and it's time to put that experience to good use for your nuclear and extended family. They need you in the now with them, not just on holidays or special occasions. Figure it out and be there for them.

Core Six – You have gaps in your skills and capabilities that you need to close. In the body of this chapter we stated that the concept of quality time was silly, and it is. You need to create room in your life for quantity time with your family. This may be uncomfortable for you as you have so much to do and likely very driven to succeed. Take the time to realize that success without your family is the classic definition of failure.

Core Seven – You now have more responsibility for your life and much more opportunity to screw it up. Your service life was scripted, and you had little control over the what and the when. That has changed. Will you take advantage of your new life and make time with your family the highest priority?

Core Eight – Life is still hard. There still won't be enough hours in the day to accomplish everything you want or need to do. You won't have full control over your life if you will be working in your post service era. It's up to you to prioritize and protect your schedule to give you and your family what you need.

Personal perspective:

Family matters; some have less fondness of family than others. Unless you are completely alienated from your family, consider staying close. As I was working in the early AM on the initial draft of this section I received a call from one of the managers in the division that reports to me. He's a good friend and sharp fellow and he was driving a hundred miles to Waco TX to be with his Father who had suddenly fallen ill. The outcome is uncertain but what is certain is that this son was close enough and caring enough to be at his Father's side in less than two hours. The wonder of jet transport can let us be almost anywhere in the world within 24 hours. But you need to ask yourself if you should be closer to your aging parents. It is the nature of the world that children leave, but should they and more importantly should YOU return at some point?

Chapter 6 – Goal Setting

This is the most important concept in this book; we've all heard it, set goals for yourself. You need goals for one, three and five years at a minimum. Even if you have set goals, how well have you executed against that plan? You must be brutally honest in your self-assessment.

In your lifetime, how many goals have you set and achieved on your own? When at, or approaching, the exit threshold of your service you will realize that most of your goals have been set for you or dictated by the requirements of the service. For this exercise, list only the goals that you set outside of the service framework.

If you did set goals, did you achieve them on time? How many did you abandon for *any* reason? Unfortunately, for most, when you look at the empirical data, you have likely been less successful with goal achievement than your ego-driven perspective thinks. The reason for this is *because life gets in the way*. Even if you have done well, there is still room for improvement. The good news is that you can and will get better at it.

In the previous chapter we emphasized the need to put family first, but you still have a lot to do. You must put food on the table, pay for healthcare and deliver on a myriad of other things. But while those things are in the present, you also need to start thinking about the future and what you want out of it. This is not advice to map out in advance, every dollar and cent spent and every decision you need to make. Think of it as a framework for those things that you want out of life. How do you go from current state A to interim state B and then to target state C and beyond?

The most important part of goal setting and realization is amazingly simple and effective with just two steps;.

> **Step One:** Create a goal and write it down.

> **Step Two:** Consistently measure your progress against your goal.

In business, you will often hear the term "SMART" goal setting. The acronym SMART incorporates the following concepts (if you haven't seen this before, don't let it overwhelm you, it becomes simple and easy to use after a just a little effort):

S – Specific: You need to define exactly what you want to accomplish along with the details of who, what, where and why.

M – Measurable: How will you measure and track your progress towards your goal? How will you know when you have achieved the goal?

A – Attainable: Is this possible? Can you actually achieve this goal? Stretch goals are encouraged, but you must have a reasonable belief that the goal can be accomplished and at least a rough understanding the critical path to the goal.

R – Realistic: Does this goal move you in the direction you want or need to go? It should be complimentary to your overall direction or passion in life.

T – Timing: All goals should have a timeframe or in other words, be time-bound. If you don't set the achieve-by date, you will never accomplish the goal.

Let's take a seemingly simple goal and examine what is needed to understand and achieve it. Set the goal of "I want to be wealthy" for this exercise. It may sound silly, but I submit that you might want to make this one of your goals.

- **Specific:** Immediately you will see that you need to add more specificity. We have the high-level concept of what (get rich), but that's not good enough. You need to specifically state what "rich" means to you. How much money is required to be rich? Is it rich as in the amount of dollars in liquid assets? Does rich mean that you have no debt and a modest income without having to work? You need to fill in the details. For this goal, you might want to add the specificity of using net worth as your prime metric. Then you might want to include the value of your car, house, or other personal items, but in that case, you have to consider their CASH value, not what you want them to be worth. In this example, skip the house, car, and personal stuff.

- **Measurable:** This is critical to achieve any goal. What is your starting point? How will you measure your progress and know when you've achieved the goal? For this example, create a measurement system that includes your current net worth, a measurement frequency for evaluation and monies available for this goal (income minus expenses). With those things we can plot our time horizon. If you find the period is unacceptable, you should go back and think about what you can do to shorten the period. Can you get a higher paying job? Can you create one or more additional streams of income? Can you cut expenses? Reviewing the data provided by your measurement process allows you to tune and tweak you next decisions based on factual information. Do your actions result in the desired outcome? Are you moving in the correct direction? If not, what can you change?

- **Attainable:** Becoming wealthy is a very attainable goal in the United States. While it might be a big stretch goal, we can now start talking about how much money we have, defining the time horizon and determining what it takes to make that goal happen.

- **Realistic:** Let's talk about the *How*. We know *What* you want, but in defining the *How* you are also examining if it is something that you can accomplish. This is different than "attainable" in that with hard work and perseverance, most goals can be achieved. Get a degree, own a house, retire early, own your own business are all realistic goals. However, some goals are not realistic: becoming the head of your favorite University next year, solving world hunger, etc. We certainly want to aim high, but can you really get there? Is your goal realistic? This is your sanity check. Can you really do this? Do you have the education, resources, time, drive and whatever else it might take to achieve something that is technically possible, but realistically out of your reach?

- **Timing:** Now it gets interesting. We've examined and set the *What, the Why and the How* of the goal. Now it's time to review and set the When. Throw out the big bang approach where your expectations are roughly "I'm a good person and if I work really hard I should automatically achieve my goals." The world doesn't care about you or your goals. You need a plan and you need to execute, which means you also need to time box your goals. Create goals, supporting sub-goals and realistic timelines that you can measure your progress against. If you are not familiar with multi-generational planning (basically up from your current position), then please take some time to learn about it.

So far, we've looked at a sterile SMART framework, then loosely mapped the methodology over a generic goal. This is not the actual framework; this is the first step in the goal definition process. Read on for a step-by-step suggestion on how to frame, track and achieve your goals. Keep in mind that you need incremental successes for both your piece of mind and those that are depending on you.

The process of creating goals is always recursive and takes a while to figure out, but it is well worth the effort. Along the way you will become the expert for your goal. The next part is a bit harder, and requires you to work consistently towards your goal(s) at every opportunity. What data do you need, how long does it take, how will you persevere and track your progress (spreadsheets are great for this) are all components of goal setting that you must follow. You should also take every opportunity to learn as much as you can about methods and techniques to help you achieve your goal as well as what not to do to sabotage reaching your goal.

Some Sample Goals

Family

- Being a good spouse
- Being a good parent
- Private school for children
- Home ownership
- Helping aging parents
- Geographical location for employment and lifestyle
- Vacations

Financial

- Net worth targets
- Owning your own business
- College expense for you and/or children
- Increasing healthcare costs Disposable income
- Traveling
- Luxury items
- Hobbies

- Financial advisor

Health and Fitness Goals

- Mental acuity
- Aging gracefully
- Managing your illnesses
- Active lifestyle target
- Exercise
- Competitions
- Activity-specific training

Knowledge and Expertise

- College degree
- Marketable skills
- Craftsmanship
- Developing artistic skills

The number of goals you should have at any given time depends on you and a few other factors. One of the primary considerations is distance over time, meaning where you are starting from, what your target state is and what timeline you have set to achieve your goal. You only have so much energy and time available each day to devote to any given goal. If you remember in Core Concept 6, we stated that it takes about 1,000 hours of practice and effort just to become "good" at a skill and as many as 10,000 hours to master that same skill. In some cases, you will have to master a skill to reach your goal, but in others you should consider alternatives. The easiest call is to engage an expert to help you, particularly with your wealth management goals. This doesn't mean you should skip taking that accounting class or ignore learning about investment options, it simply means you should buy the expertise to get started now while you develop your own expertise so you can guide and evaluate the quality of results you get from your provider.

For each goal set, you should seek out mentors who can help guide you. The less of the required expertise you have to reach the target state of a goal, the more imperative this becomes. A good mentor is one of the hardest things in life to find. When you do find one, you may have to be persistent in convincing them to take you on but don't give up if at first they turn you away. It's worth almost any effort as having an expert mentor can make the difference between long-term success and failure. Don't forget to show your appreciation to your mentor, not by fawning obeisance, but by paying attention, acting on the coaching, and intelligently discussing options. Pay it forward by becoming a mentor when the opportunity arises.

Here's a small bit of advice: when you hire a professional to help you or you are fortunate enough to find a good mentor, stop talking and listen. Ask questions, listen to the responses, and then ask more questions. The more important the decision and its ramifications are, the more input you need. Don't blindly hire someone and turn over your decisions to them. In situations where you know you have knowledge gaps; you need to listen. Listen, listen, and listen more. Take notes. Sleep on the information and give your subconscious some time to digest and contextualize. Too often we see ex-service members waxing poetically about all the things they've seen and experienced and not listening to those around who have relevant experience they need to understand. Sea stories are great and entertaining, but when pursuing any goal, you need to focus on where you want to go far more than talking about where you've been.

There are usually multiple ways to achieve a goal. You may choose to follow a single path, or you may find that managing multiple paths will help you reach your goal more effectively. Regardless of what path or paths you choose, you must continually measure your progress against your target state and the timeline you have chosen. Don't be surprised when you have set backs because life will get in the way. But given your personal history, you already know how to get back on your feet and get moving again. Continue to move forward, sometimes running, sometimes falling but always getting back up and taking another step in the right direction.

Here is another way you might approach a goal with a set timeframe. For purposes of this example, let's use five years as the timeframe. A simple three-part methodology is all you need. Your personal early-warning sensors should start firing any time someone tells you that anything is "easy," and this is no exception to that rule. There are, however only three steps.

Step 1: Pick your time frame. Done! 5 years

Step 2: Write a first draft of what and where you want to be at the end of the next five years. This is your goal so write it in a way you're comfortable; first person narrative, third person. Choose the method with which you are most comfortable and write from the perspective of having achieved your goals and are looking back. Cover all the important aspects of your life that you think of. You may find this part to be a significant journey of discovery about yourself and those you care about;

- What does the Family look like? Married? Spouse, children, mom and dad, brothers and sisters, nieces and nephews and grandparents. Where would they be in life and how would you help them achieve their dreams and goals?
- How do you define success over the last five years?
- How is your business/professional life?
- How is your health?
- What are your top three achievements over the last five years?
- Have you made new friends or reconnected with old ones? How many friends do you have?
- What routines have you established that help you with your business, family, and health?
- What do people in your community say about you, your business, family, and health?
- What has made you deeply and genuinely happy over these last five years?

Step 3: This is the hard part. For most of us, creating a private set of goals means they will never reach fruition. You need to share! Take this first draft and share it with your spouse, parents, and friends. Work up your courage, put on your thick skin and get some feedback. You were in the service for goodness sake, you can take it! Get the feedback, update the plan and then you are ready to launch.

Apply the same rules as above, be SMART, identify the gaps, the resources, and alliances you need and the LAUNCH into your five-year goal. This is not to be confused with the old Soviet Union "Five Year Plan" process. If you've never heard of that process and its spectacular failures, it is well worth a little research.

Work and review your goals list every day. Try to align your daily activities with your goals where you can. Many days will find you consumed with the myriad of tasks of life as it gets in the way. Work smart here also. Start you day by examining and prioritizing the tasks you may need to address. Sort into the following four categories codified by President Dwight Eisenhower. The concept of this sorting and prioritization has been around for a long time, and regardless of its origin, it's a winner:

1. Important and urgent.
2. Important but not urgent.
3. Not important but urgent.
4. Not important and not urgent

In the simplest example, you should sort ALL your tasks into these categories, and by focusing on the first two categories you will eliminate most of the time you waste focused on the wrong things. You should spend most of your efforts in category two "Important but not urgent." If you are spending the bulk of your time in category one "Important and urgent" then your world is out of balance and you need to take a hard look at why you are fighting so many fires. If you spend any serious time at all in categories three and four, you are letting others program your day, so stop that immediately. Be polite and change expectations but try to stop working in categories three and four immediately.

Start each day by sorting and prioritizing the work (both professional and personal) into some type of framework that makes sense to you. Eisenhower's method has proven worth, and I encourage you to give it a try. Several studies have shown that the optimal amount of time you can focus is about 45 minutes. Be organized, tackle the most important things first and most of all don't be distracted by social media.

As you work toward your goal(s) make sure you are brutally honest with yourself about your progress. The minute you start rationalizing or ignoring your lack of progress you begin to fail. You have finite resources, so manage them well. When you aren't making enough progress, explore your options and make changes.

Don't expect money to solve all your problems. It is almost pathetically easy to generate more income out of the service than what you were paid while still in. Depending on your skills, you could be banking two to ten times more income almost overnight. But if you chase exclusively after that paycheck, the rest of your life will suffer and fall apart or fall away from you. Create a balanced approach to your post service life and put family first. Don't expect your family to be happy that you are gone again no matter how much money you earn.

Execute, adapt, assess, and learn. No plan survives contact with the enemy. Expect to adjust, but keep making progress. Whatever your goal, keep doing those things that move you closer to your objectives.

Core Concepts mapping

Core One – You are NOT like the others. You have a record of accomplishments. You understand goal setting and how to achieve goals.

Core Four – You are uniquely prepared to manage your own future. You have had a lot of time to think about your future after the service. You have the drive, the will, and the right attitude.

Core Six – You have gaps in your skills and capabilities that you need to close. Unless you managed a separate business or career while in the service, you have a lot to learn and you need coaches, mentors, and trusted advisors. Start now.

Core Eight – Life is still hard. Bad stuff still happens and there are so many things you have no control over. Important persons in our lives will come and go. Your finances may suffer unexpectedly. Mistakes will be made.

Core Nine – The Republic is powered by the engine of Capitalism. You need a plan to cover basic expenses and provide for enough discretionary funds for your quality of life. If you don't have enough income to cover both, then change something. Acquire new skills, get a better job, open your own business, cut back on expenses...but do something.

Personal Perspective

I had just been promoted to Officer at a large regional bank, I was a bit surprised when I was called into the office of one of the most senior leaders in the building.

Earl, a Senior Vice President, was a small framed but very fit man in his 50s. He and I had rarely spoken, and I had heard he had been a terror to his subordinates in years past, so I was understandably nervous as I sat in his office. He sat there for a few minutes, not saying anything. His simple scrutiny was intimidating. After a bit, he reached into a desk drawer and said, "I'm going to do you a favor that no one ever did for me." The document he shared was his personal 401K statement. No kidding, he showed me his actual balances and investments. He took the time to help me understand the value of planning for my personal future. His mentoring helped me change my perspective on savings and planning for retirement. You see, I was killing myself for this company and becoming highly effective, *just like I learned to do in the service*, but was ignoring critical things I needed to be doing to be successful later in life. Thank goodness for Earl and the time he took with me.

Chapter 7 – What's next (travel or settle)

So, what are you going to do? Have you picked out a nice place to live out your days, or are you open to travel and new experiences?

In general, travel is good for you. Not the "drive by" travel of military deployments, or even the overseas duty you may have experienced for a couple of years. Even if you were extremely adventurous, made friends and developed relationships with the local culture, you probably went to work on an Americanized base (American fast food and laundromats). When we say travel, we are talking about an immersive cultural experience. Live on the local economy and work within it, become fluent in the local language, learn to appreciate the history and geography. If you do this, you will experience tremendous benefits that help give perspective that will frame your life and direction. The owners of many successful businesses traveled widely early in life and continue to do so as part of their business. The US, or whatever country you reside in, is not the sole purveyor good ideas. Not every idea in every culture is a match for other cultures and markets, but the exposure and perspective gained is immensely valuable.

Traveling and living on the local economy will give you and your family an appreciation of the world and many of the things that we've begun to take for granted in the US. In all but a rare few cases, those that travel and live aboard will eventually return to the US, realizing that your home country is the greatest of all countries in the world. The US Constitution, Bill of Rights and the effective rule of law gives us freedom of speech, freedom to practice our religion and the best legal protections in the world.

In the 19th century, the British army had a saying often quoted during my service, and I think it can be used as a compliment to this topic.

"A Subaltern may not marry,
Captains might marry,
Majors should marry,
and Lieutenant-Colonels must marry."

I believe a person in their twenties should travel if possible, particularly to culturally rich environments. They can advance their formal education and skills while doing. A person in their thirties should be settling in and should only travel if they can take their family with them. A person in their forties should travel for business and vacation and should be near their parents if possible.

Family is important. Some of you reading this book will have had less than stellar familial experiences as a child and young adult. If this applies to you and you are alienated from your family, you have become the Patriarch or Matriarch and you need to get it right for your children. At some point, that probably means establishing a place they can call home. If you don't have a home or area to return to, then pick a place and make it your own. If you are fortunate enough to have close ties to your family and to a place called "home," consider settling in close by. Your children need their Grandparents, Cousins and Aunts and Uncles. Yes, in many cases, family and friends are like fish, as they all start to smell after three days of close contact, but the rich family life for your children they provide has no equivalent.

If you know where you want to settle, make a plan about when you expect to move and get your finances aligned. Buy some land, buy a house (consider rental it until you are ready to purchase) or be creative and make other plans. If possible, home ownership should be part of your plan. At the right time, execute your plan.

Unfortunately, as our parents age, too many children reverse the parent-child roles. Under certain circumstances this is appropriate, but usually it is not. Our parents will never stop seeing us as their children. If you push too hard and try to control your parent, you will eventually meet a solid wall of unmovable force. The most important thing, I think, is that you are present in their lives and available to help.

Core Concepts mapping

Core One – You are NOT like the others. If you've traveled with your military services you already understand why living in the US is one of the greatest privileges available to the free world. That doesn't necessarily transfer directly to your family. Consider a next phase that enriches their life by letting them live in a place that is not the US.

Core Six – You have gaps in your skills and capabilities that you need to close. Even if you were stationed overseas you may not have the language or cultural know-how to blend in. Consider living in a non-English speaking country as an opportunity to develop and hone language and interpersonal skills.

Core Seven – You now have more responsibility for your life and much more opportunity to screw it up. You must make a choice about where you will choose to live. Just going with the flow is not the best choice, so be smarter than that and be very deliberate when you make this decision.

Core Eight – Life is still hard. These are hard choices. You may find that you have a time-boxed opportunity to sell your services to a military contractor or other employment entity. If you don't do so right out of the service, you may not get another chance. The tradeoffs may be significant.

Core Nine – The Republic is powered by the engine of Capitalism. Consider any job outside of the US carefully. There are places where even a high salary is negated by the cost of living on the local economy or other expenses such as traveling back and forth to the US. At the conclusion of any OUTUS period, what will be the impact on your personal finances? Net increase (fantastic)? Neutral (not bad)? Negative (less desirable but could be worth it to learn a more marketable skill set or live in a "bucket list" location).

Personal perspective:

Whether getting out or staying in, do what YOU want, not what others want you to do. If married, you must get your spouse's opinion, as both need to be happy with the decision. When I was presented with this decision, my wife and I discussed the possibilities of moving overseas and starting a new chapter in our lives. We were only three years into our marriage and incredibly happy together with our young daughter.

There were a lot of positives; life overseas would have been very educational for our daughter and would have given my wife a chance to see and live in other countries. I've always held that you can't really appreciate United States until you've lived in another country.

But there were other considerations for us, as we are both very family-oriented and have always been continually active supporting both sides of our family. My parents were a major concern. My dad was getting up there in years, already well into his 70's and not in the best health. I had always been blessed having a great relationship with my parents, and my wife understood how important that was to me. As a result, we both realized that moving so far away wasn't the best choice. We both agreed to stay put and the following year I left the Navy. Both of us were happy, we were surrounded by good friends, had good jobs, and had a new house with lots of children in the neighborhood for my daughter to play with.

This was the best decision we could have made. Our son was born shortly after and sadly mom died a couple of months after his birth. The fact she had the joy of seeing my son before we lost her was more gratifying and important to us than the opportunities missed by not traveling and living overseas. After my mother passed away, it was important for us to be there for Dad because he needed us for support as he and Mom had been married for over 58 years. Surprisingly, we found that we needed him more than ever. My father lived for many more years and passed at the wonderful age of 95. In retrospect, my wife and I both believe that being there for him was what kept him going until he was able to resume his active life after the death of my mother.

What I am trying to say is do what you really want to do, talk it through with your spouse (if married) and do your best to be happy. Remember, most decisions you make can be changed if you chose a path that doesn't make you happy.

Happiness, trust, and love are the three things that will make you and your spouse thrive for many years to come.

Chapter 8 – Your next job

The title of this chapter poses an interesting question. What will your next job be? Perhaps, if you have retired from the service, you are questioning if you will ever have another "job." Perhaps a new career, one less centric to your training and specialty and more oriented to something you've always wanted to do? Or will you stay the course and stay aligned to your training and expertise?

If you are interested in working with the government in any capacity, please review the "Veteran's Preference" information in the reference section at the back of this book. You will find information about the Veterans' preference and the administration of preference in Federal employment. (5 U.S.C. 2108, 2108a).

Competition is fierce in today's workforce and you may not be the best qualified candidate. Statistically speaking, over 70% of the US labor force is looking for a job, including people who are unemployed and actively seeking work; employed and actively seeking work and those who are employed and open to a new job.

What civilian jobs are you qualified to fill? A simple web search will provide you with multiple resources you can use for translating your expertise (officer or enlisted) to suggested civilian occupations and fields. Any links we provide to a given site would likely be broken or outdated by the time this gets to you, so when you're ready for this step our recommendation is to perform searches on phrases such as "translate military skills to civilian jobs," "military skills translator" or "civilian to military occupation." It is crucial that you use multiple resources to explore your options; find at least three sites you like to explore possible new career paths.

While searching for jobs is a challenge, the good news is the income you can generate as a civilian can start at 50% _more_ than your total military compensation. Achieving a multiple, yes, a multiple of your total military compensation is not out of reach. And for a service member this can be like winning the lottery at separation. You can affect the "multiple" by being smart and targeting your searches. You won't get the big win unless you have a valuable skill and relevant experience. The Department of Labor keeps good statistics that include salary ranges, mean and max salaries, job fill rates and perhaps most importantly, the number of jobs in a given area. The sample information below was pulled from this very well-designed website;

Occupation	Employed number	Employment per 1000 jobs	Median hourly wage	Mean hourly wage	Annual mean wage
Doctors – General & Family practice	124,810	.924	$86.63	$89.58	$186,320
Computer Hardware Engineers	76,360	.565	$52.13	$53.20	$110,650
Pharmacists	290,780	2.152	$58.15	$56.96	$118,470
Software Developers	382,400	2.83	$49.46	$50.98	$106,050
Farmers and Ranchers	4,300	.032	$32.72	$34.89	$72,570
Police and Sheriff Patrol Officers	638,810	4.727	$27.31	$28.64	$59,560
Graphic Designers	197,540	1.462	$22.07	$24.36	$50,670
Postal Service Workers	501,000	3.708	$26.01	$24.35	$50.650

http://www.bls.gov/oes/current/oessrcst.htm

Note: Annual wages have been calculated by multiplying the hourly mean wage by a "year-round, full-time" hours figure of 2,080 hours; for those occupations where there is not an hourly mean wage published, the annual wage has been directly calculated from the reported survey data.

Keep in mind that family still comes first, and anyone separating from the service should immediately consider themselves on notice if they have a family or friends that need to be held close. Your first job is to strengthen those ties. Define "strengthen" any way you choose, but realize that this is job one. Humans are social creatures and your interactions with loved ones should define your life. A favorite saying goes like this "your job doesn't love you, but your family does." Think about that. Another way to look at your relationships is to ask yourself if what people would say at your funeral if you passed today. Sounds morbid, yes, but think about it. Would someone say you were a hard worker and good employee, or would you want them to describe you as a terrific parent and spouse with anecdotes and wonderful stories from your life? During your time in service, your sacrifices for your country (thank you) have left you with limited options. You must now define who you will be and how you will spend your time.

Keep this basic theme in mind: don't be unemployed or underemployed. Try to work within your field of expertise, even if you are underemployed. It is much easier to transition from an underemployed state to a fully employed state than it is to get hired on from an unemployed state. The direct implication of being unemployed and seeking a job is that there are people with the skills and talent for that field, of which you are not included. The reason why you are unemployed seldom matters, just being unemployed seems to have a negative impact when trying to gain employment. If your last employer didn't value you, why should someone hire you? Even if you weren't terminated for cause or incompetence, your skills are rusting away. Brutal? Yes. Universally constant? Almost.

Second brutal thought; Countless books and self-help experts will tell you "do something you love, and you will never work a day in your life." The next part of their pitch is to get you to buy into a product, subscription, franchise, or something else they are selling. Let's say it again; remember these experts are selling you something even if it's just their book (no irony here!). This is pure marketing and is an absolute fiction. People who own their own businesses are the hardest working folks you will ever meet.

Third brutal thought; Be prepared to lower your expectations as you transition to civilian life, at least initially. It is sometimes difficult to find a position that matches your experience, skills, and education, especially if you want to live in a particular location. Statistics tell us that only about one-third of Veterans are employed at their skill level while two-thirds are under employed. The responsibilities of a twenty-something or thirty-something officer or NCO don't necessarily map well into the civilian world.

Remember this? Core Concept One – You are NOT like the others; You are a unique combination of hard-won skills, experience and maturity that are far ahead of your physical age and those of your civilian educated peer group. This is particularly true for ages twenty-two to thirty and for all ages when considering the direct application of military knowledge and training.

So, given that your leadership skills and experience are off the chart compared to your civilian peers, lower your expectations. Perhaps it is better stated that you should realign your expectations of your technical skills vs. your leadership skills. As you prove your metal in your chosen profession, leadership opportunities will present themselves. When said opportunities crop up, don't let them slip through your fingers. Even if you feel like they may be above your paygrade, that's your civilian normalization talking because you probably had more responsibility in the service, so go for it!

What about SMBs (small to medium businesses) and you? Abso-*insert favorite emphasizing profanity here*-lutely! Consider this a ringing endorsement for working at and/or owning an SMB. Owning your own service business (low to no inventory) is one of the fastest tracks to true wealth.

Let's go to the U.S. Bureau of Labor Statistics for some general facts about SMBs. They fuel the engine of capitalism; they employ most of the US population and they are the primary creators of new jobs. They are also the primary path to true wealth for their owners. Warning: almost half of SMBs will fail by the two-year mark. If you can get to the five-year mark you are much more likely to succeed. As the high-level statistics indicate, owning an SMB is not easy, but it is doable. Even if you love your business, you still must deal with a never-ending avalanche of details, interactions, and negotiations. It's still a job and instead of coming to work in the morning and leaving at the end of your business day, you must manage taxes, bills, regulations, laws, liability, leases, depreciation, insurance, healthcare, payroll, inspectors, customers, suppliers, supply and demand, marketing, contracts, cancelled orders, shipping, employees, theft, fraud…and so on ad infinitum.

So, is owning an SMB worth it? Well, that's up to you. You can become wealthy if you have a marketable skill and aren't a complete troll to work with, but you must live within your means, save aggressively, invest well and (hopefully) develop multiple streams of income. Remember, as explained in our Core Seven tenant "You now have more responsibility for your life, and much more opportunity to screw it up."

Don't think that because you "like" or "enjoy" something that you can be successful in running a business. Successful in this case would be defined as being able to support your target lifestyle which includes hours worked, affording time off, hobbies and the ability to spend time with your family. Jumping in without being prepared is equivalent to throwing away your hard-earned money. Many coaches recommend working for someone else in the industry for a couple of years before starting your own business. If the business you choose has a small margin for profit and depends on the careful management of lots of moving parts and expenses, then this is absolutely the way to go. You need a product or service that people will pay for. You need to market and manage the cost and quality of the product or service.

Having a mentor or coach with experience in the targeted or a related sector is literally worth a million dollars. Not kidding here, to avoid failure you need a coach-mentor. You may be particularly good with your marketable skill/service/product (as in having at least 1,000 hours of creating and delivering it) but there are masters who have over 10,000 hours and have already paid the price in lost opportunity and mistakes. Find someone who will mentor you and you will never regret it. Having a mentor doesn't mean he or she has a secret recipe for success; it means that you develop a relationship with someone who understands the business sector, can share old successes and mistakes and can be there to talk with you and have healthy debate as you work through new challenges.

Regardless of what sector you choose, be prepared to work harder than you've ever worked in your life. We're not talking about the mind-numbing effort of extended ops here, but the continuous learning in a fast-paced environment type of hard work. Trying is great but counts for ABSOLUTELY NOTHING, and can still get you fired. You need to cross the finish line. Adopt that mentality and never lose it.

Time works for you in your investments and against you in your career. Don't forget that the 30-year-old you is not as quick as the 20-year-old you, and not just physically. For example, it's well documented that scientists publish fewer scientifically relevant papers as they move into their 40's. By age 50, they are publishing more papers and may be more widely cited, but the actual innovative, ground-breaking scientific impact is lessened. A key point here is that as they age, they begin to rely on older material, the implication being that they are less familiar (pick a reason) with new papers and research and rely on data learned earlier in their career. This can become a career death spiral.

You can probably still hang with the best into your 40's and maybe into your early 50's if you work hard in your field of expertise. After that, things get much harder mentally and physically. You absolutely don't want to be doing an outside, dangerous, brutal job in your 50's and 60's because you will wear out your body. If you don't take care of your body, what should be your "golden years" will be the most miserable era of your life. You also don't want to be competing with the 20 somethings for state-of-the-art comprehensive knowledge in a very technical field as you get into your late 40s and older. Plan well and acknowledge that you are aging (body and brain) and take compensating actions with respect to your employment. Your experience is valuable, particularly your ability to manage risk-reward issues.

When coaching employees, a favorite analogy is the soldier who just wants to drive a tank. This person is happiest and most fulfilled when dealing directly with maintenance, training and operations that involves their tank. They have no desire to lead a Tank Battalion, Company or even a small Tank Platoon. They just want to drive their tank; it's what gets them going in the morning and makes them feel whole. For this discussion, it's important that you understand this concept. Our tank driver does not want any type of change that takes them away from the hands-on, day- to-day work of operating their tank. While they are certainly willing to transition to a new model, this person wants to stay in the driver's seat of a tank, period. Our soldier doesn't care about stripes, promotions or pay. The only ambition is to be the world's best tank driver.

Every military should reward and encourage this type of hyper-focus, but unfortunately, every military does just the opposite. They are not receptive to this idea of the perpetual tank driver. They don't want a 30 or 40-something tank driver. They want to see that person promote and leverage their training and expertise for a larger impact. After all, who doesn't want more responsibility and reward? Unfortunately, our perpetual tank driver will always be fighting the system and viewed as a flawed element in the command structure.

The civilian world is more receptive to the idea of a focused, experienced specialist. This is particularly true in hands-on type jobs that require specialized training or skills. As an example, effective project management can be a game changer, but most companies aren't willing to pay as much for an experienced project manager as they are for people with tightly focused skills that are considered to provide a competitive advantage. These are usually "master level" specialists (10K hours of training and solution delivery). These extremely specific skill set jobs are always in high demand and always pay a premium. Persons with matching qualifications will be hired as fast as they can get you on the phone, and at often ridiculous pay rates.

Many jobs are less specific in terms of qualifications, and pay accordingly. Hence the advice to "obtain a marketable skill" and keep your knowledge fresh and cutting edge. You can make a good living on the edges of the market with jobs that don't require specific skills, but you are always on "first to go" list when it comes time to trim the budget.

Check the latest data from Bureau of Labor Statistics (www.bls.gov) for 2013. This is a useful resource with useful statistical data for over a thousand different job types, including what each pays. We all know there are certainly persons in each profession who earn more and others who are paid less than the average person in any given profession, but the average salary data is a tremendous resource. This would have been fantastic information to have when I was in your position. Choose wisely and enjoy.

Now that you know how much you can earn in your dream job, let's talk about your "brand." Your brand is what the aggregate opinion of what others think of you and your capabilities. You personally, and no one else, must always manage your "brand." Almost always included in your brand are labels and classifications such as:

- ✓ Work ethic
- ✓ Education
- ✓ Social polish
- ✓ Overall professionalism
- ✓ Overall talent (how well rounded you are in business)
- ✓ Specific talent (job you were hired for)
- ✓ Emotional IQ (attitude, plays well with others, how you handle adversity)
- ✓ Leadership potential (within this unit, division, company)
- ✓ Flexibility (ability to adapt to change)
- ✓ Are you a compliment to the team? (team player)
- ✓ Risk management (do you make good decisions)
- ✓ Communications ability (can you communicate up, down and laterally within the org)

At the end of the day, your "brand" defines you. If you ignore it, you allow others to define what they think about you. You may have run into some class "A" a-holes in the service, but most of those were either incompetent or just poorly trained and generally they didn't really matter unless they were in your direct chain of command, and at least parallel or higher in rank. Back in the real world, you will see a whole new class and level of persons who will place obstacles in your path. Some will assassinate your character just because you are prior service person (not joking), and some will block you because they see your competence and abilities as a threat. These folks will come from every strata in a business (above, below, and laterally). Manage your brand, be aggressive, take on the naysayers and you will do fine. Ignore them at the peril of your job. Manage Your Brand.

When considering a "next" job, consider yourself in quantum job states. Why quantum? Because you can be in more than one mode at a time, depending on the point and time as well as who is observing. For this discussion, review these possible states and explore the possibilities of each:

1. Full time position within your current area of expertise

2. Full time position outside of your area of expertise

3. Participate in the "Gig Economy" part time or as a contractor

4. Transitioning to a position targeting a specific field or area of expertise

5. Full time student

6. Part time student

7. Retired, no real job

Let's dig deeper into each of these states. For each quantum job state, consider the following as mandatory:

- Depending on your area of expertise, this state should track most closely to the income vs. age recommendations
- Manage your career path to the level of responsibility desired
- Be prepared to change jobs every 2-4 years if you are not progressing
- Stay current on your skills, even if you must pay for your own training
- Build your social and professional network
- Get involved with your local community, interact and volunteer
- Start managing your money, including investments, 401K, retirement, savings, and insurance
- Stay fit, no one really wants to hire a person who is in poor health and overweight unless that person has savant-level (very rare) skills
- Look for ways to create multiple streams of income (income that does not require you to be present for every transaction)

1. **Full time position within your current area of expertise.** This should be self-explanatory and will likely be your default state. This state will likely provide you the most peace of mind and stability. It will also provide you with the most reliable income (tied to the job type). In this type of job, you have to be careful because you can lose the habit of continuous improvement and learning. Pick an "in-line" job with your current expertise and push yourself to stay abreast of advancements in the field.

2. **Full time position outside of your area of expertise.** After looking and not finding something in their specific field, many will branch out to related but slightly different types of careers. This is the time to learn a new set of skills and develop relationships outside of your comfort zone. Think of this

as a life-enriching path that you may choose to stay with. Alternatively, you may find that you are not fond of this path and can use that as additional motivation to move your career to desired path. Remember, the goal here is to stay employed and preserve an income stream. You should consider going back to school to finish your degree or complete a higher-level qualification. Consider volunteering with an organization that is related to your primary expertise.

3. **Participate in the "Gig Economy" part time or as a Contractor.** In a gig economy, large numbers of people work part-time or temporary positions. With a working theory (not completely accepted) that the impact of a gig economy is cheaper, more efficient services, such as Uber or Airbnb, for those willing to use them. The corollary is that anyone who doesn't embrace using technological services such as the Internet tend to be left behind by the benefits of the gig economy. The most prevalent gig economies are found in the mid-to-large cities. America is making progress towards establishing a gig economy with some estimates showing that as much as a third of the working population is already in some gig capacity. This number is expected to rise, particularly because the digital economy makes it increasingly common for people to work remotely or from home. This facilitates independent contracting work as many of those jobs don't require the freelancer to come in to the office to work. This leads to more flexibility for gig workers and more options to expand their working resume. Unfortunately, it also comes with downsides. One of the biggest downsides is the lack of health care, which is always shockingly expensive when we have to bear the full brunt of the cost. Additionally, not all employers chose to hire contractors, especially those outside of traditional contractor staffing models. For some workers forced into gig job, the nature of gigs can very disrupt work-life balance, sleep patterns, and aspects of a traditional life. Participating in a gig economy often means that workers have to ensure they constantly monitor job availability and make themselves available any time gigs come up, regardless of their other needs. Gigs come in all shapes and sizes, but for this section we'll go back to more traditional classifications;

a. **Part time position within your area of expertise.** This option should be considered a short-term strategy while you gear up for a full-time position. You should be maximizing your study within your current field and aggressively working and expanding your social and professional networks. Assuming this income stream is insufficient for your long-term goals, be prepared to move as soon as the next higher-paying opportunity presents itself.

b. **Part time position outside of your area of expertise.** This is the same concept as above except the need to get to a higher paying position is likely more urgent, as most of these types of jobs will pay much less than jobs in your area of expertise. Remember, the goal is to stay employed and preserve some income stream. Always do your best and leave a trail of friends and associates, not a debris field of angry, vindictive former associates. Many times, this option will find you placed in a position for which you are vastly over-qualified. This will lead to resentment and frustration on the behalf of coworkers who understand that while this job may be a temporary stop for you, it is the pinnacle of what they will achieve.

4. **Transitioning to a position targeting a specific field or area of expertise.** This type of job is intentionally sought to "get in the door" of a targeted organization or field. This job probably has the highest bar to achieving the next level, otherwise you would have been hired straight into the desired position, right? What matters is that you create friends and allies within the organization and you look for options to showcase your current or recently- acquired skills that can open doors for you. You can't afford to get caught up in petty office/shop politics when following this path. Make targeted friends and allies, work the system. Most importantly, keep your hand on the pulse of the job market and move on after X time frame (your choice) if you can't get into the position you are targeting.

5. **Full time student.** You are likely living off savings or military retirement. Either way, full time school expenses can be outrageous. You have a limited time to get this done, so be super aggressive and get through the courses as rapidly as the system will allow. Work the system at the school, make friends and allies across the organization. Also start working the job market and key professors and instructors who might be willing to help

you with your post-education job. Look for internships and other ways to accumulate experience in your target degree/certification.

6. **Part time student.** Hopefully this is coupled with a full or part-time job. Same advice applies here as for the full-time student. Stay focused on getting through the degree/certification process as you are very vulnerable to being derailed. Work the system, create allies, and cultivate relationships with those who can help you.

7. **Retired, no real job.** My favorite! Best wishes for you as you enjoy your retirement, you've earned it. But, you need to immediately and brutally assess your expectations vs. reality. Do you really have enough money on which to retire? Have you done cost of living estimates over your expected lifespan? Have you factored in the cost of healthcare and medications as part of your assessment? Have you reviewed your financial health with a real financial advisor? You need to do all these things, because if you ignore them and fool yourself, you could lose everything you've worked so hard to create and accumulate. Consider developing another stream of income. Finally, you need to stay active in your lifestyle, your community, and your faith. If you spend too much time in your chair or on your couch watching the idiot box, you will waste away years before your time. Get up, get out and be active. Hopefully you've got grandchildren to enjoy and spoil.

Never forget your job doesn't love you, but your family does. This leads us to the challenging concept of work-life balance. For most people there is no balance, only the demands of the job that must be met to keep the job and not limit your career. You need to establish a pattern of protecting your home life and only very occasionally allowing work to intrude. This is harder when you are low on the totem pole and are told you "haven't paid your dues." Some jobs require you to be available 24X7 as the on-call support person. Even so, the advice still stands that you should keep your work and personal life as separate as possible. Ignore the company double speak about how important work-life balance is for them and how they encourage that balance. The first time you spend the weekend keeping the company afloat while the managerial team leaves sharply at 5pm on Friday and doesn't return until 9am on Monday, you'll get it.

A good manager or leader will protect your work-life balance because they know that happy, well rested employees have better morale, are more creative and productive. Creativity is hugely important in ANY job, not just a "maker" or "marketer" position. Creativity is you becoming an expert in any job and making intuitive leaps of how to do some part or all of it better. If you can't sustain high morale working in a broken system (long hours, constant weekend work, unpredictable hours) you won't have enough headspace to be creative. Creativity also even applies to repetitive and grunt work. You need the ability to look forward to the end of each work-day and each workweek as a positive point where real life becomes available again. You need a level of morale to perform the work properly, particularly when it is boring and repetitive. In this type of job, you are trading your time for a sum of money that enables your real-life activities and goals. In these scenarios and all others, you need to be able to recharge and return with a modicum of good morale and creativity.

One of our favorite people once sent a great letter to his staff laying out a method for the team to approach the creativity and focus. Here's the abstract of that letter;

You must avoid the false comfort and satisfaction of doing non-critical work. In any walk of life, you earn your way by thinking critically and innovatively and then by DOING those things that matter most. If you aren't doing so now, you need to immediately start to carve out time each day to read, think and innovate as part of your daily core discipline.

At a minimum, you should:

1. Create a set of personal, family, and professional goals for short, mid, and long terms
2. Start your day earlier than your peers and your competition
3. Spend the very first part of your day on you, your finance, family, and exercise.
4. Find AT LEAST 30 minutes of your business day to read, research and advance your 5% skills
5. Review your daily goals and priorities BEFORE you open email and other documents…get your goals sorted, then adjust to the incoming demands.
6. Track and review your progress against your goals each week
7. Finally, end your work day consistently on time and spend time with your family

Follow these guidelines with good discipline and you will regularly slay the personal and professional dragons in your life.

Notice that it starts with setting goals that include family and ends with a reminder "spend time with your family." The letter also encourages you to start early, focus on yourself and exercise before you begin your "work" day. What fantastic, incredibly valuable advice. Bravo Zulu.

The next thing to pay close attention to is the promise of an annual bonus. Let's be very, very specific here. Unless you have an employment contract that guarantees a certain percentage of your salary or a specific bonus amount for an annual bonus, it is **ALWAYS** at risk. No matter what the hiring manager, recruiter or others say; without an employment contract with the bonus details spelled out, there is no guarantee you will receive a single dollar. Many companies have never embraced the concept of an annual bonus. In those companies that have an annual bonus structure, it is anything but transparent. The most important part of this concept is that while it may be customary, it's not required by law. It is rare for a poorly performing company to pay bonuses to those without a contract. The entire process of calculating the bonus pool, how much gets handed to each level and what the award criteria for getting a bonus is murky and not well governed.

I've personally seen, experienced and participated in the annual bonus process first hand. Sometimes bonus amounts are rigidly determined by the performance of the individual with strict limits are set for minimums and maximums. This is usually seen in the most professional organizations, but the bonus process still has an Achilles heel in that it is tied to an always subjective performance rating and the deeply flawed persons who determine those ratings. More on this in the Chapter "Succeeding in your new Career."

Core Concepts mapping

Core One – You are NOT like the others. You come from a rigid professional environment, much more so than your non-Service peers.

Core Two – You have been forged in fires your peers can't understand.

Core Three – There are less of us than you may realize. However, you will find allies scattered through any organization who are service friendly or former service. Treat these allies as precious resources, culture and nurture your relationships with these people.

Core Five – You have skills and capabilities that are marketable. People want to hire the optimal you. They don't want to hire the opinionated, storytelling you. Make sure you provide the "you" that they need, not the other person.

Core Six – You have gaps in your skills and capabilities that you need to close. In this section, we mentioned brand as an intangible, but important concept. Who are you? Just because you have the skills that get you the interview, do you have what it takes to learn and thrive in line of business, culture, or company? Are you willing to put in the hours to catch up the skills that are lagging, learn new skills while acquiring new knowledge to help you get ahead?

Core Seven – You now have more responsibility for your life and much more opportunity to screw it up. There are many opportunities to fail in the civilian world, no matter which path you choose. You must realize this going in, learn quickly and realize that you must be constantly on guard against the unknown. As a reminder, good mentors are a strong counter here.

Core Eight – Life is still hard. Things break. Bosses change. The economy surges and retreats. People get sick and leave us. Be prepared for adversity.

Core Nine – The Republic is powered by the engine of Capitalism. You need a minimum amount of money to live your chosen lifestyle. You may need multiple streams of income (recommended) to achieve that financial stability. Before you accept any job, you should be crystal clear on whether you are being compensated at, above or below market rates including performance bonuses or stock plans if applicable. What is your total compensation package?

Personal perspective:

Be careful what you ask for. One of my early jobs right out of the military was a bit of a disaster. I didn't get fired but it was a grind. I was going to school in the morning and working at night. I learned a lot of painful lessons about picking the right job. The company looked good from a distance, but it was full of unprofessional, half-baked leadership and managers exploiting the hard work of the employees without fair compensation. We had one guy that the managers hated but were afraid to fire since he was the only person in the company who understood the systems that generated our revenue. This guy would literally break a door down if his access card didn't work that morning. He would maliciously change things, bully people, and laugh it off when someone caught him misbehaving. There were good people there, but they weren't in charge. The final straw for me went like this; we had this process where we needed microfiche (yes, that dates the story) produced daily. This involved generating tapes that were picked up from our data center in the wee hours of the morning, (think 0300 hours), and taken to the microfiche vendor by a young man who was struggling to work two jobs to support his young family. Early one morning, this young man was leaving the building at the same time someone without an access card was trying to gain access. The young man followed procedure and did not allow this person he did not know access to a secure facility, just like he was trained. Unfortunately, the person who was trying to get access was our CEO who was so full of himself it was embarrassing. On this occasion, he was enraged that this guy would not let him pass the security access door without a valid ID or security card. In fact, he later bragged that he had the guy fired and that our vendors had been warned to educate their staff to recognize our leadership team by sight, him. It was surreal, the CEO was rarely in his office and even then, it was on a different floor of the building and not accessible for 98% of the company. There were no pictures of the CEO anywhere, and a simple courier was supposed to recognize him on sight? Recognize him at that time of the morning, trying to get into a building with no ID? That was the final straw for me, time to exit the madhouse.

Chapter 9 – Getting Hired

It's time to choose. You really should not think of this as picking a job as much as choosing a path. You need access to opportunities. What do you really want to do? This is an extension of our **Core Four** – *You are uniquely prepared to manage your own future:* You need a plan for your life, and to develop one you need to know what you REALLY want. Figure that out and take steps every day toward that goal. At the very minimum, don't allow yourself to lose your hard-won ground on your goals.

Again, think about what you really want to do. The options are endless, and you need to decide on a path, so you can start working your way up. It's easy enough to start with a list like the following:

- Military-aligned skillset
- Military contractor
- Corporate job
- Small to medium business (SMB)
- Government job

Each of these paths has significantly different recruiting and hiring methods, so it's important to understand and know how to engage. Here's a high-level breakdown (tip of the iceberg) overview of how to engage and get hired.

Military-aligned skillset – this is basically the job you were doing in the military, or one that uses the same core skills, but for a private or government entity. Many ex-service members will join Law Enforcement (LE) or First Responder (FR) organizations. Others will take their skills and just move from the military into the exact civilian-equivalent job. This type of direct transfer hiring is usually done in one of two ways:

1. Minimum experience hire: For LE and FR jobs, there is a rigorous training and certification process accompanied with constant on the job training and review. Couple this methodology with high demand and that opens these jobs to a service member with little to no direct experience in the specific LE or FR job. Veterans are particularly attractive to this mode of

hiring because of their experience with high volume learning and skill acquisition.

2. Senior experience hire: service Veterans with many years of experience, retirees and specific military leaders are hired into more senior positions

Military contractor – generally, this type of job hires requires similar experience if not an exact match to duties and usually requires a background check, particularly for overseas work. Here's an excerpt from an interview with an ex-military who has worked with the United Nations missions in Africa and in the remote regions of Afghanistan.

The best advice I can give you is that if you are currently in the military and have a security clearance, that's a huge plus for certain types of jobs. If you are interested in that the type of job that needs a security clearance, try to set it up before you separate. While these types of jobs aren't exactly common, the demand is decent. These defense contractors have web sites and they are easy to find. Go to your favorite search engine and use the search string "Defense Contractor jobs." You'll get a list of the of the major players. Job boards are basically websites that allow you to search and apply for jobs online. Do some research on several of these for the type of job you are interested in and the qualifications needed. You should also cast your net as wide as possible and consider positions that may not directly align to your specific skill set. Here's a list of job boards to get you started:

- www.monsterjobs.com
- www.vetjobs.com
- https://recruitmilitary.com
- www.hireveterans.com
- www.militaryhire.com
- www.militaryoneclick.com/job-board
- www.usajobs.gov
- www.careerbuilder.com
- http://www.gijobs.com
- www.hireheroesusa.org
- http://www.amvets.org
- http://www.civilianjobs.com
- https://clearedjobs.net
- www.linkedin.com

A security clearance will help, but it won't land the job for you. You need a strong and clear resume that is relevant to the targeted position and/or actual posting. You'll want to start building multiple versions of your resume as early as you can. You'll need at least two: one that avoids military acronyms for applying to civilian positions and one that emphasize your military experience including specifics for the defense contractors. In the case of the latter, don't go overboard on the military jargon and acronyms.

You'll want to make a decision to look for CONUS (contiguous US, or the "lower" 48 states) or OUTUS (outside of the continental US) jobs. Obviously, there's a world of difference in the job conditions and the pay. I've done both and my house is paid for because of just one deployment.

Deployments with the companies that work on government contract always required a major medical screening. If you are headed to Southwest Asia (SWA), this screening will likely take place at the military deployment base. Major medical includes getting your shots up to date and likely some vaccinations for things you've never heard of, depending on the region you may deploy to. You will be screened for drugs. It doesn't matter what state is legalizing marijuana, if you can't pass the blood and urinalysis tests, you will be booted. I watched a guy in Houston get yanked from the process because of failed urinalysis. He lost a support oriented, non-combat job that was almost tax free at $100k because he was stupid. Drug screening outside of the military is almost impossible to beat. It is usually done at a specialized facility with people who are much better at it than your friendly service medic. Don't try to game these guys with various dodges. Because they've seen it all before and with the money involved, they don't make amateur mistakes.

Expect to go through a multi-part interview process. No matter how impressive your resume or how badass you are, you need to convince the person or persons that you are the best candidate for the job. Remember, they've likely been screening ex-military candidates for a good years, so this is not the time for bullshit or exaggeration because they'll spot it a mile off and call you on it.

As most people join the military right out of high school or after being in the civilian workforce for only a fleeting time you should realize your interview skills will most likely need some work. If you're not comfortable talking about your service, skills, and accomplishments, find the time to practice until you are. Mirrors work better than spouses because of the repetition required.

If you know someone who was working as a defense contractor, that can be a huge help from the perspective of a mentor and someone with whom you can network. When filling out an application, many of the web sites will ask you for the name of the person who referred you. If you have a reference use it wisely, make sure that person would recommend you. It's a "must do" to check in with any potential references and ask for an endorsement. No one should be blindsided by a reference request. Give them a call and tell them about the job(s) you are applying for. Networking is important.

If you are still in the military, take some time to learn about the contractors who are currently on base. Create your resume and go make some friends and acquaintances. Don't drop by in your grungy utilities after a hard day. Clean up and do it right because first impressions are *always* important. Ask them who to talk to about hiring. Once you are having a dialogue with the hiring manager if he tells you they are not hiring ask him/her if they know any other contractors on post looking for someone with your skill set. Try to identify all the civilian contracting companies on the base/post. Work to develop contacts with each, even if their scope is not directly aligned to your goals. Network and make friends.

So, briefly:

1. Build *at least* two strong resumes.

2. Avoid doing ANY drugs after you transition from military life to civilian life.

3. Research jobs on-line and in person.

4. Register with state employment agency in the area in which you plan to settle. They will usually have a division that is specifically set up to match Veterans to jobs.

5. Keep your security clearance if possible. Once hired by a contractor, you can expect to need security clearance. They will want ALL the information about you for the past seven years. They WANT to know everything from addresses, to jobs to relatives, family history. pet names, blood types... ad nauseam.

6. Networking, networking, networking.

Large Corporation – Can you walk in to the office on your first day and have an impact? In other words, the best jobs don't want to train you, they want to unbox you as an employee and see you helping day one. Can you pass background checks (financial and legal) and a drug screening? Do you have contacts in the industry that you can use on your reference list? Corporations are very image conscious; if you show up in your controversial grunge outfit, don't expect to get a call back. Corporations are also extremely sensitive to business culture so you will need to fit in some degree. You don't have to be a perfect fit or clone, but there are limits. As part of your social media image check, you might want to consider blocking or unfriending your contacts who spew obscenities laden rants and other such nonsense.

1. **Low skill match candidates:** Usually hired for general aptitude in a related field, or for entry level positions, they are looking for a person with a great attitude and reasonable appearance.

2. **High skill job candidates**: Need an overwhelming alignment to the job and a great resume with a proven record of accomplishment.

3. **Individual Contributor:** There are a small number of jobs with extremely specific skill sets. At the highest tier, these folks could come into work in their PJs if they wanted, even in an image-sensitive company. They can get away with it because they generate a lot of revenue or have such specialized skill sets, usually accompanied by a PhD. The air is rare up there, and there are a lot of mid-to-high tier jobs under that glass ceiling, but you must have the skill set and you will be under constant scrutiny. Project Managers are a good example of this type of position. They have demonstrable, auditable skills and certifications. This is not a fake-it-till-you-make-it type of job.

4. **Management/Leadership positions** (low to mid-level): Buyer beware as these leadership opportunities can be a nightmare of managing disgruntled employees in dead-end jobs. The job might look good on paper, but a lot of time you will be compensating (with long hours, fewer staff than you need and incredible stress) for idiotic decisions from the senior leaders and HR. Having read the warning notice, not all low to mid-level leadership positions are bad, but a lot depends on the culture, the immediate boss, and the team. Ask lots of questions and you should talk to peers and subordinates before you take the position offered. Keep in mind that your military mindset is generally NOT what is needed here. You will need to simultaneously learn the culture, understand and drive the team efficiency metrics, keep the boss happy and use soft people skills you didn't need in the military.

5. **Management/Leadership positions** (high level): Vice President, Senior Vice President, Executive Vice President and Director level positions are hard to land in your first gig. You either need a friend or friends in high places (remember we said you should start early and build a social network that extends to friends and acquaintances in and out of the military) or you need to be a rock star with proven leadership skills and some ability to translate your impact in the military into civilian terms that impress. Generally, you need at least a bachelor's degree, a Master's degree is better and if you have a doctorate, you are set.

Small to Medium Business: Culture, culture, culture. SMBs have a different perspective from those found in large corporations. They tend to trend toward either end of the tolerance range either having a lot of flexibility and generally hiring candidates that need little direction and supervision, or they hire persons who can perform endlessly repetitive tasks reliably. This flexible end of the pool encourages employees to grow and assume authority and responsibility that matches their goals and talent. They don't tend to get to caught up where the idea came from or who is next in line for a promotion because of seniority. In contrast, some SMBs can be significantly more draconian on working hours, conduct at work and so on. This rigid end of the pool usually relies on managers and supervisors that jealously guard decision-making and leadership authority. As a result, these individuals can be petty and overbearing. Ask good questions and decide if you like the company culture. Remember, many of these companies are created by great people with a good business idea who may be lacking in their people skills. These companies can be sensitive to your social media, so make good decisions here. Find a business you want to work with and then research and learn about the company. This type of company loves to pick off disgruntled, highly trained, and experienced workers from the larger corporations. When you get your interview, have a clear message on how you can help.

Government: Entrance exams, education…you have an advantage here with points being added to any exam scores as well preferential hiring practices for some jobs. If you think you understand government because of your military experience, stop here and re-think. It's a completely different system with different requirements and management methods on the inside. Unfortunately, the government jobs are the epitome of mediocrity with tiny islands of brilliance scattered here and there. Some people thrive on the power and control that comes with these jobs and some people just want a place to work 9-5 in a predictable work environment. This is not the place for an energetic, up and coming person who wants to get ahead on the basis of talent and accomplishments. In most cases, the ladder-limbers are social engineers, most of them bright and competent at the job, but even better at working the bias of the culture. You will never find a more politically and favor-based system.

While some government work is essential, and rewarding other types, not so much. If choosing to work with any form of government, local, state, or federal, pick your field and area carefully. Politics can be vicious and savage to newcomers. Poor leadership and the "look the other way" syndrome can lead to a bad place. Just do your homework and don't go in blind. You won't help yourself in your community and circle of friends if you find out after the affect that you joined a department surrounded by controversy and considered a waste of tax-payer money.

On the upside, you will probably be surprised how many jobs are available at any point once you start looking. Identify the hiring channels and work them relentlessly. Engage and stay engaged until you get the job. Keep in mind there are simply so many applicants for the jobs that one missed phone call or late email could eliminate you from the pool.

Let's talk about resumes.

Your resume *must* be effective, it *must* be accurate and relevant.

Here's an analogy. Think of your resume, paper or electronic, as the whole of your testimony in a legal case that means the world to you. You go in knowing that you are at a disadvantage but still need to win the case. You take the stand knowing that you need to be concise, effective and cover all the salient points. You understand that you will need more time than you will ever get. Without the time to logically lay out all the details you believe are important for winning the case, you need to compress and optimize what you say. You need your statement to be extremely relevant and understandable. You don't want to put the judge in a position where he (or she) must interpret your testimony to evaluate it under the law. If your judge must "figure out" what your testimony is, you are burning down the time and focus that the judge is willing to spend on your case. You need to be crystal clear and allow the judge to spend the time evaluating your argument for the best outcome. If you fail to deliver the proper message, you fail. With resumes, it's much the same. If someone struggles just to understand your qualifications and experience they will abandon the effort and move to the next candidate.

Remember that hiring a new employee is expensive and can involve a large number of people. Companies invariably try to solve for X with the resources they have on board at the time. Hiring and integrating a new employee takes time and pulls other productive workers away from their main task. They may be asking themselves "is this candidate worth the effort?." This may sound a little self-serving, but if you are reading this book you are probably worth the effort as you've already proven yourself a life-long learner and have set your own high expectations.

Here are some of the main ways that you get an interview:

1. Through a friend or relative. In this case, the resume doesn't open this door, but it is critical to keeping it open.

2. Direct hire after applying for a job. Sometimes this is a paper application, but most jobs can now be applied for online. In this case, your resume may be uploaded as part of the application either in its entirety or piecemeal.

3. Job boards. Maximize your presence on the job boards and any specific job social media such as LinkedIn. Do your research and get your resume into to those places that have the highest exposure in the industry you are targeting.

4. Recruiter/head-hunter placement. This can become full time contractor employment or a full-time employee position. Your resume is critical to this process as you may create initial interest with job board postings or professional social media, but you need a great follow-up when engaged by a recruiter.

Most resumes will go through at least two filters before they ever get to the hiring manager. Many large companies pay human resource (HR) professionals to match external candidates to internal positions. These HR specialists will scan the jobs boards, applicant lists and work with recruiters, sometimes known as head-hunters, to develop a pool or applicants. The reality of this single or dual filtering is that recruiters and HR specialists spend less than 10 seconds on your resume before deciding to keep or discard.

The technology behind resume screening has changed greatly in the last 20 years. Resumes are now uploaded, stripped of all fancy formatting, and added to various databases. This allows hundreds, if not thousands, of candidate resumes to be screened by machine algorithms before a human ever sees them. That is not to say the human screening process isn't critical. Even though it has moved from the front of the queue to the very last step in the process, there is still a human review hiding in there. What you need to know is that most recruiters/screeners are looking for a targeted set of skills and experience. They have exact jobs and skills to match, so, they don't really care if you are an all-around nice person with tremendous potential. They want to present the smallest number of candidates with the greatest affinity to the job. This refined list is then presented to the hiring manager who selects the persons to interview. Occasionally, if directed by the hiring manager, the recruiter will have a bit more flexibility to go a little farther afield versus a strict match to job requirements.

Not every company, recruiter or head-hunter strips the resume down to its component parts. Many still manually scan the various professional social media sources. Because of this, you need to have an impressive presence on professional social media as part of your job search.

Take away lesson: Recruiters and hiring managers don't know you and don't feel any obligation to "give you a shot" unless you meet or exceed their job requirements. The job posting is the final product of a lot of internal review discussion and (often) argument. In many companies, just getting a backfill position (for someone who has left the company) approved and opened, in the face of an indisputable staff need, is a difficult, uphill process. Once they get the position approved, they need to move fast to fill it before someone takes it away and allocates it to a different division. Does this process sound absurd, bureaucratic, and idiotic? Welcome to the real world. At the end of the day, there's only so much money to pay staff, regardless of the size of the company. Job positions must be justified and must align with the company's strategy and needs, both of which can change abruptly.

Many automated processes strip out all your careful, artistic work on your resume and punches the text into someone's database. Should you forgo the professional resume? Absolutely not. You are really facing a binary process. We are assuming that you want maximum coverage and visibility for your job hunt which means using online job sites and other social media vectors, but it also means sending your resume directly into organizations that may not have a job posted online. At a minimum, you will need a professional resume to provide during a face-to face-interview. And keep in mind not every resume gets digitized, many are sent intact for the prospective HR and specific hiring manager to review and use during the interview. Even if the interviewer has their own copy of your resume, handing out a nice crisply done resume on good paper stock is a professional touch you should not overlook.

What does a resume need to be impactful? Keep it simple and focused with no gimmicks or tricks. It is critical that your resume is clear and concise, ordered and visually appealing. Always avoid pictures, graphics, and photos (unless you are applying for a job working with those elements). Your resumes "bones" should contain the following:

- ✓ Name
- ✓ Top 20-30% of resume should be a summary of why you would be a valuable hire. This is about money, revenue and cost savings linked to achievements…take your time with this part and be succinct.
- ✓ Current Job, title
- ✓ Previous jobs, years in position, span of responsibility and accomplishments
- ✓ Education, professional and college
- ✓ Technical skills
- ✓ One page in length (optimal)

Does your resume stand on its own, or is it full of meaningless acronyms and low-value statements? Avoid claiming accomplishments with no measured results. Anything you place on your resume should be there to make a point. Any accomplishment or achievement must pass the "why would a hiring manager care." More importantly, can someone read your resume without you standing by to decrypt and explain your statements? This statement does not apply to education or specific technical skills, but to things you claim to have accomplished. Too many resumes are full of cryptic statements like "improved the efficiency factor of the company gunkulators by 23%." If your accomplishment can't be tied to one of three critical factors to the company's business, then it shouldn't be included. The three critical factors are (1) speed, (2) quality/risk and (3) financial benefit and or efficiency. A better- written accomplishment might read "approved the efficiency factor of the Mark 1 Mod 0 gunkulators by 23% thereby reducing cost per unit by 5%."

Accounting is the language of business, so unless you are pursuing a job as an accountant, CPA or financial advisor/expert try to stay away from sterile accounting terms. Always include information about your experience that relates to dealing with the flow of money (revenue generation, expense management and resultant profits) through a business. Information about growing the size and success of a business measured in revenue, expense reduction and profits are good points to include on your resume. If you have worked with CAPEX (Capital Expense) and OPEX (Operational Expense) and speak this type of language, put it on your resume. Because in many companies not having responsibility for a budget can result in making you irrelevant and easily downsized; consider having budget responsibility as a critical factor as you progress through any corporate career.

Stay away from the "I was there" statements apart from the scope and scale of teams you've managed. Obviously, managing a huge bloated staff that is inefficient isn't a bullet point you want to explain. Follow the same rule as above and describe what your measured results/improvements were when managing this staff. For some positions, the primary screening factor will be the largest number of people you managed. For senior level positions, there is a direct correlation between the size of staff managed and scope of responsibilities. Staying with the large-scale multinational corporation theme, it could also be important to show that you've successfully dealt with and managed teams and individuals working in "other" countries and cultures. You may not have these accreditations right out of the service, but it is something to keep in mind.

It is impossible to stress the importance of the need to show a potential employer why they should care about your "accomplishments." Other than the staffing size and scope, each accomplishment should be tied directly to a business benefit. The hiring manager will only be impressed by your accomplishments only if you can tie them to a real-world business benefit. Stay away from "cost avoidance" type of accomplishments" like "my actions prevented the future expense of X" as they are too often misleading and overstated. Stick with hard savings and benefits. At the end of the day there's only one question, are you the best candidate to help improve the company's bottom line?

Social media matters. Some jobs request that you provide your Twitter, Facebook, or other social media account information. Don't kid yourself, even if they don't ask, you should expect them to look you up. Surveys from recruiters indicate that over 90% of them will look at your social media profile. If you are an immature ass and it shows on your personal social media exploits, then really, don't expect to get the job. With that said, if you are well-represented on social media, then it can benefit you. Over 40% of recruiters have reconsidered an applicant based on social media information. Some of those re-assessments are positive, however most are negative.

What qualifications do you really have? Did you obtain a real estate agent license, are you an EMT, do you have a commercial driver's license (CDL) or other non-military license or credentials? Rather than delve too deeply into this subject here, please take the time to review the link to the report "THE FAST TRACK TO CIVILIAN EMPLOYMENT: STREAMLINING CREDENTIALING AND LICENSING FOR SERVICE MEMBERS, VETERANS, AND THEIR SPOUSES" provided below:

https://www.whitehouse.gov/sites/default/files/docs/military_credentialing_and_licensing_report_2-24-2013_final.pdf

Mistakes to avoid on your resume

1. **Generic Cover Letter.** Goes hand in hand with resume. Take the time to create a UNIQUE and impactful cover letter for each job application.

2. **Creating a "one size fits all" resume.** You will likely need multiple opportunity specific resumes depending on the job for which you are applying.

3. **Overburdened with military jargon and acronyms.** If you aren't applying to highly technical defense contractor ask one of your non-military friends or your spouse to read your resume. If they are baffled, you need to keep working on it.

4. **Failure to demonstrate results.** Achievements are what matter. Don't get caught up in the "I was there" trap. Every bullet and paragraph needs to demonstrate results. Does it pass the "why would I care" sniff test? Here the internet is your friend; find the description of an impactful accomplishment which aligns with your experience, then modify it to make it uniquely yours.

5. **Making spelling and grammar mistakes.** Use your word processor spelling and grammar checker. If you don't have a good word processor, get one.

6. **Straying to the irrelevant.** Is your resume focused? What is your relevant experience tied to outcomes and results.

7. **Your Resume Is badly formatted.** Should show some effort at organization and formatting. don't ignore this as many resumes are scanned, and if yours is too complicated it may not scan and load.

8. **Your resume Is too templated.** Some originality is always appreciated.

9. **Lists of tasks or duties without results.** Achievements sell. This is a recurring theme here, pay attention and show that you are outcome and results oriented.

10. **Explanation of anything negative.** No one lives a perfect life without mistakes. Let's assume you've learned from them and NOT put them on your resume.

11. **A list of every job you've ever held.** No one cares that much, really. Include only jobs that have easily understood relevance to the job for which you are applying.

12. **Resume is too long.** It should be two pages maximum. You don't get the job via your resume, but it is key to opening the door for interviews.

13. **Including personal details.** This is not a dating profile, so there is no need to share your hobbies or passions no matter how impressed you are with them.

14. **Crimes against capitalization and grammar.** This is a fan favorite given how often it is crops up. Use common sense, your resume is not a blog and you should put emphasis on presenting an easy to read, easily understood description of your accomplishments. Crime and Punishment is a novel that is worth chewing through, but no one will invest that much effort in your resume.

15. **Incorrect contact information.** Really? Get this right.

16. **Don't inflate or exaggerate your resume.** Be very precise when describing your experience. Do not claim anything that you haven't achieved.

17. **Avoid diploma mills.** You know what they are, and every company will fact-check your education.

18. **Avoid tired old and overused phrases and concepts.** Keep terms such as "hard worker" and "thinks out of the box" statements out of your resume.

19. **Don't put in an "objective" on your resume.** Your objective is to get hired. If your "objective" doesn't exactly align with the hiring company's expectations, you won't get the interview, so it's best to leave it off.

20. **Never, ever put your current salary or target salary on a resume.** In fact, be very cagey with this information. Salary is a negotiation so avoid early attempts to get that information from you. This should only ever be a discussion of what the employer is offering. Any other dialog is a losing proposition for you.

21. **Don't include your graduation date(s) from college.** If you don't have a degree, don't put anything, certainly not your high school info.

Let's talk about the interview.

You've managed to pass all the screening processes, or you have a friend or relative who has helped, which by the way, has a much higher success rate. This is usually where you land the job or blow it and there's really nothing in between. Very few companies will keep your resume on warm standby for the next job. This might happen in the small to medium business (SMB) space, if you particularly impress someone, but don't count on it. Most hiring is done in small increments of one (1) person for a specific job. Even if there's a bulk hire (more than one) you still need to pass the interview. Did I say interview? I should have said interview process.

Remember that every interview is a learning process. You will likely have to go through many interviews in your civilian career and you will learn something new from each one. Take notes immediately after each interview about what went well and what didn't. Keep these notes forever and review before your next interview.

One of the most effective openers in an actual interview comes from the hiring side. If we pose the same question to ourselves in advance, it can be a very powerful tool and may give us a competitive advantage. The question?

"What did you do to prepare for this interview?"

What did you actually do? Can you describe the process, actions, and results in a professional manner? You should ask yourself this question each and every day, starting 5 days before the interview. Write down your answers each day and look for progress, gaps, and opportunities to improve your narrative.

Being prepared for an interview of any type is incredibly important, and you should do everything in your power to be ready. The perfect interview would result in the perception of you already working for the company with a clear understanding of the business' challenges, culture, market and why they are hiring for this position.

Technology has changed some business processes dramatically. The old-school method of paying for you to fly to different city for an interview is rarely invoked these days. It still happens, particularly for more senior positions, but don't count on it. Today, some positions are hired without any type of face-to-face interaction. Some positions are hired with a hybrid approach of phone, video and in-person interviews. The hiring manager may be in a different state or country. You may face a process that is conducted completely over the phone with no video, or the process may conduct a meeting via video using Skype or some other internet-connectivity tool. Many of the recruiters who want to represent you will request a video interview.

For a telephone interview: Sometimes this is a preliminary step and in other situations, it's the only interview method conducted before hiring. Treat it seriously. Have a backup means of communication, at a minimum have your cell phone and a Bluetooth headset, with the numbers of the companies preset if you are dialing in to a specific number. Make sure you have a quiet place to conduct the interview. No kids, no dogs, no distractions. Lock down your interview location and use the best quality phone you have. The use of speaker phones is usually a huge mistake, because the sound can be spotty. Use a headset if you have one. Do not try to look up answers on the net while conducting a phone interview. The interviewers are looking to catch you at that. I've seen it done and it still boggles my mind that people think they can get away with it.

For a video interview: This method is becoming more common. Treat this very seriously as you have much more to manage than in just a telephone interview. You are being observed and judged harshly. Double and triple check your image. Wear clothes and present your image just as you would for an in-person, on-site interview. Double and triple check your connection. Scrutinize the background in the video and present the most professional setting you can create. Check the lighting and make sure it's complementary. Don't get too close to the camera. Scrutinize your appearance, shave, brush your teeth do the hair thing just like a formal inspection. Details count, and it's harder than it sounds to make yourself appear to be relaxed and confident. Here's a trick, ask a friend or family member to do a mock interview with you either over the net or face to face and record it on video. Spend at least 15 minutes responding to questions (formal dress not required, but you should still look your best). After you're done, review the video and examine it for any distracting elements, lighting, or body position. Then, do the interview again, but this time run the video in fast forward and look for any annoying, repeated mannerisms. Almost everyone has some type of unconscious or nervous tell that can be very annoying to others. Learn to manage it.

For an in-person, on-site interview: This is the old-school, *"we're taking you seriously, let's see who you really are"* interview. Do a drive-by test, make sure you know where you are going, plan for traffic and have an alternate route ready. Arrive early, be ready and have multiple copies of your resume printed on quality paper. Have a copy of the job description and a good blue or black pen with some paper to take notes on if necessary (think small portfolio). Have your interview uniform on. Please make sure it fits and you have all the pieces in place. Eat a healthy meal before the meeting. Hydrate and accept if a beverage of any type is offered. You could be there for hours and you may be in a wait state as business issues interject themselves into the interviewer's day.

Always greet your interviewer with a firm handshake and look them in the eye. Treat every person you meet with respect and dignity. I've seen too many people assume that the person that signs them into the building is some type of low-level admin, but in many cases this person can be a senior HR person who is going to shepherd you through the process. In other cases, that person could even be the hiring manager. Don't be shocked if they are much younger than you. Don't dismiss or underestimate anyone you meet. Don't try to pick the person you need to impress. Everyone you meet will get a voice in your evaluation. Be clear and concise with your answers. Don't fidget or display any distracting or annoying physical habits (foot tapping, hair adjustments, playing with your pen). Be confident and composed. These types of interviews usually occur when the candidate pool has been reduced to a few top candidates. Expect to have some buttons pushed. Expect to be asked "what if" questions. Expect to be challenged on your skill set and area of expertise. Expect personal questions. Never become combative or annoyed, remember it's a test proctored by people who are usually full of themselves. This type of interview includes a severe *"will this person fit into our culture"* element. Don't worry if the interview seems to be heading downhill, expect that you will screw up in more than one interview, it's a learning process. It's not a disaster, don't try to rescue the interview if this happens, that makes you look desperate. Finish up and go on to the next person or exit as appropriate.

Expect the hiring process to flow through the Human Resources team. They will most likely be your primary contact and will schedule various technical or specialty interviews with other teams. Face-to-face interviews could be with one or more persons and could take hours. If you claim to have a specific set of skills or area of expertise, expect to be challenged about your knowledge and experience. A favorite technique commonly used is to bring one or more experts to the interview with the hiring manager. Don't be intimidated if this happens, take your time answering these questions as they are looking for the depth of your knowledge. Ask for clarification if necessary, speedy answers are not necessarily your friend. But don't dwell overly long on technical or specific expertise questions. Expect to be tested. Do some internet research by looking up "interview questions and how to answer them." You will be amazed at how many variations there are of the "tell me about your strengths and weaknesses" questions. Some of these questions don't have a right or wrong answer, they are just used to see how you approach a problem.

Always dress for success for any meeting where people can see you, particularly face-to-face situations. Don't settle for "good enough" out of your closet. If you are chasing a sales job, you need to look like you just stepped out of a fashion magazine, because being a salesperson usually equals fit and extremely well dressed. For most other jobs you need an interview "uniform" that doesn't have to look like it cost a month's pay but says "take me seriously." If you aren't sure how to put your look together, then go to a medium to high-end clothing store, grab a salesperson and ask for help. Tell them that you need something to wear to an interview. Then enjoy the process. These people live for opportunities to dress someone, just be sure to tell them your budget up front. Spend some time putting this together and have more than one outfit you can wear.

Men should buy at least one new suit with a couple of shirts and matching ties. Single breasted black or blue are best. Don't forget the new belt and new shoes, and pay attention to your socks. If you aren't wearing new shoes take a moment to look at the shoes you intend to wear. Don't show up in scuffed shoes, but a spit shine is not required, just a decent polish. Pay attention to fingernails, they should be clean and trimmed. Even better, consider getting a manicure, no polish.

Women have more options (mid-length skirts to longer dresses and slacks), and don't overdo the make-up, be conservative. This is also not the time to put on the most expensive and full set of your jewelry, again be conservative. Create a simple, elegant look that shows you are taking the interview seriously.

Keep these clothes on ready standby; have them cleaned and pressed professionally and DON'T wear them for any other reason. Think dress uniform that only comes out of the dry-cleaning plastic for specific occasions.

For both men and women, please don't overuse perfume or cologne, but don't show up "au natural" either.

You want to look in the mirror and see someone who looks professional. Expect everyone who is interviewing for the position will bring their "A" game, so you don't want to look like a slob or, as you learned in the military, someone who doesn't pay attention to details. It's not just about how you answer the question, it's also about the image you project while you are answering those questions.

Each company is different, you will just have to adapt to the style as it is presented.

Do your homework. This can't be stressed enough. Your ultimate goal is to figure out why they need to hire you, if possible. Learn about the business, learn about the industry, and review legislation that affects the business. Research the company online and see how it has been performing. If it's a publicly traded company, read the annual reports and understand the company's stock behavior. If it's a privately held company, what can you learn? Often the founders of successful companies have biographies published and those can be full of insight into both the executive and the company. Call the main office number, speak to the communications director, and *ASK* about what you should know. There's a plethora of information that you need examine; stock reports, annual reports, trade journals, industry trends, management changes and news coverage. If you have a financial advisor (and you should!) ask them for guidance. Ask your friends and relatives for any insight they might have. Compile any and all intelligence you can gather. Ask for the names of the people with whom you will be interviewing with and Google them. The bottom line here is knowledge is power and the more you know, the better prepared you will be.

Speaking of being prepared, have your resume, job description and any notes ready as references in electronic or hardcopy format. Re-read all the information you have (including your resume) twice in the hour before the interview. Review all your notes, particularly your notes on the persons with whom you will be meeting.

Be ready well in advance of the interview date. Even if the interview is done remotely (phone or video link), be in place and ready at least 15 minutes before the interview. If this is an in-person interview, arrive at least 20-30 minutes before your interview is scheduled to start. For a face-to-face meeting, there's always a check in and greeting process, and you may get a glimpse of the competition. You may have a chance to introduce yourself to the greeter and gently probe for advice on the company's culture and information about the interviewers. For this type of meeting, be prepared to sit quietly and wait patiently. Do not schedule your time so tightly that you end up with no flexibility to run beyond your scheduled time.

Salary discussions are always a bit awkward. One golden rule that you should adhere to is to try to *avoid* discussing salary on the first call. It's not necessarily a "trick" when someone asks you how much you are currently earning on the first communication, but buyer beware. At some point in the future if the hiring process continues, you will have to negotiate a salary and possibly other compensation, but generally not on the first call or interview. However, some companies will request this information if you apply on their website, or in the initial interview.

If possible, defer the question about current salary or salary requirements as long as possible. In a very polite and professional manner, reflect this question with a response along the lines that asks, "what is the compensation range for this position"? In the extremely rare case that the interviewer provides this information early in the process (don't be afraid to ask), you should respond in kind and provide your information. Don't game this this part. But go in with a clear understanding of what your current job should pay and what the pay rate should be for the one you are interviewing for.

Here are some sites that will help you with getting line of sight on the salary ranges;

www.payscale.com

www.salary.com

www.LinkedIn.com/salary

Sharing your current salary information will put in you a box with hard boundaries. The interviewer could make assumptions that may not be in your favor. They are looking for two things. In the first case, if your salary is too high they want to screen you out early in the process. It's not just about the salary, but the good business decision to avoid someone who would abandon process when they learn the position pays much less than their current pay rate. The other half of this situation is concern that an over qualified person will be looking to move back to a closer pay rate. To alleviate their concerns (maybe this is your dream job) then make it clear that you are willing to negotiate. In the second case, if your pay rate is significantly below their range, this would indicate that you may not be as qualified or recognized as you want them to believe. If you are currently working at a much lower pay rate than the target position, be prepared to make a solid case as to why you took the current job and why you are still the best candidate.

Compensation is always a negotiation. In almost every case, there is a range and you want to max out your starting point. Notice that the term "compensation" is used repeatedly. Not all compensation is salary or bonus. You might consider the other benefits so attractive that you will take a lower pay rate. Even so, initial interviews are NOT the place or time to have this discussion. This may sound harsh, but you should not disclose current income information if you can avoid it. Try to keep the topic on a salary range that the company offers, and only talk specifics when you are actually being offered the job. It is up to you to learn as much about the position, customary compensation, and other benefits as you can to make sure you are getting a good to great offer.

Some generic but extremely important truths to remember;

>#1 Maximize your presence on all hiring vectors/channels
>
>#2 No one gets hired without an interview
>
>#3 You must impress all your interviewers at every step
>
>#4 You must really impress the hiring manager.
>
>#5 No one wants to train you, they want to on-board you, integrate you and put you to work.

If you have a security clearance, it is one of the most valuable assets from your time in the military! Don't let it expire if you want work in any related field. Your clearance will be deactivated at separation but can be reinstated within the first twenty-four (24) months as long as you are in one of the cycles for each type of clearance. Confidential clearances must be reinvestigated every fifteen (15) years. Secret clearances must be reinvestigated every ten (10) years. Top Secret clearances have the most rigor and must be reinvestigated every five (5) years. If you hit one of these thresholds it can be much harder and more expensive to get back to the target clearance levels. Figure out your current clearance cycle and plan around it. Companies will certainly pay for a full investigation and reinstatement if they need or want you enough, but it takes time and positions have a way of evaporating. One of the easiest ways to keep your clearance is to take a job that requires the clearance (even if it's not your dream job). The company that employs you will maintain your clearance while you are there.

Did you know that many jobs require fingerprinting, background checks and of course, the drug screening we mentioned earlier? While this varies from job to job, if you are going to make serious money you should plan for these. The greater the compensation, the more thorough the screening will be. In some cases (high level positions) you will be required to complete a psychological evaluation. Some jobs require you to be "bonded" implying a position of serious trust and exposure to the hiring company. This all happens AFTER the job offer has been made and accepted. No company is going to spend money on performing a background check until they've decided on the hire. There is no arbitration, mediation, or negotiation if something shows up in your background check. Just like social media, your past behavior particularly related to legal, finance and drug use can come back to haunt you.

The best closing advice for this subject is for you to mentally recalibrate your perspective of yourself. Take the time to remember who you are and all that you've done and seen. You are an unusual person. You have experiences that make you extremely valuable as an employee. Before each interview, take some time to review you. Do this not to reinforce an over-inflated ego, to think hard about how you got here. Remember and review those things at which you succeeded, as well as the lessons you've learned from your failures. Go through the successes and failure you've seen of others and the lessons they learned. You get to own that information and make it part of your professional portfolio. Observational experiences automatically become integrated into your professional perspective. This is particularly important, as you are sum of the experiences you have had to date. It's part of you. Reconstruct your mental image of yourself by reviewing and affirming all that you've experienced. Be confident and current in your self-image. If you take the time to do this, you'll find the review process less stressful and might just give you the edge you need.

Core Concepts mapping

Core One – You are NOT like the others. Capitalize on this and leverage to your benefit. Find the best job and income match from opportunities that value your background and experience.

Core Four – You are uniquely prepared to manage your own future. Simply by reading this book, you are orders of magnitude more prepared than your competition. But don't be complacent, look to other sources, mentors, and coaches to help you prepare and get the job that you really want.

Core Five – You have skills and capabilities that are marketable. Not every job you want will come your way, but you are valuable property and you need to remember that. The process of reviewing who you are and what you've experienced will build your confidence and help you through every step in this process.

Core Seven – You now have more responsibility for your life, and much more opportunity to screw it up. If you don't prepare properly, you could miss the job of a lifetime. Or conversely, you can land it and live happily ever after.

Core Eight – Life is still hard. Sometimes, no matter how well you prepare, the dragon wins. You may be the best candidate by an overwhelmingly large margin and still not get the job. When, not if, this happens, keep moving. The fact you didn't get the job is a blessing for reasons you can't see from where you stand. Count it as a win, not a loss.

Personal perspective:

Always prepare for your interview. The time I went for an interview and didn't fully prepare was awkward and embarrassing. Seriously interviewing a candidate face-to-face usually involves multiple managers and experts. I didn't make it past the first HR screening. She simply asked what I thought about their company and products. I drew a blank, I didn't do my homework on the company and wasn't sure what their flagship products or services were. Huge mistake as every company is proud of their premier product and service offering. She took pity on me and let me gracefully exit the process. I never made that mistake again. While my bruised ego was healing, I decided to turn that failure into a lesson learned success. In fact, I created a business that was very profitable as a direct result. I offered resume services to help build and target said resumes to land specific interviews. For an outrageous sum, I guaranteed to help the candidate get an interview and offered a 50% refund if what we produced didn't at least get them in door. I was never asked for a single refund. Why? Because I researched the target company and tailored the resume to the job posting, the product and service niche for that company. Lesson learned.

Chapter 10 – Owning your own business

Owning your own business is the most highly recommended path, but only if you are motivated and are willing to do what it takes to be successful. Pick the most insanely intense military qualification you can think of, one that taxes the mind and body to the point of failure. That's what owning your own business takes. Wash, rinse, repeat, over and over again.

Skeptical?

Maybe a better analogy is that of having a child, a toddler who can't really walk yet, who gets into constant trouble, isn't toilet trained and needs constant supervision. In this analogy, the child never grows up and the attention required is a permanent. The mischief may change, but the need to be vigilant never ends.

The hard truth is that it is very unlikely that you already know how to start, operate, and grow your own business. I say that because this topic often requires extreme specialization wrapped around a core of fundamental behaviors and methods. Those with experience in running their own businesses learn lessons every single day the business is in operation. Some of those experiences are common while many are very specific to the type of business. You just can't get the requisite experience out of a book or college course.

So, let's go back to the opening statement. Owning your own business is the most highly recommended career path. You can certainly earn a good living in any of the other career paths and may want to pursue those while you get ready to launch your own business.

Did you know that privately held businesses are the largest employers in the US?

Did you know that owning a service company is one of the fastest paths to becoming a millionaire?

Did you know that owning your own company gives you the most control over your personal life and more flexibility than any other employment option?

Having a desire to own a business is a good start but consider it the first 2% of what you need. Cleaning out your savings and opening the business of your dreams is a sure path to bankruptcy, failure, and crushed dreams. Did I say failure? Let me say it again. Failure. Having spent X years in the military, you aren't accustomed to failure. Failure can be soul crushing and career ending. Or, it can be just another lesson learned. Let's take a look at the rough statistical data for sole proprietor businesses:

- About half of these businesses will fail in the FIRST year
- Roughly 10% of all small businesses close their doors each year
- Only about 30% will survive to the 10-year mark
- Overall, about 90% of startups will fail

Why do they fail? That's a list that is as long and varied as the numbers and types of businesses that are created. But there is some data available to answer that question also:

1. New owners think they can do it all themselves past the point when they need expert support
2. Picking the wrong mentor and getting bad advice
3. They fall in love with concepts that never convert to sales because concepts don't sell but products do
4. Not understanding the competition in the local market, ecommerce or globally
5. Using marketing strategies that just don't work
6. The team has critical skill gaps
7. Poor location choice for brick and mortar stores - location, location, location is key
8. Inadequate start-up funding
9. Lack of a business plan, incomplete business plan or just a bad business plan.
10. Not mentally tough enough. Unable to adapt and overcome. Failure to drive their businesses through the challenges that will inevitably arise.

A weakness in any of these areas (and many more not listed) can create a fatal flaw in your new business that will siphon off your savings and leave you in a less than desirable state. In most cases, when the business shuts its doors, there are still debts that must be paid off.

Many individuals who start their own businesses will raid their savings, make a ridiculous number of avoidable mistakes and shut their doors within the first year. They will also be broke, with no real leverage or funding to try again. Having lost all your money in a failure because you didn't plan well puts you in a predicament. It is very unlikely that anyone will invest in you with their money when you have that type of track record, and without funding you can't start over.

Thinking about crowdfunding to get started? Unless you have fantastic concept or product, it's not likely to happen. Crowdfunding companies like GoFundMe, Kickstarter, and Indiegogo (the top three at the time of writing) only really work when you can capture the imagination of large numbers of individuals who can provide funding. You need people who want to see your product brought to market. You need something innovative and rule-changing to really leverage this method. If you think you've got that then what are you waiting for, get started! Just keep in mind that most small, privately held business wouldn't get a dime from this method because their idea or product is too local or not differentiated enough to catch the imagination and the money in other people's pockets.

You might ask that if owning your own business is such a great idea, why the doom and gloom? Because I'm a huge proponent of preparing properly and being realistic. An older warfighter friend of mine always says that fair fights are for idiots. What a great analogy! For someone just jumping into to something without being ready is worse than being in a fair fight. It's like pouring all your money into a wheelbarrow putting on a blindfold and then walking at night through the streets of (insert worst place you know of here). This blind faith that you will not only complete your journey but have fun while doing it AND thinking that your money will have doubled or tripled when you take of the blindfold is an asinine perspective. Look in any direction and you will find too many good people who've lost everything they had because of a good idea poorly executed. Even worse is a bad idea that has become a dream but never had the slightest chance of success. Empty 401Ks and savings accounts don't magically replenish themselves.

You need to have expert knowledge about the business you want to start or have the funds to run the business and grow into the necessary expertise over a specific period.

Let me say that again a little differently. Jumping into your own business with most of your savings and little to no real-life experience in the business is like taking 90% of your wealth and buying lottery tickets. Some people win, most don't. Sure, you will have a few $5 winners, maybe a $50 or something even larger, but the odds against winning big are so bad that math is literally depressing.

You need to plan well and have some financial resilience. This means more than having a little money set aside. You need to pay the rent, the electricity, the water, the grocery bill, the insurance, your car payment AND have enough money to invest and run the business. Sound daunting? It should. This is probably why so many individuals start their business while fully employed elsewhere.

If that concept is not as appealing to you as an "all or nothing" kind of person, then you need to prepare extremely well before you launch.

That advice is a little misleading. You need to prepare extremely well to launch under any scenario.

Chances are, you don't have a clue what "preparing to launch" really means. Let's see if we can help with that. Keep in mind that there are a multitude of books on this topic that you really should read. Consider this a high-level primer to get you started *thinking* in the right direction.

Your primary mindset should be to dream big and plan for failure. This is not doom and gloom. Ignore all the *"feel good-power of positive thinking-it will all work out if you try really hard"* idiot perspectives. In the military, we trained hard and often to be able to continue when things inevitably went wrong with a mission or operation. You need that same mindset here. Remember, you will have minimum to no resiliency if one of your business components or employees go down. Even though it's hard to think about your business that way, you need to plan for failure first. In most cases, you're going to suck as a business owner the first time you try. Prepping for failure will keep you honest, will keep you on your toes and hopefully make you realistic in your assessment of how you are doing.

Take the time to learn about liability and the types of corporations. Yes, you absolutely need to be a corporation. Too many people take a shortcut and don't learn what they should in this area. Too many people take a second shortcut and create a do-it-yourself limited liability corporation (LLC). Be smart and realize that this is not often the optimal type of corporation. Make an informed decision.

Minimum funding. Plan for six (6) months of no income being generated by the business. During that time, you need to live, pay your mortgage, and manage other expenses necessary to promote and run your business.

What are you selling? How do you produce it? What supplies do you need to produce your product or service? What is your supply chain? What is the profit margin for each product or service? What staffing do you need to support it? How do you gain customers? How much does it cost to acquire each customer? How do customers find you? What forms of payment will you accept? Do those questions sound daunting? I came up with them in less than 30 seconds, and those are just the high-level types of framing questions for which you will need detailed answers. When you get those EXACT and SPECIFIC answers, then you need to go back and ask how you optimize each action. Wash, rinse, repeat and challenge yourself ten times on each topic. Can you figure out a way to do each one better, faster, or cheaper?

Will you buy your supplies from or your current country of residence or will you buy from the lowest-cost supplier? Right now, very few first world economies supply components or finished products at prices that let you maximize your profit. Think low volume initially, plus the need to create a trusted brand with loyal customers. Very few businesses can survive on new customer business only as the cost of acquiring a new customer is often significantly higher than customers giving you repeat business. Back to sourcing, let's just lay out your supply chain from an overseas source and what that might mean to you. Disclaimer here please. Yes, the online ordering process can and does radically simplify this process, but you can't count on your supply chain being capable of producing and delivering your order in a just in time mode. You need to understand how your order is produced, what lead times are involved and any vulnerabilities or variables in the supply chain. Ignore this at your peril:

1. Specific component or finished goods at price X based on volume price, lead time, tooling, manufacturing (assembly or transformation), cost of supplies to make, package and prepare for shipping

2. Source country shipping to port

3. Overseas shipping (container ship)

4. Drayage costs and truck pick up from port or intermodal warehouse location to your general area

5. Shipping to retailer (you) or directly to your customer (e-commerce model)

6. Can you unbox and sell directly or is there some additional manufacturing step required? If so, do you need different components or supplies to complete this step?

7. Where will you store your inventory? How much space do you need and how much will it cost?

This is a model of a supply chain. It is grossly oversimplified. You must understand the overall costs and risks associated with each element in your supply chain. You must know the people involved in each step and have some way of tracking your order. While sites like Amazon do a fantastic job of this, if you are dealing with bulk items or component materials, you're not likely to be buying from Amazon and shipping next day service with FedEx or UPS.

So, how much does it cost to buy and procure your finished product or product components and get them to the right place at the right time? When should you re-order? How much inventory will you carry? Can you create a reliable just-in-time supply chain? Can you run your business completely as e-commerce and skip the whole inventory on-site management complexity? Will you run a hybrid retail presence with e-commerce offerings?

Every single business in operation today has four things in common:

1. The production of product or service which can be sold

2. A process for gathering customers

3. An exchange process where products or services are delivered, and revenue gathered

4. Multiple accounting methods and processes to track sales, inventory, efficiency, profit, payroll, and cost of goods sold

Again, pardon the oversimplification, but hopefully you are starting to get the picture.

Without a clear and well-defined business model, you might as well send me your savings and I'll help you write a resume for the job you'll need after you fail. Your business model creation will be a journey of massive learning and insight. You'll need to learn aspects of business management that you don't have any expertise with.

Find a mentor, court experts, and befriend them. Learn your business. Build a business model, tear it apart and critique each element until you don't think it can be improved upon. Then find a willing and intelligent friend, coach or mentor and do it again with them. Expect to be humbled by the experience. Expect to learn and plan to succeed. Every entrepreneur in the world (except your direct competition) is pulling for you.

Owning your own business is one of the most direct paths to true wealth and living a self-directed life. It does require tremendous commitment and effort that may be intimidating. Where do you start? What are the pitfalls? What can you do to maximize your chance of success? These questions do have answers and there are things you can do to help yourself if you are motivated. Even if this option seems to be something is not for you, please read the chapter "Succeeding in your new Career." It might change your mind on this topic.

One last thought: don't be an ass. Before you open your business, drop the mindset that your opinions outside of your business focus and area of expertise are relevant or interesting. Your customers won't come to your shop to listen to your latest theory on how to solve the world's problems. You don't want to alienate your customer base. You want all the paying customers, regardless of their politics or philosophies. You certainly have the right to refuse to serve a customer, but that's a slippery slope. Remember, living well is the best...well, simply the best everything.

Core Concepts mapping

Core Four – You are uniquely prepared to manage your own future. Even though this chapter was a bit brutal in trying to point out what you don't know, remember that's exactly how the military taught you. Huge, complex systems were broken down into digestible parts and you learned how to deal with the subcomponents and the overarching system. You can do that here. Don't be intimidated. Get started now on building your dream business.

Core Five – You have skills and capabilities that are marketable. The examples provided in this chapter were for more traditional retail and e-commerce models. If you remember, one of the chapter's opening statements was that one of the best ways to become a millionaire is through ownership and management of a company that provides services (vs. goods). What skills and capabilities can you apply to that business model?

Core Six – You have gaps in your skills and capabilities that you need to close. You need to be a life-long learner. Get started now. Start reading, taking classes and above all FIND A MENTOR. If you are lucky enough to find a mentor, stop talking, start listening and taking notes. Honor and respect your mentor by learning from them.

Core Seven – You now have more responsibility for your life, and much more opportunity to screw it up. If you don't prepare properly, you could lose everything you've worked so hard for in life. This can include your family if you aren't careful. It's not just about putting your material possessions and bank account at risk. Clinging to a failing business model obsessively can and will negatively affect your relationships with friends and family. Be smart, prepare and be your toughest critic. Don't fool yourself that somehow, next month will magically become what turns your business around.

Personal perspective:

A friend of mine has a successful grading and construction business. He runs it full time when not working at his "real" job, which is firefighting (and he's no slouch there either). His real job provides a formal retirement plan and insurance. He has his priorities straight and has turned down multiple offers for promotion, more pay and responsibility within one of the largest fire departments in the country. His focus is on his business and his family. He's not rich, but lives comfortably and more importantly, happily. What would you do? Would you be able to avoid the temptation of more pay, recognition, and responsibility? What are your priorities?

Chapter 11 – Succeeding in your new Career

This first thing to remember is that you are not in Kansas anymore because this ain't the service. A new career means new rules, new idiots, new experts, new friends, and most of all an entirely new system to learn. Beyond your training, experience, or formal education, you are the FNG; that really new guy who no one trusts, who doesn't fit in, who might have authority but no wisdom or insight into the current business culture, process, and system. Even if you are hired into a managerial, senior individual contributor or C-level position, you are still the FNG. You have a lot to learn and a brief time in which to do so.

You are just starting out, so don't shoot your credibility in the foot. Keep your sea stories and/or war stories to yourself. Your civilian peers don't have the context to digest or give credit to your stories, even if you dumb them down for their consumption. They are also watching you with a critical eye, looking for flaws and weaknesses. When you take a new job, there is so much to learn and much of it comes all too much and too soon.

By the way, congratulations on beating back the competition and landing the job. But buyer beware, you won't know what you've gotten into until sometime in the future, so always yourself a favor and keep your job search active . Don't get complacent and don't stop looking for your next great opportunity.

Expect to work through a transition period that can last from two weeks to six months, and plan fora longer period of adjustment because there is much to learn. Depending on how technically advanced the company is, you'll learn about methods and processes associated with specific jobs. Many companies will outsource (if they are small) or provide in-house technology and computer systems to help them run their business. As part of coming onboard, you could be required to get access to various computer applications such as administrative systems for HR, payroll, and timekeeping as well as various applications that are used for training, providing information about safety and security and a myriad of other information. . Once you have been onboarded, you've got to learn the actual job as specified by your new manager and others.

Do you have a target level of compensation? This should be tied to your goals, your timeline, and your target lifestyle. How does this job help you accomplish want you want? No one expects life to be scriptable and predictable, but if you have a plan then you have a framework for evaluating your progress and adjusting as necessary.

One of the biggest open secrets of being an employee is that you have the greatest leverage for salary negotiation at the point of hire. You need to be ready to negotiate carefully to maximize your starting pay.

After you've been hired, you may discover that you did amazingly well with your pay rate or that you have significant room for improvement. This chapter will focus on the success factors for managing the job after you've started.

Remember our earlier review of the minimum level of compensation?

Core Nine - The Republic is powered by the engine of Capitalism

- Minimum annual income: *Your age X $3,000*
- Net worth check baseline: *Your income X Your Age / 10*

How do you stack up?

Remember that income from your primary job is just one source of wealth and to increase your odds of success, you need multiple sources of income. Also remember that we want to focus our financial health on true wealth and not income, but you need income to allow you to grow your wealth. We'll dig more deeply into the topic of multiple streams of income in the Money Management chapter.

This chapter will focus on maximizing your measurable performance, your intangible reputation, and the impact those factors have on your compensation.

If you own your own business, then you are in full control of how much you get paid. You should understand and be an expert at managing cash flow, and gauging the health of your business. You may go through a few lean years as you grow your business, but hopefully you'll achieve the goals you have set for your personal wealth and lifestyle.

If you are an employee, you have fewer options. Other than negotiating your salary when you start, your compensation will be decided by persons and factors which are at times beyond your control. Think about that statement because it is important. When you work for a paycheck, you are in reality contributing more to someone else's financial bottom line than you are to your own. The math is simple, to have you as an employee they have to make more money than they pay you.

Though the previous paragraph seems to imply it's a bad thing to have a job instead of being self-employed by owning your own business, that's not the intended message. If you are reading this book, then you are already an exceptional individual who is looking for ways to excel. It's not a huge leap to assume you are, or could become, one of the top performers in your company. The target message is that you may find you have undervalued your contribution and now must find a way to negotiate and get the compensation your experience demands. Part of this is a continuous process of managing your brand. You can't just wake up one day and decide, "hey, I'm an important person and should get paid more"! It doesn't work like that. You need to understand a multitude of factors and create a framework to evaluate the goals of the company along with your contributions compared to the company bottom line. If you are buried in the bowels of an organization doing menial tasks, your compensation will reflect that. If you can handle the risk and pressure, the big money is always closest to the point of sale and customer-facing jobs.

By the way, your employer has little to no loyalty to you. Some of this is corporate indifference, after all there is always someone else to hire. Let's dig a little deeper into that last comment, as it sounds kind of snarky, shallow, and over-simplistic. In many companies, top and mid-tier managers have grown up under a common method called "top grading." If you search the web for that term, you will see various explanations and exultations about what a wonderful managerial "secret weapon" it is. The basic principle is simple: fire a certain percentage of your lowest performing employees every year and hire the best you can afford to replace them. The most famous proponent of this management practice was Jack Welch, CEO of General Electric.

If we can all agree there is no perfect management structure and no perfect staff alignment, you can understand how the constant churn of employees leaving and joining is accepted as a part of the management equation. People and businesses come and go. Popular managerial wisdom (that should make you cringe) says there are only three types of employees; average, hero, and under-performer. It has been my experience that there are four types. There is a high-performance group that is often overlooked; a group of workers who perform consistently and significantly above the average, but don't quite rise to the level of hero status. These four rough groupings break down like this:

(1) Average: This group makes up 80% of the work force, keeping the lights on and performing the majority of the day-in and day-out work

(2) Subject-system matter experts: approximately 10% of the population responsible for executing change and innovation as well as directing the average performers even when not in a supervisor role

(3) Hero" less than 2% of the workforce, literally high-level experts including some of the smartest people you will ever come into contact with.

(4) Under-performers: between 5-8% of the population who don't pull their weight and should be replaced.

There is also "the management team" or "senior leadership team." These individuals have to keep the lights on and revenue flowing. In some cases, "the management team" will come to rely on the "hero" class elements to such a degree that it creates a toxic environment. In cases like these," the management team" and the "heroes" lose touch with the other team elements, becoming increasingly hostile in their interactions with various areas, groups, and individuals. Often the "heroes" will work to create perception that only they can be trusted to solve the issues at hand and thus become irreplaceable. Unfortunately, due to the hoarding of information about process, method, and contacts they can become irreplaceable *at a given point in time*. It takes a strong management team to break this type of stranglehold when it occurs, and the process is called eliminating "key man dependencies," a concept you should master before ever thinking about becoming a manager. Some people can succeed at the "top performer toxic bullet-proof" dance for years, but eventually someone will see through this situation and manage through them or around them. If we have a core of competent persons and a minimum of "toxic heroes" (we would of course move heaven and earth to keep the non-toxic heroes) then it sounds like a solid practice to move out the lowest performers, right?

Find those under-performers and root them out, every year. This should be done with no hard feelings, good luck to them, it just didn't work out. Sounds simple but a bit ruthless, right? In all practicality, getting rid of under-performers is usually a train wreck for most businesses. The problems arise when the evaluation process is flawed, relying on the subjective, not objective input provided by individuals. Add in the variations and the absolute gaming of the system by various decision makers, evaluators and reviewers and the process can be dead on arrival (DOA) before it ever has a chance.

Please note the language "can be DOA" used in that last statement. There are companies that have been successful in implementing a system for fairly evaluating employees. These companies are usually run very efficiently and have very disciplined methods to measure success at all levels. They also have multiple independent reviewers to prevent favoritism biases from corrupting the process. If you can find one of these companies then you have added incentive to stick around…if you keep performing.

There is a fundamental concept here that you only owe your employer loyalty as long as they are taking good care of you. This means you need to pay attention and note various biases, undeserved promotions, compensation inequality for the same type of work you're performing. Look for other preferential treatments that others may be receiving that you aren't. Keep your eyes wide open all the time. If you are getting paid adequately, are treated as a valued member of the team, and can maintain your quality of life, then you are winning. When any of those factors start to slip, you need to take notice immediately and act.

What does this pessimistic, cynical perspective have to do with managing your success and compensation?

Let's start with a bit of realism. Think about this statement: *"Blood relation and access will trump hard work and ability every time."* We certainly don't want this to be true; we want the good guy to win, and the bad guy to fail publicly if possible. But some truths in life, like this one can't be and shouldn't be ignored. This is a fundamental truism, ignore it at your peril and better yet embrace it so you won't be surprised. You must continually assess your position and be prepared for your next move.

With this in mind, realize you need to start planning for your next job from the very first day you start the current one. If you understand today's businesses have only one imperative and that does not include taking care of you like the corporations of yesteryear did for our grandparents and parents, then you understand you always need a plan. The company has little or no loyalty to ANY employee at ANY level. The company is loyal only to itself. It's not evil, but the company is in the business of creating wealth for its stockholders and owners, not you. You need to plan to learn what you can from this company and be ready to move on at your convenience and on your timeline. Unless you have a specific tradesman-like skill, you need a resume that shows movement and growth throughout your career. Optimally you should work through each position in two to three-year blocks. With each move, you should take on significantly more responsibility and work to expand your experience with diverse types of business and business elements. You should also see significant pay increases with every move. So, harvest and integrate the lessons, knowledge, and wisdom you learn from each employer, make lasting friends and respected business contacts but plan to move when the time is right for you. Let's say that again a little differently. Don't burn your bridges, make lasting friends, and show respect and professionalism as you move through your career.

When important things begin to change, you need the ability to detect negative trends and be prepared to take steps that will benefit you. This is hard, and you must pay attention so you can identify changes as early as possible. Skipping over the obvious trends of market collapse, declining product sales, downsizing, going out of business, offshoring, corporate raider, and such, let's focus on you and the subtler internal politics. This awareness or early warning radar will help you sense when things may be shifting to a sub-optimal condition for you. There can be huge warning signs such as when a manager starts closing their business goal gaps with your quality of life while not expecting the same from others on the team. Cliquish behavior, undeserved promotions, over-socialization with select managers and lowered output by select individuals can be significant warning signs. There are also more subtle signs that you should pay attention to, like being excluded from various meetings or suddenly having your access blocked to decision. Excessive scrutiny of your working hours, work product and even something as simple as being asked to explain a common expense report item that should be self-explanatory can be warning signs. We can't be exhaustive here due to the complex nature and variation in s businesses and business practices, so pay attention to your employer, manager and how you are perceived. When things begin trending towards "sub-optimal" be ready to make a move. Be proactive, not reactive.

Secondly, paying close attention to the performance and behaviors of your peers and others will give you a basis for evaluating your contribution versus your pay versus the contributions of others. For this, you need to review and understand the market pay median and ranges for your area and your job. This is more complicated than expressed here, but it is something you want to develop a feel for. It would be great for everyone's compensation to be posted on the break room wall, but that just isn't going to happen.

At this point you're probably wondering why I should bother if the company has no loyalty to me and the deck is stacked. Let's create a framework for analysis based on statistics. You've probably heard about the "the curve" at some point in your life. Think about a normal statistical distribution and even if you haven't, read on and you'll understand what I'm referring to. Here's a normally distributed data set for reference, often called the "bell" curve. You will see this type of distribution in a "normal" system; in other words, a system that has normal behaviors and is mature. This mathematical tool is used to analyze data of all types. It's a good working tool that allows someone to assess the behavior of any given system and its elements. In a normal distribution the mean, median and mode are the same. Don't worry if you don't understand these terms, you'll learn more about them as you read on.

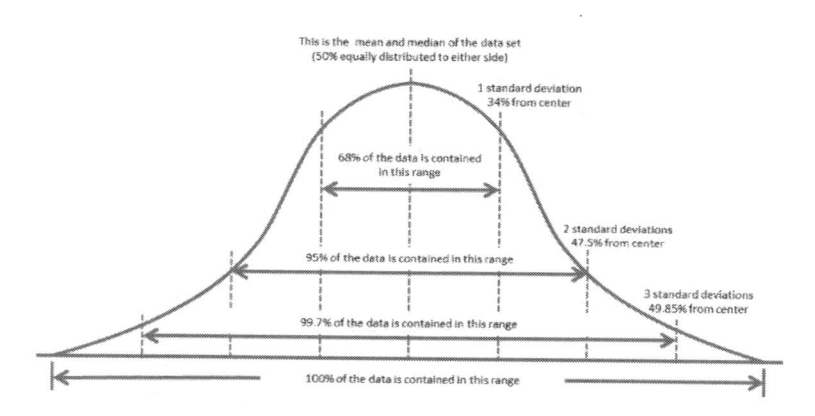

Most of us dwell within the first standard deviation from the normal. In other words, about 68% of any normal data set is within 34% of the average, positive on one side and negative on the other. This is important to understand as most people, processes and expectations are centered around the average. Moving too far from center in either a positive or negative direction will elicit a response from systems that are designed to manage to the average.

A statistician, or data analyst would plot the data and look for systems that are skewed to one side or the other. This skew would indicate a positive or negative bias. For example, a positively skewed distribution may look like this:

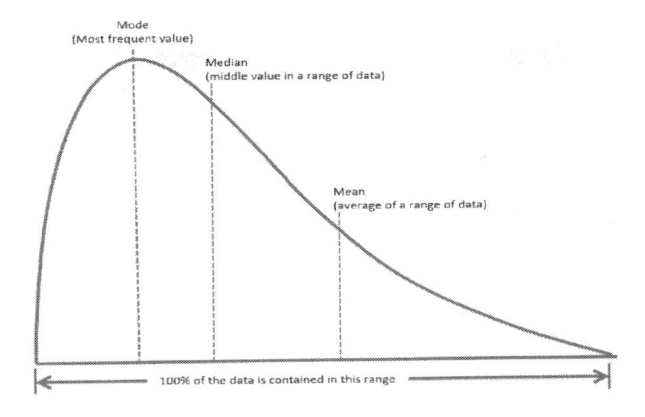

Though a gross simplification, this type of data chart is generally read from left (bad) to right (good).

Positive is good, right? No. In this case it indicates the majority of the data is to the left of the mean (average). If we saw this data in terms of defects per employee, this means a majority of the (those to the left of mean or average) workforce is producing significantly higher numbers of defects per unit of work than the top performers. As an employer, we might want to take this data and use it to determine performance-based compensation ranges. Assume this is tied to some real-world measure of performance, in this case defects per unit. Those individuals to the right of the mean (average) are producing the least number of defects per unit produced. In a perfect world, assuming that defects per unit is our key quality indicator, these folks would get pay commensurate with their contributions.

An analyst might recommend that the employer introduce some type of compensating mechanism, perhaps several, to correct this skew. You want a "normal bell curve when possible.

It is unlikely that you will ever get all the empirical data to fill out this type of statistical analysis unless that is specifically your job. However, if you can get your head around this as a framework for evaluation, you can certainly apply it to your workspace. Who is contributing the most? Are these individuals respected and rewarded appropriately? If so, you want to get into that group. If not, look more closely at the reasons the top performers aren't celebrated as such. You may find reasonable explanations for this including too many toxic heroes, poor management or simply lack of training.

Be particularly alert for an intentionally skewed system. This generally indicates a weak or compensating leader who is protecting their turf and friends. Don't try to "fix" this type of system, just be aware of it and learn the rules until you can move on. If the compensation is good enough, you may be tempted to stick it out for the long term but that's generally a mistake. Eventually something breaks the fragile balance, and everyone gets swept out.

If it seems as though this chapter is focusing on the more negative situations you can run into, you've gotten the message loud and clear. You are walking away from an environment where a simple glance at a sleeve, collar devices, fruit salad and badges can give you almost all the information you need to know about everyone in the room. At a very minimum you can get a read on the experience and rank. Of course, not everyone wears every badge and ribbon all the time, but you get the point. You can get referential data from the uniform. You get NONE of that from the civilian world unless your next career is within the First Responder or Law Enforcement ranks. Sometimes the most influential persons are those that least look like they should be making decisions. Even worse, some of the people who have enough influence to do you damage aren't even in your command structure, or to use the civilian term, on the organization chart in a leadership position. There is a power structure, and you are not part of it.

If you've done the full ride or even had more than a couple of years in the service, your first reaction may be that it's more complicated than I'm describing. This is more a of reminder that most of the referential framework and data that you are accustomed to having in the service simply will not be available in civilian life. You'll need a different set of lenses through which to look.

In the Chapters "It's not always about what you know" and "Your Next Job" we talked about building your personal brand. Understanding the culture and expectations of your current job is key to creating and managing your brand. Remember the part about not being bulletproof? You can't slay every dragon, and even if you could, eventually you'll be taken down by someone out of professional envy, jealousy, or competitiveness. There will always be someone better, faster, and cheaper or failing that, there will be someone who can whisper a better story into the right ear.

So, you come to your current job and learn the culture. Every company wants to succeed and to see their mission statement and culture embraced and executed faithfully on a daily basis. In short, they want the win. Unfortunately, every system ever designed is corrupted and gamed by the people in it. There is no Uniform Code of Military Justice (UCMJ) to declare and enforce the rules. By the way, if you have ever actually read the Uniform Code of Military Justice you would likely be appalled at its archaic, draconian language and approach. However, it has stood the test of time and provided a strong functional framework for managing behavior and discipline. Out here in civilian-land, it's more about lawsuits and illegal acts and to that end, you'll really want to understand the rules, regulations, and laws that are applicable to your current employer and business. It will only be a matter of time before someone asks you to do something that may cross over into a "grey" area. If you don't understand the black, white, and grey boundaries, someone could use you to do their dirty work and eventually being assigned the blame.

This happens all the time in the service. You may not have had direct experience with cronyism, nepotism, favoritism, and other malicious behaviors, but they were all around you. However, you were protected by multiple layers of formal and informal reporting, detection, investigation, and reprimand including punishment. Unfortunately, corporate rules, federal regulations and civilian laws are no substitute for the Uniform Code of Military Justice.

Take a moment and think about the concept of a "lawful" order. How many times did you debate the meaning and application of a "lawful order" while still in uniform? By comparison, it is a poorly documented concept when so many other military traditions, rules and regulations are made crystal clear. You may not have realized it, but you were probably given multiple illegal orders in your career (likely nothing that would rise to the level of a felonious offense). Skeptical? Look up the concept of duty hours, liberty and think back how many times you were "ordered" to work beyond normal business/duty hours when in CONUS and not deployed or under emergency/alert conditions.

Think about working in a new world without the institutional framing of the UCMJ to safeguard you. There is a legal framework of rules, regulations and laws that protect you in your civilian life, in much the same way as the UCMJ did, at least in theory. In practice, receiving the guidance and protection you are entitled to is often a huge miss. You may not recognize being given poor guidance until it's too late. You can go from hero to zero in the blink of an eye, ending up out of a job and being interviewed by a state, federal or industry regulator or law enforcement. You might have been following precise instructions, but if you are kicked to the curb with no cover from your former employer, you would be in an unfortunate situation. Dozens of real-world behavioral examples from corporate America can be summed up in this simple strategy when dealing with a complicated issue; "go ahead and fire them today, we can deal with any legal issues if and when they decide try to sue us." This is neither a joke nor an exaggeration.

So, take all this with a grain of "worst case scenario" salt. But realize that if you don't spend some of your energy learning the moral, ethical, and legal boundaries of your chosen profession you are likely going to run aground at some point. Be as smart as you were in the military; learn the system and the culture, and build yourself a brand of success and trustworthiness.

One of the most powerful mitigating actions you can take is to find a mentor in the business, within the company, where you are employed if possible. Honor the time your mentor spends with you; don't waste their time, ask them all the tough questions and listen to their answers.

Keep your eyes wide open at work. You still get full credit for the successes and failures you observe and integrate. It is important you understand this point. You don't have to personally drive each event to get the experience. It's just as important to learn from the mistakes of others as well as your own. Pay attention because class is always in session. Your next job or profession expects to benefit from the totality of your previous experience so bring as much with you as you can.

To be successful, you need to understand the power structure or your organization, as well as who the decision makers are. You need to help make them successful. To do that, you need to understand the goals, objectives, and timelines of the company, division, and unit that of which you are part. How can you contribute to obtaining the target state? Make friends and acquaintances, not enemies. You know the drill; tap into the various subcultures (not the toxic or negative ones) and make sure that your new coworkers see you as professional and human. Spend some time learning key persons and roles. Ask for advice and clarification if you don't understand something, and listen. The advice to be a good listener can't be emphasized enough. Watch out for the manipulators who want to monopolize your time and have very toxic perspectives.

No matter what job you land, you'll need to learn about the company and culture and how success is defined from the inside. Here are some ideas on how to identify, acquire and master the information needed to be successful.

General business integration

1. **Get ahead of the competition.** In a world where your competition is looking for reasons to slouch and come to work in their pajamas (not a

joke), you should always dress for success because it matters. This recommendation does NOT mean "spend all your money on clothes." You should dress appropriately, attractively, neatly, and most importantly you should make sure your clothes compliment your body type. Don't wear clothes that are too tight; if you gain a few pounds (and 99% of you will gain a significant amount of weight post service), buy some clothes that fit until you can shave off the extra weight. There are numerous ways to describe the Zen of dressing appropriately, and I think that elegant is the word which best describes you should strive for. With that said, while most of us aren't model material and will never grace the cover of Vogue or GQ magazines, the right clothes are particularly important. Keep your military uniform discipline: you had more than one uniform you to wear daily, so extend that habit to your civilian life. Try to maintain at least a week's worth of clothes that are appropriate for your working hours, and keep them at the ready in your closet. You should always have some options available to turn up your style a notch or two. If you travel as part of work, always take extra clothes for an unplanned extension of your trip.

2. **Learn the company.** Get a clear understanding of the major efforts underway. What is the company particularly good at? Where does it have room for improvement? Where does the management team WANT to invest in next? Where are the company's other locations? What really matters to the leadership of the company? What regulations and laws dictate behaviors, methods, and processes? How mature is the company in terms of process and methodologies? Basically, you should gather all the data you can and leverage it to integrate into your world (business) view.

3. **Learn the culture.** You need to map the cultural behaviors and expectations. Figure out who can help guide you. Your boss/manager/team lead can help, but you need input from outside of your department. Take all "advice" with a grain of salt. The longer the advice giver has been with the company, the more likely the input may be flavored with personality conflicts.

4. **Where is the "center of power" located.** Figure out where the center of power in the corporation resides. Some very large companies have multiple centers of power focused on specific product lines or customer bases. In many ways, these act like independent companies and the more profitable these "lines of business" silos are, the more independence they have. Be aware that strong personalities can be found in the bastions of

profitability. Once you understand where the power center is, make a conscious decision on whether you want to be part of that. If you do, then you need to be walking the halls of the "center" every day. You need to be visible and accessible. Remember, people do things for people, but only for those people they like, respect and can work with.

5. **Be deliberate.** You really do need to slow down and take things slowly. Transitioning from the service where everything came at a "drinking from the fire hose" pace, you must realize that most businesses are not organized to move that rapidly. You may show up for work and not get admin access, logons, or assignments for days or even weeks. You may be more capable than the person assigned to train and help you get on-boarded. Don't chafe, don't be impatient. There are cultural clues and lessons to be learned and you should take this opportunity to learn as much as you can. Make new friends, but don't alienate your coworkers with your crisp military expectations. Above all, don't create adversaries. Practice patience and kindness; don't start telling sea stories and tall tales. Be a considerate, careful listener and thoughtful new employee. Think before you speak.

6. **Who is your manager and what do they expect from you?** This is where it gets very real, very quickly. You need to manage this relationship better than any previous leader-to-subordinate relationship you've had at any point in your previous life. While you work for the company, your working loyalties must be aligned with your boss. Usually, you can't grill this person on their expectations and get them to give you a perfect set of instructions. Instead, you must pay close attention during the time they give you; make note of how they operate, as well as what are their expectations and leadership style. Some managers will micromanage, some will fire off objectives and ask you to report back at certain intervals, but most will fall somewhere in between these extremes. You need to get this right. Learn their business language and meet their expectations. You can and certainly should ask what they expect from you. In the early days of your job, they may not know exactly what they want until they understand what you are capable of. Think of it as a period of learning for them before they hand over a critical, large or highly visible deliverable. One of the most important conversations you should have early-on with your boss is about success. You need them to tell you how they will define success for you over what timeframes. For example, how will they measure

your success over the first 30/90/180 days? What must you do to become their top-rated associate a year from now? Be prepared to hear you can't get achieve that top job slot in a year, because it may take longer to get there and there may be other blockers. As was stated earlier, you may not get a completely coherent answer when you ask these questions about success beyond 30 days. Don't worry about the less than complete response as most managers don't necessarily think that clearly and that far ahead. Instead, try to establish a productive dialog you can revisit as you grow into your position.

7. **Learn the chain of command and their idiosyncrasies and expectations.** The greatest sign of your success comes when someone above your manager's level contacts you directly, or asks you to fill in while your manager is temporarily unavailable or out of office. You need to know what you are dealing with before that day comes. Who hates a certain delivery method? Who wants everything in writing? Who wants to have control of the people and the process as part of the conversation? Who has relationships embedded in the lower ranks? What about personalities, who's a great person and who could care less about you and your career? The farther up the food chain you go, the more abstract the conversations are and generally the level of expertise goes vertical on the plot. These are not the guys you baffle with BS. They generally know the answer before they ask it. Expect to be tested, judged, and evaluated on everything, from your knowledge of the company, major efforts and how they relate or depend on your department all the way to how well you stand up under pressure.

8. **What is the product?** What does your company produce? How good is the company in the market? How do you measure the market? How can you really contribute if you don't understand how your company sells to generate its revenue? This may not be relevant to your immediate job, but understanding the company's products, market share and consumer opinions are good things to know over the long run.

9. **Who are your customers?** Who are your largest, most important customers? You may not have direct responsibility for a customer relationship (that's a whole different book), but you need to understand some customers are more equal than others. It would be nice if you could grab the order book and general ledger for the business and map out the customers who spend the most money on the most profitable products

and services to get that "ah ha, there you are!" insight. Unfortunately, customer relationships can be complex and may have layers you initially can't see or understand. Personal relationships can come into play, complex business-to-business (B2B) exchanges can be involved, there may be a joint marketing relationship; the list of relationship complexities is infinite. You must be patient, ask a lot of questions, listen to the explanations, and integrate the details into your knowledge base. Remember that without customers, regardless of size, you are instantly unemployed. If you make a customer unhappy, you end up with the same results while someone else repairs the relationship.

10. **What challenges does the business face?** This is another complex topic which requires an understanding of the product, the current economic state, product sales, regulatory and legal requirements. Has there been a recent exodus of the founders, the company's brain trust or perhaps just some of the most experienced people being picked off by a competitor? Is the product line aging and in need of a redesign or a facelift? Some topics, particularly issues related to legal, regulatory or employment problems, are usually held as confidential, available only to those on a need to know basis. Other issues are easier to discover and learn about, possibly offering you a great opportunity to help the company resolve. Don't try to inject yourself into all the issues in play, but do find a way to add value and materially contribute to the resolution.

11. **Learn the specifics about revenue and profit for your company.** How does your company make money? What are the fixed and variable costs? If your company is publicly held, then a version of this data is publicly available. That doesn't mean it's absolutely accurate or in a state that you can decipher. This is where you need to find a mentor to learn from, as this is topic most leaders in the company will talk about with you. Your questions may get an occasional rejection to the effect what you're asking is "above your paygrade," but if you've been building and strengthening relationships you'll get quite an education when you start asking. Be prepared, most companies revenue to profit equations can be extraordinarily complex, involving business issues you've never heard of. Accounting is the language of business, and if you understand the numbers, you are in a rare and select group because typically less than 1% of employees (considerably less in larger companies) understand the bottom line. Becoming one of those rare individuals will give you deep

insight into business in general and may provide a line of communication with the decision makers in your company.

12. **How do you get promoted?** We will assume you want more responsibility and authority to get things done. Now you need to define what "promoted" means to you. There are managers and individual contributors, and you need to decide which of those paths you want to drive toward. In most cases, the main path will be chosen for you, but you can influence it. Some promotions come from simply being in the right place at the right time. When that happens, take the promotion even if you feel you are under qualified. There are times when you will be offered more responsibility and perhaps a nice new title without being offered additional pay. This brings us back to the definition of promoted. Sometimes you need to take a step sideways to get to the next level. Sometimes you need to say no to a job that will just grind you up, or perhaps get an agreement to fill the role for a certain amount of time while the company finds a permanent hire.

13. **How well are you paid?** The civilian world works off a concept called "total compensation." It may sound unfamiliar, but you certainly understand the concept. You no doubt applied it calculating all the benefits you received from the military when you were working through your decision-making process about if or when to leave the service. In that scenario, to calculate your total compensation you should have included Basic Allowance for Subsistence (BAS), Basic Allowance for Housing (BAH), Variable Housing Allowance (VHA), thirty days paid leave, Healthcare, even base commissary access. Across the services there are over 50 different military bonus payment categories, covering everything from hazardous duty such as hostile fire or exposure to toxic substances and other categories including flight pay, submarine duty, medical corps, and other bonuses too numerous to list here. This means you really do understand the concept of "total compensation" but just need to understand the civilian framework. When a company makes you an offer of employment, their cost is much higher than your pay. The rule of thumb for the personnel expense is approximately salary plus bonus plus 30%. This 30% generally includes vacation and other paid time off, healthcare contributions, 401k contributions and other balance sheet items that benefit you. Combining all those components results in total compensation. Increasingly companies are moving to that concept of total compensation versus the

"what is my pay" only conversation. This concept is fair and relevant, and you should be prepared to evaluate any offer, raise, or bonus in terms of market rate or in more simple terms, what is the going pay for the job you're doing. What you need to determine is are you going to be compensated in the lower, middle, or upper ranges of the going market rate for your job?

14. **How are raises and bonuses determined?** This is a significant, appropriate and relevant question. Every company is different, and in most cases, you won't find this information clearly spelled out in any human resources manual because base pay and merit increase information s is highly confidential. While there may be a compensation system which tries to pay competitively, there are always outliers that are hard to see from anywhere on the normal distribution curve. With that said, you need to take personal responsibility for negotiating your base pay by understanding the market and you value within it. Sometimes a person can get a compensation adjustment if they were hired at a below-market rate and proved they could deliver. However, this is such a rare event that you should never count on it. Make your best deal going in. Once in the system, there may be caps and increase limits about which you will not be told. Some companies automatically give a cost of living raise like you've seen in the service, but this is also becoming less common. You may find yourself capped in a certain job and going without a raise for one or more years; the only way out being to move up to a new level internally or out to a new company.

15. **Bonus.** In some businesses, bonuses may be expected and customary for many of the employees, however these types of bonuses tend to be small. In other situations, the bonus can be as high as 50% or more of an individual's salary. On Wall Street, you will see an annual job shuffle just after February, when everyone has received their bonus for the previous year. In the best run companies, bonuses are tied to individual performance and the company's overall performance. In others, the bonus structure is secret (can't even ask) and the vast majority are paid out to the senior managers who "are taking all the risk." That might sound like bureaucratic doublespeak, but it is not. This term is often associated with successful, well-known industry players who leave a large successful company to help a smaller company achieve success. In that case, they have taken enormous risk by leaving a well-established position (usually

also highly compensated) and moved to a new job for an even higher level of compensation. Bonuses can usually come in two forms: cash or company ownership. Sometimes a bonus will include both, providing a certain amount of immediate cash and a deferred method of company ownership. Examples of company ownership are stock grants or options, and they are typically set up to vest over a three-year period. What does that mean?

Example: Total Bonus $100,000 (yes, these do exist, and they are obtainable. Would you be shocked to know that some companies will pay much higher bonuses?)

> **Cash:** $50,000, sometimes paid in lump sum, sometimes paid incrementally.
>
> **Stock:** Valued on the day of the grant, 33% will vest in 12 months, 33% more in 24 and the last 33% at the end of 36 months.

One of the best situations you can land is a good solid salary with an aggressive (not impossible) set of goals that will result in bonuses (cash and/or stock) as you achieve them.

What about taxes on your bonus? This can be tricky and while it's not really a negotiable item, you should learn how it works at your company. The IRS "recommends" withholding a flat 25%, but most companies don't do that. Instead they will combine the bonus and pay in the period it is paid out and tax you at the higher combined rate. By the way, the same applies to any stock grant received, you will pay taxes when you vest or activate.

Small-to-Medium Businesses

1. **Culture is critical in SMBs**. Unless you are hired to help turn around a business that is in trouble, you have entered a culture of success or at least stability (mediocrity). It's important to remember that, because you don't mess with success or stability. The company has a plan, a method and the bottom line to prove it. SMBs are often an extension of the owner's personality. Figure that out quickly, hopefully as part of the interview process.

2. **Many SMB owners don't want to become the next IBM or AT&T**. They took this path for their own reasons that can be as simple as they are anti-big company. Many started with big companies and found them toxic for different reasons. There are reasons not to grow beyond a certain size and it is a choice, not because the business has been blocked or stunted. Learn as much as you can about the company's strategy so you can align with their expectations.

3. **Some SMB owners are absentee owners and they like it that way**. They have one or a few trusted employees who run the business for them. They may be on semi-permanent vacation or starting another business, which is consuming their time. Usually they understand the foibles of those they put in charge and are willing to live with them in return for the business running smoothly.

4. **Consider trust as a component of culture, but different enough to merit this paragraph**. Trust is paramount in SMB land. The landscape is too small and highly populated for any type of misbehavior, including lowered performance, to go unnoticed for long. Everyone tends to know everyone, and everyone understands a portion of everyone's jobs, deadlines, and deliverables because they are all so intertwined. Aberrant behavior is quickly spotted, trust erodes, and the individual is usually terminated with haste. In the SMB, you can't afford toxic or criminal behavior. Occasionally, a fresh set of eyes will identify theft or fraud. If you come across that situation, don't confront the individual you've found doing something illegal, take it to the management chain and the owner if necessary. But before you do anything that serious, be very sure of your data.

5. **That one person who doesn't play by the rules.** There's always that one person who seems to violate all the stated and implied rules and expected behavior of the SMB. Generally, this person will find you after you join the firm. They work on the basis of fear and intimidation. In almost every case, this person will have built an image of themselves as being irreplaceable to the point that their firing or resignation would permanently damage the business. They have usually found a key part of the business, performed some fairly innovative work, and then refused to share. Don't underestimate this individual, they are always extremely bright and can walk the walk. Despite their toxicity they are a real part of the business and you must figure out how to deal with it.

Large/Government/Multinational corporations

1. **Variation is the enemy.** Very few large companies have found room for the variation and personal differentiation you see in owner operated or small-to-medium businesses. In many ways, large corporations are very military-like, and a lot of this has to do with the fact many that were created or heavily influenced by the large numbers of military that joined the business world after World War II, emphasizing the pyramid type organizational structure. This anti-variation can extend from the smallest item (types of pencils or detailed dress codes) to more broadly defined guidelines.

2. **Don't underestimate corporate culture.** The most common rule seems to be something like "have all the differences of opinion or approach or method or anything but reach a conclusion without escalation." More simply put, solve your problems at your level and don't bring them to the next level or you will be perceived as anything but a team player.

3. **The business model is very rigid and reinforced.** Your job will likely be to support the current model/process, not fix it. Remember, these large businesses aren't in the habit of hiring the lowest common denominator. They hire top talent and constantly evaluate their market, supply line, manufacturing processes, customer base, costs and revenues. If you have an innovative idea, refine the concept then ask around to see if it's already been tried. If you think you are onto something new, then keep it to yourself until you've fully developed it. Ignore this advice and you'll find that someone has picked off your idea and run it up the food chain ahead of you. Did I mention that large corporations can be vicious?

You were hired for a reason. Hopefully, as you integrate with personalities and the culture and goals, you can demonstrate you are capable of more than the role for which you were brought. This takes us back to goals and timelines, and I am not talking here about silly "mission statement" stuff. What are the real goals and how are you materially affecting them. Sometimes your job will be to provide stability or risk mitigation while others work on the revenue-generating aspects of the business.

Whatever your role is, work with your manager to get it clearly specified and documented. This is so important that I simply can't overstate the need. If you can get your goals and delivery timelines in writing, you will have a basis to evaluate your progress throughout the year. What does your management really need from you? How do they want to be updated or informed?

Written goals also protect you from inept, poorly organized managers as well as other processes and people you can't control or influence directly. With written goals in hand, you can be both proactive and reactive. One of your top priorities should be to constantly review your current workload versus your goals. Your workload should have your running at about 80% utilized in an optimal goal-driven system. This gives you the ability to pick up temporary short-term tasks without derailing your primary goals. If you are assigned a large scale, long-term task, you should immediately and professionally sit down with your boss and talk about it. This should never be some snarky, passive-aggressive dialog to ask which of the written goals can you defer or drop and replace with the new one. Instead, you should be very prepared to discuss your time and resource constraints. Explain and/or remind your boss-manager-supervisor what you still have on your plate and what will happen to those objectives if this new project is prioritized. This should never be about avoiding work, rather it should be an open and honest dialog about priorities. Your boss-manager-supervisor is always under pressure to deliver against compressing timelines and shifting goals. They get to set the priorities and you have to react and help deliver. Remember, you work for the company but as long as you are not being asked to do something unethical, illegal, or immoral your "real" job is to make your boss successful. To do that, you need to know what they expect of you and when and how they expect it. Being able to have this type of prioritization conversation is usually only possible if you have established goals and delivery timelines. If you mismanage that, or you don't have the capacity and prioritization reviews, you will likely be buried with non-critical work that is not aligned to your pay for performance equation.

If you have a bonus structure based on meeting your goals, then you must manage your work carefully and constantly. Everything you deliver and take ownership of in your job should have a component that delivers against your bonus structure. Even if you don't have a formal bonus structure, you should always be working for your next raise. Review your current work versus your written goals every week. Stay on track. Speak with your manager and update your goals as necessary to meet changing business requirements. Document ALL the work you do. In fact, you should create weekly, monthly, quarterly, and yearly updates of your achievements versus your goals and any additional work you do. Even if your management team doesn't take the time to review your work and accomplishments with you regularly, create this data and keep it for later use. You should be aware there is a point, sometimes well in advance of the end of fiscal year, where performance is reviewed, and bonuses are awarded. In large and small businesses, the leadership team has to make decisions about salaries and bonuses for all employees. If you are a self-starter (which almost all of you reading this book are) you'll want to provide your boss with the information they can use as part of this compensation process. Figure this out ASAP and make sure your boss has all the information he or she needs to match your compensation to your performance level.

In this small summary, remember it is your responsibility to manage the job, don't let it manage you. Find mentors, identify toxic members of the team, and have a plan to deal with them if the need arises. Your biggest mistake would be to ignore or antagonize. Be aware and make good decisions.

The good news is there are so many jobs that paying so much more than your service income that your compensation more than makes up for the whole "new guy" thing. Again, the compensation makes it worth your while to survive your early months in a new job. If you happen to be one of those persons who pursues a rewarding but non-compensatory career in service and volunteer organizations, you will find your fulfillment in the service, not the money and you have our deepest admiration and appreciation.

Core Concepts mapping

Core Six – You have gaps in your skills that you need to close. The purpose of this book is to help you identify the differences in the world you are leaving behind and the one you are entering. Make no mistake, you are not fully prepared to succeed in this new world. It's not just about working hard, delivering and being honest; you might be the top performing employee in a company and still be underpaid while lower performers are compensated at a much higher level. Remember that "blood and access" will trump ability and hard work every time. You may have an allergic reaction to that statement but let me assure you it is a fundamental truth of your new world. You need to develop the professional and interpersonal skills, required for you to thrive in your new career.

Core Seven – You now have more responsibility for your life and much more opportunity to screw it up. You must learn how manage to the culture and the people in it. While there are no perfect recipes and this chapter was focused on how to spot the toxic elements manage around them, you CAN figure out the rules and the decision makers. You must do these things, otherwise you are surrendering your quality of life to people and processes you don't understand. You need to take this seriously. Hopefully, you will never have to manage in a toxic environment of any type, but don't count on it. The first time you go in with both guns blazing, calling out all the things wrong with any team, process, or solution, you will likely be disappointed in the results. It is a rare business culture that doesn't protect its own. Take your time and learn the culture and the decision makers. Realize that it is not your job to solve every problem and the more simplistic the solution might appear to you, the less you probably understand it. Learn, watch, and listen to your peers, superiors, and others. Pick your battles; pick those that can be won AND will benefit you.

Personal perspective:

Once, a very capable young man that I know who was just out of high school and starting college had to make a decision. He had just started a new job at fast food restaurant and was called to come in for a second interview at a big box hardware store with a strong hint that he would be offered the job at a higher pay rate and benefits. He was two weeks into training at the restaurant. He did not want to be irresponsible and leave the restaurant in a lurch and after two weeks of training, but he felt like the other job could be better for him. He received conflicting advice from the people in his life he respected. Most told him that he "owed" the restaurant some type of loyalty and should stick it out. A small minority told him that he should explore the other option. The smaller group of advisors said he should at least see what the second employer would offer. The majority convinced him that he shouldn't even follow up with the big box store. Six months later I ran into him as he was getting off work. He was tired and splattered from head to toe in deep fat fryer grease. His shoes were literally coated in flour, grease, and raw animal fat. I didn't ask but will always wonder what he would have done if he had a "do over" opportunity.

Chapter 12 – Do THIS instead of THAT

Maybe you want the abridged version because sometimes we just want people to net it out for us. Is there a formulaic way to approach your transition? Are there Cliff Notes for life after the military that will keep us on the path for success? The answer is an absolute, emphatic NO! There are so many moving parts in your new life you need to stop, think, plan, write it down and then do it again and again and again. Please keep in mind that you MUST have a plan. Don't expect your plan to be perfect the first time you come up with it. Our life plans must be flexible for we certainly don't control all the elements. You can jump in and ride the chaotic waves of those who fail to plan, but if you do so you can expect to pay a high toll in lost money, lost time, lost opportunity and most likely the loss of your family's sense of safety and security. In other words, if you don't plan you are intentionally adding significant risk to your quality of life. We all know the old adage about plans and contact with the enemy. This still holds true. Without a plan, expect to encounter delays, obstacles, unforeseen complexity, confusion, and frustration. With a plan, you may still experience some of these challenges, but you will always be able to find your center and get back on track. You can adjust and overcome rather than being swept around by the surf.

Having said this, you must know there are no shortcuts. So, for those of you who like to skip to the end of the book thinking you're now ready for your new life, here are a few of the guiding principles followed almost religiously by leaders and those who transitioned successfully:

Absolutely Do THIS: Manage your time, your focus, and your day. You need routine, ritual, and personal focus to manage your life. Create and protect these essential elements.

1. Remember, character is what happens when no one is looking.
2. Expect curveballs, derailing events and disasters. Keep your character through all of them.
3. Learn to forgive. It is the most powerful force in the universe after compound interest.
4. Put your family first. Your service absolutely got in the way. Make up for that.
5. Find quiet, uncompressed time for yourself every day. Think deeply and quietly.
6. Find quiet, uncompressed time to share with your family

7. Establish goals for you and your family. You should personalize and prioritize this list. You should not wait until you get out to adopt this "in your face" reminder. You must set your goals and then post them where you see them every day. (Sample list provided):
    a. Family first
    b. Education and training which moves you towards your goals
    c. Home ownership
    d. Creating a second income stream
    e. Creating a third income stream
    f. Creating a fourth, fifth and sixth stream of income
    g. Creating a second career
    h. Target age of actual retirement
    i. Expectations for retirement
    j. Investment strategy
    k. Savings strategy
    l. Create and act on a bucket list
8. Find a mentor for your business goals.
9. Find a mentor for your other goals.
10. Did we say, "find a mentor"?
11. Take steps EVERY DAY towards your goals.
12. Prioritize your goals, attack, and complete the tactical steps, but always work on the end game.
13. Exercise daily.
14. Live an active life.
15. Get engaged in your community.
16. Volunteer and find ways to give back to your community.
17. Celebrate the achievements of your family and friends.
18. Create a traditional get together for family and/or friends.
19. Attend every party to which you are invited.
20. Throw a party.
21. Work on your weak areas, you know what they are so take a chance and put yourself out there.
22. Find a hobby, or break out that hobby you've put on hold.
23. Find a second hobby and enjoy it.
24. Create a routine and stick to it.
25. Start or end each day with exercise and personal time.
26. Create a social media presence for your personal life.
27. Create a *different* social media presence for your business life.

28. Protect your personal and business data. Buy a shredder for your documents and use it.
29. Protect your personal and business data. Backup and encrypt your data and critical emails.
30. Outsource tasks and goals that require skills mastery.
31. Create a will and keep it current. Make sure those affected know what is in it.
32. Create a medical directive and health care proxy with your wishes clearly spelled out.
33. Buy as much life insurance as you can afford.
34. When you have a professional problem, hire a professional and take their advice.
35. Realize you can't do everything.
36. Realize you can't please everyone.
37. Surround yourself with people you admire and look up to. You haven't had that option for many years, and you need to be careful and intentional about doing this.

Instead of That:
1. Don't lose focus.
2. Don't stop running, walking, crawling or even clawing your way forward to your goals.
3. Don't let barriers stop you.
4. Most of all don't get caught up in those activities that siphon your time and energy away from family and success.

Fact of life; as you get older, you start losing the capacity for physical and mental work. However, you can perform at your peak if you avoid things which impact your performance. Once you make yourself aware of what you want to avoid, it becomes much easier redirect your focus, so you don't get sidetracked. Unfortunately, most people make the mistake of filling their day with wrong activities; it's almost like an addiction. Perhaps you've heard the phrase "people's problems often become their hobbies." Here are a few things we've seen derail goals, careers, and daily life:

1. Don't feel guilty about enjoying your life, you've earned it.
2. Don't worry about the past, you can't change one second of history.
3. Don't let your past define your future.

4. Don't let others program your day. Ignore email, reading the news, surfing the net, and listening to voice mail until you reach that part of your daily routine.
5. Don't sleep in, get up as early as you can.
6. Don't skip your daily physical conditioning. Even if you're past your glory days, this is essential.
7. Don't mindlessly surf the Internet. Sure, it's fascinating and a true wonder of the world (no sarcasm), but it's also a ravenous, time wasting, soul-rending beast that will consume your productive focus.
8. Don't get into online confrontations, you won't change the world and you might pick up a psycho stalker. Read and move on.
9. Don't gossip. It is evil, hurts everyone involved and is a waste of time and energy.
10. Don't try to master a specialist skill for one project. Outsource it.
11. Don't treat every problem with equal priority. The squeaky wheel should never automatically get priority.
12. Don't start projects and without finishing them. Stay focused and get things done.
13. Don't enter into unprofitable, time-consuming relationships with others. Pick your professional and personal circles carefully.
14. Don't hang around with toxic, negative, gossiping people
15. Don't fool yourself. Understand your capabilities, strengths and weaknesses and plan accordingly.
16. Hope is not a strategy. While it is a crucial part of life, substituting hope for planning is a recipe for disaster.

Core Concepts mapping

Core Eight – Life is still hard. Life is what you make of it. Plans fail, others will let you down and everyone makes mistakes. People and pets die, accidents happen. Plan for the worst and hope for the best. Life will fall somewhere in the middle. Forgive those that wrong you, but never forget. Live a full and optimistic life, and laugh and cry as the day requires. Find joy in every day to carry you through the hard bits. Live a responsible life of no regrets if you can. Most importantly, enjoy your life and be proud of who you are.

Personal Perspective:

I left the service with no real plan. I drifted from job to job for a few years before I got serious about my future. Too many very capable persons exit the military with no plan, and for you some part of that life is behind you now. No matter what you decide, make it YOUR decision, not just something that randomly happens to you. Be that person who lives the life important to you, not someone else. Create a plan and take action every day to move yourself in the direction you want to go. Failure to plan is something that can be avoided. Too many vets fall victim to lack of planning, so don't be one of them.

Chapter 13 – Technology and You

The older you are, the less likely you are to fully embrace the latest technology, particularly if it requires some effort on your part. When you go to the doctor, do you ask them to skip things you may not be familiar with like an MRI or ultrasound? Of course, you don't, and similarly as you age, you should make learning and using innovative technologies a major part of your life. It will literally make the quality of your life better.

Technology moves fast, and the rate of change is accelerating as we noted in Chapter 3. Have you ever heard of Moore's law? Gordon E. Moore, a co-founder of Intel Corporation wrote a paper in 1965 that noted a trend in computer hardware capabilities that compute power would double every two years as a result of a combination of more efficient manufacturing and the miniaturization of the transistors providing the actual compute power we use in our computers. Case in point, in a few short years, we've gone from slide rulers to smartphones functioning as computers which have more processing power than NASA had at its disposal when they put the first men on the moon.

Personal technology has surged in the last few decades. Social Media, staying connected and other modern personal technologies and conveniences have benefited from demand, consumption, and profitable markets. There are products you can buy today that did not exist five years ago.

Technology has revolutionized multiple professions and accelerated the retention and expansion of knowledge. Before we had modern technology with its multiple backups in multiple locations, a simple fire could result in the loss of information that might take a generation or more to rediscover.

Disruptive technology is a term that you should become familiar with, as it fundamentally changes the way things get done. It "disrupts" existing business models at one or more levels, and can change the supply and demand model, or the accounting methods or the way products are marketed and sold. The introduction of a disruptive technology can render existing products and services obsolete almost overnight.

Here's a limited list of major disruptive innovations from history:

1. Gunpowder

2. Vulcanized rubber
3. X-rays
4. Electricity
5. Flight
6. Combustion engine
7. Antibiotics
8. Nuclear fission
9. Integrated circuits
10. The microprocessor
11. The Internet
12. Smartphones

Disruptive technologies in our lifetimes:

1. **Mobile Internet.** Everyone loves access, all the time from everywhere! The adoption and innovation in this space just going to continue to accelerate. In current and future generations people will live and die without ever owning a PC or laptop by simply accessing the Internet and apps via handheld devices.

2. **3D printing.** The combination of 3D scanning and 3D printing puts an incredibly powerful tool directly into the hands of innovators across the world, and is literally shaking the foundations of manufacturing. Expect this technology to accelerate and eventually provide the ability to print metal and compounds with high tensile strength.

3. **Drones.** Drones will change everything. This hugely disruptive technology, individuals and governments now have the ability to fly drones so small as to be virtually undetectable. Amazon is experimenting with "last mile" package delivery by drone. There is a video on the 'net of an apartment dweller in a large city sending his drone down with money to the local coffee barista and returning to his windowsill with a very fresh cup of java.

Tesla and Google's self-driving cars are another example of drone technology. Imagine the possibilities.

4. **Cloud Computing.** It's here now and continuously disrupting business models. Not just the specialized cloud computing for high performance computing (HPC) or analytics, but the ubiquitous deployment of data, services, and connectivity everywhere, all the time, for everyone.

5. **Cloud Storage.** This is a derivative of cloud computing, with several powerful services to enhance and protect your personal and business data. If you aren't backing up both your personal and business data to the cloud, you should look into it. For the cost of your pocket change, you could back up every digital document, spreadsheet, and irreplaceable picture. Don't rely on removable media technology as it decays over time; yes, even a DVD will lose bits. Data stored online is constantly checked for accuracy.

6. **Artificial Intelligence.** This is one of the few things that scares renowned British physicist Stephen Hawking. In a 2016 interview with the BBC he said that AI will be "either the best or worst thing" for humankind, and he is right because there is the potential for huge upside and downside here. Only time will tell, and this is technology you might want to keep an eye on.

7. **The Internet of Things (IOT).** We're seeing this happen in real time. Small microprocessors and wireless technology are connecting relatively simple devices together. This technology is moving rapidly into our daily lives. Our refrigerators can now show us what's inside, we have thermostats we can control from our mobile devices and our cards have loads of sensors to monitor components. The capability to share information about device status, behaviors and unexpected issues with manufacturers, maintenance providers and you as a consumer will likely create new businesses and services that don't exist today.

8. **Removal of the Communication Barriers to Language and Distance**. Facetime and other video chats are just the beginning. Real time language translation (during a conversation) will allow two or more persons to speak in their native language while the listener hears a zero-lag translation. Did you know that you can take a picture of a menu, a sign, or anything else that's written in a foreign language and get any one of several search engines to translate for you in real time? Tools like Skype and Facetime

(and many others) have already removed the barriers to communicating from afar.

9. **Evolution of Mobile Search Engines.** Expect the limited, often a single topic search capability of today to make huge bounding leaps in effectiveness. In the near future, you will be able to string together multiple questions, concepts, and search parameters for a mobile phone voice search.

10. **Augmented Reality and Wearable Technology.** Hold on to your hats because we're just getting started here. Google Glass 1.0 was an eye-opening experiment. Google Glass 2.0 in Apple and Android watches is much less disturbing, and just as disruptive. Expect much more in the next few decades.

11. **Free and Open Source Software (FOSS).** This is a major game changer which is in progress, and is the easiest and most rapidly producing open source vector. People around the world can collaborate, enhance software, and innovate new features without ever meeting face to face. Did you know that the Linux operating system (OS) is open source? How about Google Chrome or Firefox? Do you want Microsoft Office features and compatibility, then try the Open Office product…for free!

12. **Free and Open Source Hardware (FOSH) Open Design.** This is an open source (software) for the physical world. Physical products, machines and systems are developed through the use of publicly shared design information.

13. **Open Design (FOSS + FOSH**). This is a "2 + 2 = 97" equation. Engage a group of smart people who want to change the world, and you get a force multiplier effect, resulting in an incredible game changer that leverages the power of the open source community to produce physical products. Both software (FOSS) and hardware (FOSH) benefit from common DNA including:

    a. Open source designs with no-fee licenses

    b. Open to do-it-yourself

    c. Open to end-user dialogue

- d. Open to peer-review
- e. Open to collaboration
- f. Open to cradle-to-cradle analysis
- g. Open to viewing as an ecosystem of processes
- h. Open to democratic participation
- i. Open to new design ideas
- j. Open to new economics
- k. Open to the future

14. **Crowdsourcing.** Do you need funding for a great product? Access to this method of funding is easy and helps fund a wide range of ideas. Thankfully, this has the potential to obsolete the monopoly venture capitalists have had, as they often get far more control and benefit from their investment than they deserve.

15. **Quantum Technology.** Scientists continue to unravel the underlayment known as physics. As they learn more about the quantum level of the universe, expect to see major shifts in computing and communication technologies.

16. **Alternative Power Cars:** Electric cars have come a long way in the last few years, with significant improvements in range and reliability that have changed the automobile market. The battery technology that enabled this market is spinning off into home power and other markets. Hydrogen fuel cell cars may one day replace the combustion engine.

This is certainly an incomplete list. As always you should be asking yourself the question why should I care?

The answer is you should care because this will be the world you live and thrive in. You must be engaged, and you should become a power user of technology and embrace innovative changes. Both will enhance your productivity and your connectivity; they will lower your expenses and someday may save your very life. Any one of these disruptive technologies could literally be a gold mine for you, resulting in a new job, or your big idea and the business you've always wanted to run. Disruptive technology empowers individuals. Where can you take it?

Case in point: many small-to-medium businesses would not exist today if it were not for the internet and internet-based services. Amazon Web Services (hosting), also known as AWS is a prime example. In fact, did you know that many Cloud companies offer services free or charge for the first 6-12 months? While you may not know about them, you can count on the fact your competition certainly does. Why should you care if your business isn't a web, software services or other internet-based company? Because every business can use at least a subset of these services, purchasing them from a hosting provider at a lower expense than can be developed and supported in-house.

Behind us are the days of having to buy or lease technology and proprietary software packages that could leave your business in a lurch. These hugely disruptive and enabling technologies accompanied by the experts to support them are a not-so-secret requirement for your business at some point. The total cost is now far less than before. Amazon (AWS) applications and hosting is an impressive set of services, and it's just one among many.

If you are bewildered by the emphasis on this topic or maybe just not sure how it applies to you, you're not alone. Think of the availability of custom business tools with the most sophisticated and mature services available for you a la carte. These services, and others like them can help you create services to enable your business. You can snap these things together like building blocks. It's easy to get caught up in this technology, but remember they are only tools, and remember a fool with a tool is still a fool. Your business is your customer and just as importantly, your data. Don't forget that if you are leveraging these solutions, you are likely not to be their biggest priority in the event of an outage. Design redundancy into your business that allows you to continue to conduct your business servicing your clients in the event of an internet provider or service provider outage.

In our personal and social lives, interactive and connectivity technology has exploded. The use of social media has become an obsession with our young people. It's entertaining, useful, and insidious, as it is always asking for our contact lists and then selling that to the insatiable maw of electronic marketing.

Social media, cell phones, free to almost free voice over IP telephony, instant messaging, texting, tablets, Bluetooth headsets, video calls...wow, the list grows while we sleep. This technology is fantastic, you can find long lost friends, maintain current friendships, and reconnect with loved ones with minimal effort. You should use and leverage these technologies to your advantage when they make sense.

Social media can be part of your new safety web, particularly when you first get out and may be away from home, and you need a safety web as you rebuild your contacts, friends, and associates. The easiest way to start is with a simple social media presence, but don't forget they will sell your descriptive data. In fact, be skeptical about any service that promises not to sell your information. Don't share your contact list to access some silly tool or game they offer. Don't forget that data persists forever, and your internet activities and social media presence will linger for decades. Realize that some employers are going to ask for access to your social media accounts. There are some great sites out there that provide "good enough" services in their free offering. LinkedIn is probably the best example, and I strongly recommend you create a LinkedIn presence and manage it carefully if you are looking for a job or new career.

Texting is great! Use it! Did you know that most smart phones allow you to create a text message with a voice command? It allows you to have multiple conversations with the delay between messages managed by you according to your priorities. Texting allows for simple updates, the sharing of photos and links, and can be a tremendous enabler for your activities. Parents and children now have an extra channel with which to stay in touch.

As a parent, you absolutely must monitor your children's use of the internet, social media, and texting. Did you know there is an entire genre of mobile applications designed to automatically delete message texts or pictures? How about applications that can track your child's smartphone location in real time? One of my favorites is an application that "locks" a phone and only allows it to dial 911 or an approved number when a parent or guardian calls or requests a response. No texting, no internet, no games allowed until a parent provides an "unlock" code.

The statistics available for adolescent exposure to inappropriate images and porn are alarming. While it's difficult to come up with fully accurate statistics because of the nature of surveying children about the topic, many experts place the exposure at +60% before age 16. That estimate goes up to +90% by age 17, so please go the extra mile and pay attention to this. It is almost guaranteed that they will be exposed to this before they have the mental capacity and discipline to deal with the easy access to inappropriate materials.

Even Social media can be destructively addictive and is almost always trivial. Be careful about how much time you invest in personal connectivity and social media, and set boundaries for you and your children. Not allowing phones or tablets at meal times is an absolutely required limiting behavior, in my opinion. Realize that your brain needs to "cool off" to go to sleep and must be fresh to allow your creative processes to work. Don't fill up your mental processes with silly updates and obsessive social media. Instead, create interactions with real people starting with your immediate family, your extended family, your friends, neighbors, and business acquaintances. Unless you are trying to create an online presence for your business, stay the heck away from Twitter and other *minute by minute* social media (#wasteoftime). If you don't understand the pound sign (#) reference, then good for you!

Another personal productivity recommendation is for you to avoid electronic reminders or to-do programs. Too often you will find you are focused on getting something on the list rather than clearing it off the list. Please note no one is recommending that you don't use your phone/tablet/PC for productivity and convenience, because honestly most of us could not function without our electronic calendars. This advice is the product of many years of using the latest electronic gadget or app to help with managing our goals and productivity.

The ability to stay connected over long distances of time and space is truly a wonder of the modern world. You should learn to leverage this technology to maximize the quality of your life, but do not let it dictate how people access and interact with you. There are times when should be present for important interactions. Make the decision to be present for key meetings and discussion consciously and deliberately. Don't default to remote technologies for everything.

What about your next computer? Well, one of the first things you do when you leave the service is buy a good computer. A good computer is something that is reliable, affordable and meets the use cases you need. Though there is tremendous hype, the decision-making process is straightforward:

1. Can you meet all of your personal and business requirements with a smartphone?

2. Can you meet all of your business requirements with a phablet (large smartphone)?

3. Can you meet all of your business requirements with a tablet?

If you answered no to any of the questions above, you will need more than one device. Most of you will enjoy having a real keyboard to work with, which means you will need a desktop or laptop and a cellular/mobile device. In fact, it is recommended that you have both a type computer (of some flavor) and a smart mobile device that can be synchronized for emails, contacts, and other application data.

Assuming this is the most likely scenario, you then must decide what type of technology you want to adopt for your computing needs. The path of least resistance is to buy a laptop because it's mobile and it can act as a home and work computer. You can buy a large monitor, a separate keyboard, and (optical) mouse to get even more use out of it at home. Now, what type of operating system (OS) do you need? This is important as it often affects the type of hardware you need. For example, Apple is easy but expensive, but having both an iPhone and an Apple laptop (Mac) can simplify the technological aspect of your life. For less expensive solutions, others will want to stay the course with a more traditional Windows-based PC, which makes the choice of phone less relevant. Lastly there's the Linux-based computer.

Think it through. Focus on the software and how you will be using the computer. When you've thought it through you are ready to purchase your hardware.

Tech recommendation #1: At a minimum, get a mobile, even if you have some kind of computer. To be absolutely clear here, get a SMART phone. If you are gadget-focused and like to tinker, you may find the Android OS appealing. If you want a plug and play device requiring minimal effort to leverage calendars, email, and contacts, get the iPhone. But get a nice, large-format SMART phone. Buy the largest format you can afford, it may seem awkward at first, but soon you will wonder how you ever survived with the smaller format. Be sure to have a big enough data plan so you don't have to worry about overages. In our modern world, you will be at a severe disadvantage without it.

Tech recommendation #2: Find an online backup service that fits your budget and USE IT. You need a service that will encrypt your data (no peeking by intentional or inadvertent access) and consistently backs your data up. No action is required on your part unless you want to exclude some data (like the OS data). All your devices and all of your critical data, including photos and emails should be backed up.

Tech recommendation #3: Keep a local backup. Purchase a detachable drive that can hold all of your data and update it monthly or quarterly. If you have followed the recommendation to use an online backup service, why do you need a local copy? That's a good question and the answer is simply the time factor. Restoring Gigabytes or Terabytes of critical data over an internet connection can take a significant amount of time. Grabbing that removable disk and pulling your data off of it takes minutes, and while the data may not be as current as it is in the online backup, it may be good enough to keep you going until you can restore the most current version.

Tech recommendation #4: Make sure your surfing, social media and generic passwords are different from the passwords used to access your financial accounts. In fact, though most of you will ignore this, you should have multiple unique passwords so that no one can get access to your important data with a single password. The best advice that you will get and most likely will ignore is to change your passwords frequently.

Tech recommendation #5: Use your mobile phone as part of a two-part verification for your sign in to critical apps. If you are an iPhone user, consider your Apple password a critical application and religiously follow this rule.

Tech recommendation #6: Password-protect all of your devices and all of your accounts. Use a sophisticated method, and make it one you can remember. A short search online will give you several examples, like taking a favorite saying or bit of advice and using the first letter of each word followed by a number sequence which makes sense to you. In this example, you don't have to memorize a random set of numbers and letters, but a phrase that is easily recalled and almost impossible to guess.

>Example: *There is nothing so powerful as truth; and often nothing so strange.* Daniel Webster (1782-1852), American Statesman, Lawyer, and Orator

1. Becomes: TINSPATAONSS

2. Add in some numbers to similar shaped letters, looks like this; T1N5P4T4O55.

3. Mix in some non-capital letters t1N5p4T4

4. Add in non-alpha characters is can look like this T!N5P$4t4*55

Note that in step 2 we used a zero for the "O" when we started mixing in numbers; you don't have to, but it is recommended that you pick one ("o" or zero) and stick with it, saving a lot of confusion later. You can even add a space at the beginning or end, but be careful because that can be confusing!

Tech recommendation #7: Keep a hard copy of your passwords in your house somewhere safe (under lock and key, a safe is preferable), and keep them updated. As you get older, you will eventually find it exceedingly difficult, if not impossible, to keep the logins and passwords straight in your head. You will likely be surprised how many places you need to log into to manage your retirement, prescription, medical, insurance and other touch points in your life.

Tech recommendation #8: Get a shredder. You need to shred all documents, credit offers, insurance, utility bills...you name it. Identity thieves will grab any information from your trash and try to use it.

Tech recommendation #9: Get your finances online, and don't put any form of payment into your mailbox as it has become a prime target for thieves. Pay your bills online via a bank, not some other bill pay service. Banks will cut a check to individuals and businesses if they aren't set up for electronic funds transfer (EFT). They will literally print a check and mail it for you. If you need to send a physical check, drop it in a regular mailbox or at the post office.

Some other good, but not-so-absolute, recommendations:

1. Buy the largest monitor you can afford Your eyes aren't getting any younger.

2. Even if you buy a laptop, consider using a wireless keyboard, a mouse, and a large monitor for access at home.

3. Wireless printers are GREAT when they work, but they are not a lot of fun when they don't.

4. Even though wireless internet connectivity is great, use a wired connection when you can, particularly at home because there's simply no comparison to the speed of a hardwired connection.

5. Always encrypt and secure your wireless internet connection at home. It's a pain, but a technology "must" have for the modern tech user.

6. Don't grab just any Wi-Fi connection when you are out and about. Some criminals set up hot spots for the specific purpose of capturing your data. The Wi-Fi will work just fine, but if your data and transactions aren't secure, the crooks will get it all.

7. Turn off guest access to your home Wi-Fi system. You should know how to turn it on for a guest to use it, or you can just give them the password and change it after they leave.

8. You don't need your landline phone anymore. You can get great service from your internet provider or you can buy a voice of Internet device and set up a low cost or free (Google Voice is free) connection to any regular phone.

9. Invest in a good quality Bluetooth headset/earpiece.

10. Set up your phone to work with your car's audio. Most cars after 2010 have integrated Bluetooth allowing you to use your phone hands- free for both making calls and listening to music on the stereo.

In summary, you need to be a life-long learner when it comes to technology. If you don't, you will become more isolated and disconnected from the world around you. Technology will never and should never replace face-to-face interpersonal interactions, but when important people are distant, technology can bring them closer. Technology is not a panacea; it is a tool and you should become the master of your tools. You wouldn't avoid technology in other areas of your life, but for some reason most of us are reluctant to really learn how to use it in our personal lives. I challenge you to do an honest assessment. Have you ever really read the manual for any critical device on which you rely? Try it and become a super user, not a two-percenter who only learns the smallest part of the capabilities of a given technology tool.

Did you know? Many companies will allow you to bring your own device (BYOD) for your work computing needs. Sounds great, but there's a huge catch. The company will load their apps on your device(s), but they will require (this is usually policy and non-negotiable) you give them complete control over it. This means that after you have agreed to their BYOD terms, they can "inspect" all the data on the device at any time, without your specific permission. More alarming is that the fact that they can also wipe (delete) all data from the device at any time, so think carefully about allowing that access. This is the reason many professionals still carry two mobile devices, one paid for by their employer and one for personal use.

Core Concepts mapping

Core One – You are not like the others. You've been exposed to technology, and likely consider yourself as an apt tech user and consumer. However, the technology you came into contact while in the service is nothing like the cutting-edge technology you can purchase with your own money. Military tech is usually very dated and has a narrow and specific range of function. This should not dismay you, instead it should empower you when you realize you were surrounded by technology in the military, including everything from your supply chain (logistics) to the ability to coordinate ops of all sizes. You may have even been exposed to technology that hasn't made it to the public sector just yet, which means you are a power user of technology and have been for years. This is not a new concept for you, it's simply a matter of shifting your usage patterns and skills to a new set of technologies.

Core Six – You have gaps in your skills and capabilities that you need to close. Realize technology can help you in your personal and professional life. Realize also it can give you a competitive edge or, in the case of social media, become a distraction or addiction that weighs you down. Embrace technology and accept the fact it moves on a curve which will require you to become a lifelong learner. Don't imagine you are at the top of your game just because you have a smartphone, a PC, and a social media presence. Don't overestimate the current level of integration of technology or its effectiveness in your life. You might be one of those persons who has it all figured out, but if so you would be in the vast minority. Exploit technology and technological advances at every opportunity.

Personal perspective:

I once met a very nice woman who was very unhappy. She was a friend of the family who had just lost her job, and she was hurt, angry and afraid for her future. She had been a typist for her company long past the point where typewriters were obsolete. Her company offered to train her on PC software and word processing skills, but she refused. She was certainly bright enough and was not too old to learn, she just did not want to move out of her comfort zone. At some inevitable point, there was no place for her with her long-term employer. Even the least demanding positions in her division required the ability to use word processing, spreadsheets, and electronic calendars, so she was let go. Her prospects for employment were grim. This was a hallmark experience for me. I was still in the military (home on leave) and was stunned by her situation. I was up to my eyeballs in the latest office technology and could not fathom her antipathy to technology. I loved technology; how could anyone turn away from it? Technology was, and still is, the crown jewel of the future. Don't be this person, there is *never* a point in your life where you can decide to stop learning, and personal technology is an area where you should continually strive to learn all you can.

Chapter 14 – Faith and Religion

Have you ever heard the saying "there are no atheists in foxholes"?

This concept goes all the way back to the time of Plato but it's such a universal concept that it is likely even older than that. Various historical figures, including Dwight D Eisenhower, have used the phrase, but its use in modern times is most often attributed to Ernie Pyle, the famed U.S. World War II war correspondent.

The question the "foxhole" statement begs is does what you believe in when you are safe change when you are in imminent danger.

Some of you will have made a decision to turn away from the concept of God and religion, perhaps because the things you've seen and experienced were too horrific for you to reconcile. Yet the person who was standing right next to you may have had just the opposite reaction and found themselves bound more closely to their religious beliefs. In times of stress and danger, it is not unusual for individuals to react in the direct opposite of the beliefs they hold to on a daily basis.

Initially, I had grandiose plans for this chapter, but after a lot of research, reading, and discussion with many well-educated persons on both sides of the argument, I decided to table the debate. A discussion that has spanned all human history is too big for any single book, much less this one. All I can say is I would challenge you to do your own research on those beliefs opposite to your own. In the military, you were taught to look at all the angles and options and to never underestimate your opponent. Take a hard look at the other side's perspective, cast your net wide for information and see what you find.

Regardless of your choice, this is such a personal, polarizing decision, let's simply talk about a moral framework for life.

Another wise man once said, "if you don't believe in something, you will fall for anything." Experience and observation tells us that this statement is an important truth which we need to incorporate into our daily lives.

How do you govern yourself? What framework of legality and morality do you live by? What do you expect from your fellow man, or from strangers? How will you raise your family? What type of moral ground will you give them to stand on to rise to their potential?

You are coming from a world that has ceremony and regimen fully instantiated into your daily life. Though you may have chafed under some aspects of that daily rigor, you will find that you will miss it. Building a strong moral framework into your new daily regimen will help you replace some of that missing element.

Having this solid framework and personal support network for you may be more urgent and important than you think. As a former service member, you probably don't realize how much stress you endured, it was just part of the job. Please read and re-read the chapter "The potential downside of your military service." There is important information you need to know about the risks to your health and wellbeing. For example, did you know that suicide rates for veterans are 50% higher than for our civilian counterparts? It's a complex issue you need to understand, or at least be aware of.

You will hit rocky shoals (pun intended) in your post military life. Plan for these times, as you will need many positive, optimistic people in your life that you can lean on. How you find that support group leads us back to the moral framework you choose and the ceremony and regimen that comes with it (if any).

Find your personal position of strength and framework and stand fast. If you don't feel strong, then keep looking and challenging.

Core Concepts mapping

Core Seven – You now have more responsibility for your life, and much more opportunity to screw it up. You need a plan for this; you need to find a place of strength for you and your family. If you don't provide a moral framework for yourself and your family, you will be unhappy with the results. Children will seek stability and safety, if not at home, then where?

Core Eight – Life is still hard. No matter what you chose, Life will be lobbing grenades and mortars at you for all your days. Create a network of family and friends you can depend on, and create and foster deep relationships with the people you trust. There is no single panacea to solve all our problems. Defense in layers is your friend.

Personal perspective: (point)

I served in the US Navy for eleven years active with two years active reserve. I am writing about my faith and religion, as I believe it is the most important part of my life, what has been and what will come. Please don't get the impression that I am trying to sway your beliefs in any way or that I come across as an irrational religious zealot, this is not my intent.

I married a wonderful woman after my first hitch in the Navy, and I am blessed in that we are still together after so many years. She came from a strong Southern Baptist background and I was raised Methodist. Prior to our marriage, I did not attend church on Sundays. My normal weekend schedule consisted of watching ball games, drinking, and having fun with my friends. Once my wife and I were married, I settled down and found something missing in my life. We wanted to start attending church, so we started visiting several local churches. Neither of us cared whether it was Baptist or Methodist. It took some time but eventually we found a church we liked and joined, shortly after our daughter was born. Since my wife and I were raised religiously, we thought our daughter should also be until she could make her own decisions.

My military life went on much the same as anyone's. Through various deployments away and time together between them, my wife kept the fatherly side of things running until I got home to take over. When our daughter was about three years old, we decided to get out of the service, and while I had no idea what I wanted to do but knew I wanted to be with my family every day. We were so fortunate to have so many people in our church help us out both spiritually and physically, and I believe that without their help and support it would have been much harder.

Our daughter is now married and has a good career, and we have a son in college. They both face their own challenges and we do what we can to help, but it is up to them to deal with their own life issues. The only thing (and I mean the *only* thing) my wife and I can do is pray that He will keep us strong, watch over our children, help them make the right decisions and keep us all safe. I believe this from the bottom of my heart and try to live that way every day.

The best suggestion I can give anyone is to 'keep the faith," no matter how hard you think it is, God has a plan for your life. Let your spouse be your partner, make her a part of your decisions whether to stay in the service, get out or retire. Pray about what you want to do in your life, be specific when asking God. He will answer your prayers, maybe not in the exact way you want them answered which means you might have to work harder than you hoped, but He will pave the path and make it smoother for you.

Personal perspective: (counter point)

I was raised in a deeply religious family, so I know what it's like to be in a family that believes in attending church regularly. Our friends and family were regular church-goers, and in our community, to date someone, you had to regularly attend church with their family. Now don't think that this put me off religion, but today, I am a different person. I don't go to church and don't force my family to go either.

I don't have a lot of patience for those who try to help a poor lost soul like me find their brand of religion. I just don't want to be pulled into that.

I don't know if I believe in a higher power. I've just seen too much of what people will do to each other for power and control. Seeing too many little one's suffering was what made it hard for me.

I haven't closed the door on the topic, and I certainly don't think less of my friends who are religious. I can see it is a big part of their lives and it is good for them. I don't have quite the same number of friends as I did when I was in church, but that's ok. I just know I've made my peace with this for now.

I still believe in right and wrong as well as the pursuit of happiness, and I will still stand against those choose the wrong thing.

Chapter 15 – Money Management

This is a vast subject, in fact, there are whole sections of libraries devoted to this topic. It is also a topic with amorphous boundaries and content. Should we approach money management from a Certified Public Accountant perspective, or how about from the eyes of a Certified Financial Planner? Maybe we should examine this from a tax burden perspective, or perhaps we should focus on types of investments and returns. How about from a self-employed business owner's view? Investments are important too, so maybe we should cover stocks and dollar cost averaging investments. Mutual funds versus individual stocks and portfolio diversity is another great topic. This list is not exhaustive or complete, and eventually you should learn something about all these areas and even more that haven't been mentioned.

This subject is like a vast river of information, swiftly moving, wide and deep, constantly changing. Check out your favorite online bookseller for financial advice and then take a break while the website pulls up page after page of listings. To master this subject takes years of general study, intense focus on specific areas and real-world experience. Unfortunately, there are no shortcuts or cheat sheets.

This chapter is not intended to give you specific financial advice on how to invest your money. Instead, consider the framework, guidelines and data provided to help you form your own specific financial and money management methods.

Given all those caveats, what is money management? For the purposes of this book it is defined as the block of best practices that help you manage your income (hopefully from more than one source), savings, investments, insurance, tax burden and wealth. This concept also includes the requirement for estate planning.

Future value and present value of a dollar are major financial concepts you need to understand. Simply stated the future value of a dollar invested in some instrument or method that gains value will be worth more in the future. The present value of a dollar (no investment) sitting in a box or safe storage somewhere will have less value at any point in the future (missed opportunity for growth) than it has right now. Keep this in mind as you read through this chapter, it is a critical component to building wealth. Keep asking yourself if your money is working for you the way it should.

Spoiler Alert: *The next 300 words or so may dramatically change your perspective on wealth.*

Money management IS all about the accumulation of wealth. Income does NOT equal wealth. We introduced the rough concept of net worth and how to evaluate your progress in the Core Nine: **The Republic is powered by the engine of Capitalism.** To put this in proper perspective, please take a moment and re-read that Core concept.

Net worth value baseline (don't include your home equity):

Your income X your age / 10

For example, a 30-year-old making $75,000 a year sounds sweet but would:

1. Not meet the minimum of $90,000 income
2. Needs a net worth of ($75K X 30 years) / 10 = $225,000

This calculation of net worth is tied to your income and is a very rough approximation of several factors, but it's more than good enough for our purposes. It anchors your baseline to your current lifestyle, savings and various other metrics that will eventually coalesce into what you need for retirement to support a given lifestyle with expenses.

This gives you the target, so now let's ask again how you are doing. This math is simple. You just need to add up all your savings, your 401k's, retirement, and everything but the equity in your house. For a simple and straightforward calculation, use this formula:

Total Assets - Total Liabilities = Net Worth/Wealth

How do you stack up? Do the math and no matter where your current calculation puts you, be brutally honest. Then, form a plan to close the gap.

If you are a typical service member, then you aren't becoming wealthy off your pay, the various subsidies, plus basic and variable allowances. You've probably seen the two types of lifers: one group has done amazingly well and is looking forward to retirement, while the other group (the majority) vary greatly in skill, motivation and intelligence but have one thing in common, they've not looked beyond the next paycheck. You don't want to be in that last group, or if you have found yourself in that category, you desperately want out. That's why you picked up this book. You are motivated and want to do better, not just a little better, you want to do much better.

Having a positive net worth is fantastic, and the higher the value the better. Almost all debt except for that associated with your home's mortgage is bad. Notice we are including lines of credit against your home equity as bad, bordering on evil in relation to your overall financial health.

You need more income (not to be confused with wealth) to create high net worth. Where should you begin?

Here's a good rule of thumb to start with, applicable to everyone except those living in cities with a very high cost of living; when you make $150,000 in a year, you have basically arrived. This doesn't mean your primary job has to pay that much, but by creating multiple streams of income (more on that later in the chapter) your total income of $150,000 sets the mark for the "no one can argue with your success" threshold. You can pretty much buy any size home, any car and so on. You certainly can't afford the top-tier luxury items, but you would be considered to have the financial freedom to live a comfortable life.

Let's start by getting your attention, the next section is crucial, and you really need to get this. You have unconscious bias that you don't realize exists. Is this bias good for you? No, absolutely not, and it has probably impeded or slowed you on your path to financial independence. Please understand you don't have one unconscious bias when it comes to money management, your perspective is likely littered with dozens of toxic, anti-wealth building perspectives working to prevent you from achieving your goals.

Bluntly speaking, you have been brainwashed. How about we start unwinding that condition here and now.

Real-life example: John Military has owned many vehicles in his life, including some brand-new vehicles from manufacturers such as Ford, GMC, Mercedes, Chrysler, BMW, Chevrolet, Honda, and Volkswagen. He has also owned used vehicles of various flavors, including his all-time favorite which was a 1977 Corvette with a sweet black-lacquer paint job. However, needs changed as his life did, and his most recent purchase was a brand-new Ford 150 Super Crew (4 door). After lots of research and test drives, he selected an XLT model without all the bells and whistles. He admitted it was very tough not to get pulled into the "for just a little more" pitch from the sales team. The only modification he had made to the truck was the spray-on bed liner and 5 years later, it is still performing as advertised. The truck is now paid off, looks and drives almost like new. He had to fight through enormous pressure from friends, family, and the dealership to upgrade to a more luxurious model. He had to fight through his own biases and perspectives. Didn't he deserve the best truck on the market? Shouldn't he drive a vehicle that impressed others? The point to take away from this is that he made a conscious decision to buy a particular model with specific features. He saved thousands of dollars by doing so, and he couldn't be happier. Admittedly, he still occasionally pines for the Corvette of his youth, but when he can pile his family and dog into the truck for a long trip or even a local outing, it's all good. He overcame his unconscious biases and made a conscious decision. He had a specific rationale and purpose (new reliable truck at the lowest price) in mind and that's what he bought. Every day, John looks at his truck with a smile and reminds himself that he made a great choice.

Over-selling is the American way, and while most products offer relatively the same technology and materials, there is some product differentiation delivered though quality control and manufacturing methods. The pitch rarely varies from the script of how someone's product is so much better than that from the competition. Unfortunately, the added value is relatively minimal from a quality perspective unless you are comparing the lowest quality item to the highest (luxury) quality item. The spin often involves the "experience" or "esteem" from being seen as a consumer of a luxury brand versus the product that simply delivers real boots on the ground performance. In many cases we are not buying something for its value and usefulness, but for some other esoteric part of the transaction and user experience. And that is perfectly all right, if you are making a conscious decision to spend your money for ANY reason you choose, and you understand the implications of that choice. The problem is that you often don't recognize the bias you have towards making these less than optimal choices. If you have satisfied yourself that you are spending your money on something that meets your requirements, go for it, and enjoy the fruits of your labor. But, ask yourself, how many times have you had buyer's remorse?

The previous paragraph might be insightful to you or just restating the obvious, and you might be wondering what does this have to do with money management? Pardon the lack of sophistication, but it has a helluva a lot to do with it, as our parents might say.

The byproduct of being under this constant over-sell pressure is that we "over-buy." Americans are conditioned to listen to the "payment" aspect of a sales pitch versus the "debt" aspect. How many times have you silently calculated how much of a payment you could afford, whether it is an extra $49, $99, or more per month as you consider your next "must have" purchase. Stop and think about that, as this is the crux of unwinding your unconscious biases that do huge damage to your financial well-being.

When we think in terms of payments, we are basically trying to convince ourselves to over pay for goods and services. We are materially harmed when we make decisions based on our ability to make a "payment" rather than thinking about the debt implications.

Unfortunately, most of us are so conditioned to think and make decisions about how much of a payment we can swing it is hard to conceive there is a better way. We don't want to consider a different method because anything other than buying today delays our gratification. After all, we can save when we are older, right? We all understand that to have a good credit score, you must use your credit. There is even an industry that provides you the ability to monitor and manage your credit rating. So, why shouldn't we take advantage of the credit we are being offered. You only live once, right?

Wrong, wrong, wrong!

This is consumerism at its worst, and the consumer debt issue in the United States is ugly. This a topic you need to spend some time researching and learning about. Here's a small primer to whet your appetite:

- American household debt hit a record $13.21 trillion dollars in 2018.

- Unsecured debt was $4 trillion dollars in 2019 vs. a population of 329 Million citizens, works out to about $12,000 of consumer debt for every man, woman, and child alive in the US. Does not include mortgage debt.

- Approximately 25% of this staggering debt consists of revolving credit, the majority associated with credit cards

- Approximately 75% of this number is money borrowed for things such as cars, education, boats and unfortunately, even vacations.

    - http://www.money-zine.com/financial-planning/debt-consolidation/consumer-debt-statistics/

Let's talk about credit card portion of consumer debt; approximately $1 trillion divided by 128 million U.S. households is about $8,000 per household.

In 2019, per the Federal Reserve, the average credit card rate on that $1 trillion was 16.9%. That equates to $169 million interest owed per year for these households.

Add to that the remaining unsecured debt of approximately $3 trillion at an average interest rate of 10%. That equals another $300 million dollars in interest owed in a calendar year.

The 128 million U.S. households will incur almost $470 million dollars in interest each year for unsecured lines of credit (non-mortgage). This means the average household is paying around $5000 in interest and fees per year that could be put to much better use in their lives.

Those of you who have less than the assumed average debt, please take a moment and congratulate yourselves. Lower is good, but zero is best. Realize that you want no consumer debt and any debt you carry for more than a month should be considered a failure of money management. Is this harsh and over the top? Maybe, but the purpose of the section is to begin to break down the conditioning you've been subjected to. Having credit is good for life's emergencies. Using your credit is for luxuries and non-essentials is bad. Acquiring consumer debt that takes months and years to pay down is worse

Remember that story about your parents, older friends or relatives who are so weird because they only pay cash for things they want? How crazy is that? Those people could have so much more if they would just use a little credit. Maybe they wouldn't have to drive a 10-year-old car, or they could update their furniture in the living room. Perhaps they could borrow some money to update that kitchen, or buy a nice boat on credit. It all seems so reasonable if you can manage the payment, still have enough money to cover the basics and leave some spending money.

You are wrong again if that's what you're thinking, because this is consumerism plus financial stagnation jammed into a single action. Everyone wants your money, and they also want your interest from the payment plan. Think about it, you are usually paying retail price for an expensive item that's been marked-up, and then you agree to pay interest on top of that. The most open secret in the world is that your creditors never want you pay off your debts. They source their wealth from your poor decision- making, and you are siphoning off your financial health. Your money should be working for you, not paying for other people's luxury vacations, expensive houses, and cars. They are laughing all the way to the bank and their expensive meals while they work less hours than you.

The "cash only" philosophy is near extinction. People who practice this have given up trying to convince others it's the right thing to do because they understand you don't want to hear it. In fact, if they try to make their point, they are often ridiculed and treated like some type of zoo exhibit. Outdated, out of touch and living a sparse, non-consuming life in the land of plenty. We, as a society have ostracized and pushed to the fringes of our civilization those that live without credit. In a better recognized reality, these people should be part of an honored elite in our family and circle of friends, not the opposite.

But people who live by cash-only standards are not the only ones who are considered limited in mental capacity, as hybrid cash-credit users are also frowned upon. These are people who bought something expensive on credit and are working to pay it off before taking on additional expenditures and purchases. How do you spot them? They are a little harder to pick out of the crowd, but you can find them, as they are focused and passionate and choose how and when they spend their money.

There is some good new, many individuals and families have decided to use credit wisely, managing it rather than let credit take over their life.

Let's take a look at some very high-level things that you may be doing wrong:

1. **Managing debt incorrectly.** Too many Americans accumulate debt to the point that it becomes unserviceable. This means that they can't pay off the principle in a timely manner because of the interest that is accumulating. For young people, student debt is a huge issue, with more than 65% reporting owing more than $30,000 in student loans when they graduate. Students with secondary degrees have even more debt. If you have debt, you should do your best to pay more than your minimum payment, thereby reducing the length of your loan and amount the you pay in interest.
2. **Using credit cards to provide income.** Credit cards should be used sparingly and paid in full each month. Unfortunately, too many of us received a flood of "pre-authorized" cards early in our adult life, which makes the misuse of credit cards nothing short of seductive. Having a single credit card with a good interest rate and relatively high spending limit can be useful. It allows us to respond to unexpected, emergency-type

scenarios without having to carry around a backpack full of cash. Having several department store, gas, and low limit bank cards with high interest is the anathema of financial health.

3. **Not having a budget.** Simply put, having a budget means you are paying attention and not letting your money trickle away when you aren't focused on it. Life is hectic and complicated, and you need a budget to keep your focus, making sure you understand where your money is going. You will see repeated recommendations that you evaluate your progress each month towards your financial goals. It's a practice worth following and therefore about which worth reminding.

4. **Overspending.** Having our own money is both intoxicating and dangerous, and we all experience this when we first set out as adults. Not having good spending habits is like a flashback to those first few paydays when you had money and then it was spent. If you overspend and don't take on debt, you'll find yourself living paycheck to paycheck, and over time, you will fall victim to a situation called "lifestyle inflation." This is where your purchases tend to creep up along with your pay increases until you have no money left for emergencies, savings, or investments. If you are overspending and accumulating debt, you will eventually find yourself in a situation where all your lines of credit (with their outrageous interest rates) are maxed out, and you have no savings or other way to service your debt.

5. **Buying junk.** In the previous example, we watched John intentionally purchase a new truck that did not have all the luxury items. He bought only what he needed and wanted, but, buried in that example was an important concept that wasn't specifically called out; John paid for quality. He bought a new truck with his eyes wide open and purchased only the functional add-ons that were important to him. Leather seats were not important, but the size of engine and towing package was. There are so many opportunities to end up with low quality junk when we make our purchases, and impulse buying is one of the leading causes. Inexpensive doesn't always equal low quality, but buyer beware. Make solid, informed decisions on each of your purchases. There are times when it makes absolute sense to purchase items that are both of excellent quality and new. This including items such as mattresses, computers, trade specific tools, clothes, and shoes. With that said, one of the most important pieces of advice any of us can get is to buy used when it does makes sense. Pawn shops and yard sales are great ways to create a family adventure and occasionally find a much-desired treasure. Another fitting example is that

you should strongly consider buying a three-year-old, low mileage vehicle instead of a brand new one. Most cars today last well into the 150K-200K mileage range and the interiors, when taken care of, will last as long. This is pure gold advice when thinking about a luxury vehicle that will have lost 50% of its value with more than 80% of its usable life still available. Think outside of the box and buy quality when you can afford it. Don't skimp on the important things you expect to use for many years because these choices will pay for themselves.

6. **Not planning early enough for retirement.** Multiple surveys have shown Americans don't really get serious about retirement savings until their late 20s to early 30s. This is a terrible thing because you miss out on the compounding benefit of the various financial and investment options that can make you wealthy. Of those employees 25 and under, less than a third take advantage of the offered 401(k) savings and investment plans. What a terrible miss.

7. **Waiting too long to start investing.** Considered by many to be the single most effective way to build wealth, investing should be a core part of everyone's life. We'll discuss this in more depth later in this chapter, but the bottom line is you should get started now if not yesterday. There is lots to learn and lots to do because you want to "win" with investing.

8. **Not establishing an emergency fund.** Having an emergency fund is a key component of your life as well as your financial health, and it doesn't matter how much money you make or what lifestyle you've chosen. Over sixty percent of Americans don't have an emergency fund. What is it, and how much money should I have in my emergency fund? Very simply put, it is ready cash that has no withdrawal penalty, doesn't come out of long-term savings, and can cover 100% of all your living expenses for six months when you have no other income.

9. **Living without health insurance.** You should have insurance coverage 100% of the time regardless of your age. When we are young and healthy, we tend to minimize the risk of needing medical care, so we avoid the expense of insurance. With the current healthcare law those days are over, and unless the law is changed, it is mandatory that you carry some type of health insurance. You are not bulletproof or invincible, you can and will become ill at unpredictable times in your life. While we wish you the best of health and hope you never fall seriously ill, hope is not a strategy. You can check the details about required coverage minimums at Healthcare.gov. At last check, those who choose not to have insurance are

required to pay a fee of 2% of your annual household income or $325 per person, per year — whichever is higher.

Hopefully you are learning to avoid or have avoided the multitude of bad financial practices out there. Now let's turn our focus to becoming wealthy and having an income that allows for our desired lifestyle at every age. What's the secret? If it were the matter of a simple secret, we would all be wealthy. The truth is complex and multi-factored. Instead of a single magic pill, it should be thought of as a daily exercise, a framework for life if you will.

Three ideas worth repeating:

1. **Live within your means**
2. Maximize your primary income
3. Create multiple streams of income

Starting at the top, it all starts with this simple concept.

Just live within your means. This is the STARTING point, as just living within your means alone will never make you a wealthy person, but it is indeed the place you need to start.

Key point, income is NOT wealth. Income is a stream of money coming to you from various jobs, businesses, and investments. I know Doctors and Lawyers with a lower net worth (wealth) than some friends who work for hourly wages.

This is worth repeating until it pushes at least one of the bad biases out of your perspective. You won't get wealthy on minimum wage or day labor rates. You need to increase your income as much as you can. The best way accomplish that is by creating multiple streams of income.

If you are just separating from the service, it is likely you have lived paycheck to paycheck for an awfully long time. If you've been able to save, it is likely that it is much less than you should have at this point in your life as the military pay scale is substandard and we all know it. The same or equivalent job in the civilian world will pay far more than the military scale. Hopefully you will land a job that rewards you properly for your skills and work ethic. You may feel like it's time to splurge, and maybe it is, but only if you have a plan and live within your means.

What does that mean anyway, live within your means? Let's do some quick triage on your finances and see how well you manage:

1. Are you saving 30% of your income? This is a huge factor, and if you can get into the habit of saving 30% before you do anything else, you can change your life.

2. Do you have emergency funds? This can be part of your savings plan, and the first step to being financially responsible.

3. Are you spending more than 30% of your income on housing? Not just the mortgage, but figure in the insurance and maintenance.

4. How well do you manage your credit card? Carrying a balance is bad, having more than one credit card is bad, not paying attention to the interest rate is bad, and taking cash advances is even worse.

5. Are you spending more than 10% on transportation? You are probably paying more because you've been conditioned that only a new car will make you happy. That's fine, if you can pay cash for all or most of it. Some advisors say you should finance a vehicle for no more than three years of payments, and you should plan to use any car you purchase for at least 10 years.

On the next page you can do a quick check.

So, how did you do? Let's score your money management skills:

For each question, give yourself a maximum of 20 points.

1. Savings Evaluation
    a. 20 points for 30% savings
    b. 15 points for 29%-20% savings
    c. 10 points for 19%-10% savings
    d. 5 points for anything below 10% savings
2. Emergency Fund Evaluation
    a. 20 points for six months of living expenses
    b. 10 points for 2-5 months of living expenses
    c. 5 points for at least 1-month of living expenses
3. Housing Expense Evaluation
    a. 20 points for no more than 30% expense
    b. 10 points for 30-39% expense
    c. 5 points for 40% or more expense
4. Credit Card Evaluation
    a. 20 points for 1 credit card with no balance (emergency use)
    b. 10 points for 1 card with less than 25% balance
    c. 0 points for all other scenarios
5. Transportation Expense Evaluation
    a. 20 points for 10% or less (including insurance)
    b. 10 points for 11%-20%
    c. 0 points for all other scenarios

100 pts	Better than 95% of the population, fantastic job!
99-80 pts	Better than 80% of the population, medium progress to becoming debt free
79-60 pts	Better than 60% of the population, treading water and possibly making some progress
59-40 pts	Better than 40% of the population, you're in trouble and you need to fix the situation
39-0 pts	You are bleeding out financially and need to make immediate changes

No matter what your score is, you need to immediately start tracking your financial health. In Chapter 6 we discussed goals, you need to revisit and review as necessary, and you need to map your financial health against your financial and life goals.

Every month you need to map out your financial health. You need to determine if you are first making *any progress* and second making *enough progress*. For many, the hardest part of starting this monthly habit is being honest with themselves. Document your income and expenses candidly and accurately and evaluate the results. There must be no rationalization, no slant, and no justification. Just the facts please, no spin. Use a notebook or a spreadsheet and map out your income versus your expenses. Where is your money going? Is it moving you forward, sideways or in reverse? You may be surprised to find what you are spending your money on.

Do this mapping and evaluation every month, each month. Skipping this is worse than skipping six months in the gym.

For the "any progress" result, you must ask yourself multiple questions:

- Are you servicing your debt properly?
- Are you meeting your savings goals?
- Are you eliminating debt effectively?
- Do you have a plan to pay off the highest interest rate first or clear multiple small debts?

Plan for and expect life to get in the way. Expect some months where you won't make any progress, but make this monthly evaluation a habit. Track each month and be honest with yourself regarding your progress. The results will be rewarding, as it is quite exhilarating to see your net worth grow over time.

At a minimum, see you should have the following incorporated into your minimum financial goals:

- Home ownership (mortgage ok, no apartment or lease)
- Six (6) months emergency expense fund
- 401K or IRA savings
- Stock portfolio (outside of 401K/IRA)
- Automatic payroll deductions for savings and investments

- Health insurance

A more complete picture would include, but not be limited to:

- Fully owned vehicle of your choice
- Whole life Insurance
- Accidental Death and Dismemberment insurance
- Short term disability insurance
- Long term disability insurance

For the "enough progress" result, you need the data from your monthly "any progress" evaluation. Then you must add a time dimension. If your goal is to save $X for goal "X" and you want to be done by date "X," calculate how long it will take you. Will you make it? Will the progress you are currently making get you across the finish line by your target date? If not, then you need to re-assess.

We don't abandon goals just because they are hard. We reassess our actions, our strategy, and our implementation of the plan. What else can you do? Stop spending money on something that is a nice to have versus a need to have. Give up some other luxury or hobby that bleeds off your time and money. That's all under your control. Sometimes our leisure pursuits are what keep us sane. but sometimes, when we do the math, the money just isn't there.

Sometimes, hopefully not for you, bankruptcy is required. Some holes can be too deep to dig yourself out of. As a service member, you may have fallen victim to some very predatory lending practices. Other factors, including divorce, job loss or overwhelming medical expenses may lead you consider this option. If you need to take this path, then hire a good attorney and do it right. Everywhere you turn you can find stories of bankruptcy filings which have gone bad. The worst of these scenarios is that a critical step in the process was missed, leaving you exposed to something that should have been covered. This usually happens when people try to file bankruptcy without professional advice. When you are facing a legal or bureaucratic process, or even worse, a combination of the two, you need to hire a professional.

When the money just isn't there you can consider it an A or B equation. If you continue with your current level of income, then only those items affordable on the

A track are available to you. If you refuse to be limited by your current circumstances, then track B opens a world of opportunities.

Three ideas worth repeating:

1. Live within your means
2. ***Maximize your primary income***
3. Create multiple streams of income

Track B is simple; to generate more income, the first critical action is to maximize your primary income. At an absolute minimum, you must determine if you are being paid adequately for what you are currently doing at work. Are you at, above or below market prices? You need to be at the top of the pay scale for your current job. If you are reading this book, you have already proven yourself to be an unusually motivated and driven individual. You should be paid according to your contributions. Many times, a person will accept a job at a lower pay rate not realizing what the job should pay. Sadly, service members often fall victim to this hiring practice, particularly when fresh out of the service.

Remember that EVERYTHING is negotiable. If you are underpaid, then create a dialog with your management. The golden rule here is you must be absolutely professional when conducting salary negotiations. This is often an awkward conversation, particularly in the early phase. You need to learn how to identify the decision maker versus the decision delayer.

If you weren't born with or have not yet acquired a talent or skill that generates a six-figure income by the time you read this book, then consider getting on that path today. Don't have a degree? Get one, but get one from a college that is properly accredited. And to that end, the chapter "Education" is a particularly important part of this book and you should read it carefully. More importantly, acquire the knowledge you need to be paid at a higher rate. That means you need to understand the market and what employers are willing to pay for a given skill set and experience level. Be realistic, if you plan to generate most of your income permanently or temporarily through your primary employment, make smart choices here.

If you already have a degree, consider jobs that may not be directly associated with your education. Some jobs require specific technical, legal, or financial education and certifications. For most of the rest of the job market, you can find a plethora of companies looking to hire individuals who are motivated, educated and want to be successful. However, as we will cover in the chapter "Education," you should consider pursuing the next higher degree that you have targeted to make yourself more marketable so you can land a higher salary and total compensation package.

Unfortunately, even if you successfully negotiate a salary/pay increase, it is not likely to provide you with an overwhelming excess of capital to fund your dreams. It is likely that at some point in time, you will have to change jobs to see a significant increase in salary. It is expected in most industries that a person will change jobs every 2-3 years early in a career, getting broader experience and moving to the income level desired.

What do you do if you can't negotiate a pay increase, or the one you got isn't enough? Create a secondary source of income.

Three ideas worth repeating:

1. Live within your means

2. Maximize your primary income

3. ***Create multiple streams of income***

The income you receive from your primary job is your FIRST stream of income.

The most important concept here is not to become a *wage slave,* or its counterpart meaning don't let yourself become locked into a *velvet handcuff* scenario. Both conditions make it difficult for you to reach your true earning potential.

A *wage slave* is when someone gets locked into a decent hourly wage. This level of compensation is far from poverty wages and comes with overtime, decent benefits and is usually a huge improvement over their previous military compensation. The problem is the job benefits your employer more than you. The occasional overtime pay sweetens the pot, but you are bracketed into a tightly controlled environment where you can be summoned into work on demand. Often these positions are associated with jobs where you are exposed to the elements, second or third shift work in less than optimal health and safety conditions.

The *velvet handcuff* scenario is much more insidious. These are generally salaried positions that provide a huge boost of income over military compensation. This type of job seems like a dream come true. However, buyer beware because these jobs often come with high expectations of commitment to the job from the employer. You will likely find yourself frequently required to work long days, weekends, and holidays. While these jobs may provide a huge boost in pay over your service pay rate, the compensation can be significantly below market rates. In the previous scenario, the pay is less, and overtime helps but the general working conditions can be miserable. In this case, the working environment is usually superb, the pay damn good along with unfortunately long hours. The learning curve for corporate culture is steep and the work is very, very demanding.

The real downside to either scenario is that they will likely turn you into a zombie. The wage slave is often physically depleted at the end of the day, and the velvet handcuffed employee is mentally wiped to the point that they have little or no creativity or ability to think clearly. Both conditions leave our employees in a condition where they are often unable to service the demands of the rest of their life.

I'm not telling you to pass up these jobs, because given time and circumstances we all experience jobs of these types in our careers. The key is to *pass through* and not get hung up. You also need to protect a certain amount of physical, mental, and creative energies to care for your family's needs as well as work on creating those multiple streams of income.

We all need multiple streams of income to ensure our success, the question is how do we get these streams up and running?

Well, start by recognizing you need to do several things simultaneously.

Your very first extra stream of income comes from retirement savings. That sounds confusing, and really, we should call it your SECOND stream of income. You need to save a certain portion of your income and create a retirement savings plan. Implement a repeatable, reproducible method that deposits part of your income into your retirement account each month. Then stand back and watch it grow.

Start your retirement planning right now. Don't include Social Security in your equation as you should be very pessimistic about the value and pay-out of that plan as time passes. It's already out of money, and redistributing incoming money to the current pool of beneficiaries. This redistribution model won't hold forever, because in the future there will be fewer people contributing to Social Security than there are people drawing from it. If you do make it to retirement and get your full benefits count yourself lucky, but don't plan on it. Plan for the amount of money you believe you will need without including Social Security benefits and you will be safe. It is also unlikely that you can live a quality life on just your military pension if you retire out unless your house and cars are paid off, but that would have required advance planning and execution. How much money do you need?

Start by identifying the lifestyle you would like to have. Don't make the mistake of thinking you can live on 50% of your current income. One major disruptor of any retirement lifestyle is the increasing cost of health care. With 90% of healthcare expenses coming in the last twenty years of life, the cost of prescriptions alone can blow your budget. Don't blindly assume the Veterans Administration healthcare system will cover you. Did you know that if your income is too high, you won't be able to get VA healthcare? If you make more than $45K (gross income) per year with four dependents, you are out. The federal poverty level for a family of five was $28.4K in 2015 so if you make $17K above poverty, then you are ineligible. Even with just you and a spouse, the income cap is about $38K, which again are really poverty wages. Start early, save as much as you can and plan for retirement, don't let it just "happen" to you.

Military retirement pay is complicated these days so we won't dig in too deeply, except to say you must become an expert. There are different rules for those who joined prior to 1980 (not too many of those folks around at this point), those who joined before 1986. Then you have to add in the High-36 calculation or the career status bonus (CSB) and the REDUX retirement plan. Unfortunately, there are no simple tables for the modern military retiree, so make sure you understand what you are entitled to, including any additional benefits and how your cost of living adjustments (COLA) are made.

To really maximize the money your putting away for the future, you want to get better results than from a simple straight savings account. While savings accounts are part of a strategy to ensure you have quick access to a portion of your wealth, they won't help you build wealth. Brick and mortar banks pay the lowest interest (1% or less) while some of the new internet bank (still backed by FDIC) can pay 2-2.5% interest.

Earning 1% interest is not a good thing except in the context that the money is secure, and you won't lose any money while parked in a savings account. Here's a simple table showing 20 years of monthly contributions at different interest rates, assuming you could save $100, $200, or as much as $300 every month.

Int Rate	Years	Monthly	Results	Monthly	Results	Monthly	Result
1.0%	20	$100	$26,678	$200	$53,356	$300	$80,034

| 1.5% | 20 | $100 | $28,103 | $200 | $56,206 | $300 | $84,310 |
| 2.0% | 20 | $100 | $29,628 | $200 | $59,257 | $300 | $88,886 |

Certificates of deposit are paying up to 1.3% and require a 2-years commitment and a minimum investment of something around $2,000. This scenario isn't even worth a table or chart; lock up your $2,000 for 18-24 months and get a whopping $20-$26 return.

What about savings bonds? They were constant in your grandparent's and maybe even your parent's savings portfolio.

Here' a little information from the US Treasury Department website; (http://www.treasurydirect.gov)

Treasury Securities & Programs

U.S. Treasury securities are a wonderful way to invest and save for the future. Here, you'll find overviews regarding U.S. Treasury bonds, notes, bills, TIPS Floating Rate Notes (FRNs), and U.S. Savings Bonds. Here's what's available:

Treasury Bills

Treasury bills are short-term government securities with maturities ranging from a few days to 52 weeks. Bills are sold at a discount from their face value.

Treasury Notes

Treasury notes are government securities that are issued with maturities of 2, 3, 5, 7, and 10 years, and pay interest every six months.

Treasury Bonds

Treasury bonds pay interest every six months and mature in 30 years.

Treasury Inflation-Protected Securities (TIPS)

TIPS are marketable securities whose principal is adjusted by changes in the Consumer Price Index. TIPS pay interest every six months and are issued with maturities of 5, 10, and 30 years.

Floating Rate Notes (FRNs)

Interest payments on an FRN rise and fall based on discount rates for 13-week Treasury bills. FRNs are issued for a term of 2 years and pay interest quarterly.

I Savings Bonds

I Savings Bonds are a low-risk savings product that earn interest while protecting you from inflation. These bonds are sold at face value.

EE and E Savings Bonds

EE and E Savings Bonds are secure savings products that pay interest based on current market rates for up to 30 years. Electronic EE Savings Bonds are sold at face value in TreasuryDirect.

There are many options that can be confusing, but the net-net is that none of these instruments pay more than about 3.5% interest and many pay much less than that. Can you say 0.10%, that's no typo, that's $1/10^{th}$ of a percent per year. They do, however, come with the payment guarantee of the US Government and have tax free benefits. They are worth looking into learning about, as it would be a bad idea to put all your money at risk of loss.

Let's see how that looks over our 20-year horizon:

Int Rate	Years	Monthly	Results	Monthly	Results	Monthly	Result
2.5%	20	$100	$31,262	$200	$62,524	$300	93,786
3.0%	20	$100	$33,012	$200	$66,188	$300	$99,322
3.5%	20	$100	$35,008	$200	$70,017	$300	$105,025

You must be saying by now that these low rates are crazy, no one can accumulate wealth from the bottom up with this type of return and you would be very correct.

What are your other options?

Let's go back to basics. If you land a job at a company, you will likely be given the option to participate in a 401K plan, you should absolutely take advantage of that. The remarkable thing about these company plans is that they often come with a matching amount paid for by the company. If you contribute X% then the company will contribute some matching amount. Take FULL advantage of this and if you don't contribute the maximum allowable to generate the maximum matching contribution, then you are leaving cold, hard cash on the table. If you work for yourself or as a contractor, establish your own Roth and/or 401K.

The 401K/Roth should become your first "real" savings effort. Get started ASAP, by learning about both methods, particularly how much and when you can contribute. The first difference (lay terms) is that the 401K has a maximum total contribution of around $24,000, including employee and employer contributions. In contrast, the Roth IRA is maxed out at around $6,000 annually. Another difference between the two plans is that the Roth gains are tax-free after 5 years of opening the account and when you are at least 59 ½ years old. In addition to the 401K and Roth IRAs, there is also the traditional IRA. Seriously, this gets complicated so here's another simple table to help you better understand: (*please note these limits are constantly changing*)

Characteristic	Roth IRA	Traditional IRA	401K
Contribution Limits	• $6,000 • $7,000 age +50	• $6,000 • $7,000 age +50	• $19,000 • $25,000 age +50 • $53,000 employer contribution
Income Limits	• $135,000 for Single • $199,000 for Married	• No limit, but high incomes limit tax benefit • $72,000 for Single • $119,000 for Married	• Employers can contribute matching % up to $265,000
Tax Treatment	• No Tax break for contribution • Tax free earnings • Tax free withdrawal in retirement	• Tax deduction for contribution	• Contributions are pre-tax
Withdrawal Rules	• Contributions can be withdrawn tax free at any time • After 5 years and age 59.5 earnings can be withdrawn tax free • No required withdrawals • Beneficiaries can withdraw over many years	• Withdrawals are penalty free at age 59.5 • Distributions must begin at age 70.5 • Beneficiaries pay taxes on inherited IRAs	• Withdrawals are penalty free at age 59.5 • Distributions must begin at age 70.5 • Beneficiaries pay taxes on inherited IRAs

Extra Benefits	• After 5 years, $10,000 penalty free withdrawal for first time home buyers	• Contributions lower taxpayer AGI $10,000 penalty free withdrawal for first time home buyers, but must pay normal taxes on distribution	• Contributions lower taxpayer AGI

The other important thing about IRAs is they come with the ability to diversify your portfolio by holding stocks and mutual funds within your account. You can set up your IRA so that you are contributing certain percentages for certain types of investments with varying levels of risk, and you can rebalance your portfolio at will.

It should be noted that, as a rule, if you have a financial adviser (and you should) they will NOT be able to manage any employer-based investments for you. They might review your investment options and give you advice on how to allocate your investments, so always ask.

To sum up this topic: create a retirement saving/investment strategy and stick to it. It will become a source of wealth and eventually a stream of income when you need it most.

Three ideas worth repeating:

1. Live within your means
2. Maximize your primary income
3. *Create multiple streams of income*
   a. *Primary income is your first stream*
   b. *Retirement savings is your second stream*
   c. *Creating an investment portfolio is third stream*

Let's move on to your third stream of income. You are strongly encouraged to create a separate stock portfolio outside of your IRA. You can do this. What you need to do is set aside some portion of your actual cash flow to channel into a stock portfolio. Over the long haul, with dollar cost averaging, this is a fantastic method to build wealth. Create a repeatable, reproducible method that does this for you, then stand back and watch it grow.

But where is this "extra" money coming from? If I follow your recommendation then I'm already contributing to either an employer- matched 401K or an IRA I set up on my own.

Because of the contribution limits and the fact that you generally have fewer investment placement options within an IRA, you should have some percentage of that 30% of savings available. In fact, many employer-matched programs only allow you to contribute up to 6% or so to maximize the matching funds from the company. This should leave you with something around 20% of your after-tax income that should go to savings.

Is thirty percent the maximum? No, hell no, 30% savings is the *MINIMUM* you should save and invest.

Is the stock market a good place to invest? Adjusted for inflation, the Dow Jones Industrial Average (DJIA), is *the* major baseline on how the stock market is doing, returns about 10% year over year. This does not mean that every year delivers a 10% profit, it means the long-term average, and with stocks, you need to invest for the long term. In some years the market can and does lose money. For specific data, please review the chart of the DJIA and S&P performance from 1979 through 2016:

Year	S&P 500	DJIA	Year	S&P 500	DJIA
1979	11.59%	4.19%	1998	26.67%	16.10%
1980	25.77%	14.93%	1999	19.53%	25.22%
1981	-9.73%	-9.23%	2000	-10.14%	-6.18%
1982	14.76%	19.61%	2001	-13.04%	-7.10%
1983	17.27%	20.27%	2002	-23.37%	-16.76%
1984	1.40%	-3.74%	2003	26.38%	25.32%
1985	26.33%	27.66%	2004	8.99%	3.15%
1986	14.62%	22.58%	2005	3.00%	-0.61%
1987	2.03%	2.26%	2006	13.62%	16.29%
1988	12.40%	11.85%	2007	3.53%	6.43%
1989	27.25%	26.96%	2008	-38.49%	-33.84%
1990	-6.56%	-4.34%	2009	23.45%	18.82%
1991	26.31%	20.32%	2010	12.78%	11.02%
1992	4.46%	4.17%	2011	0.00%	5.53%
1993	7.06%	13.72%	2012	13.41%	7.26%
1994	-1.54%	2.14%	2013	29.60%	26.50%
1995	34.11%	33.45%	2014	11.39%	7.52%
1996	20.26%	26.01%	2015	-1.63%	-1.80%
1997	31.01%	22.64%	2016	9.50%	13.40%

Over this period, the S&P 500 averaged 10% per year and 405% gain. For the same period, the Dow Jones Industrial Average averaged 10% per year 394% gain.

You may be asking yourself; how do I get started and what should I invest my money in? The absolute best advice on this topic is to hire a financial advisor. Meet with more than one and consider these meetings as interviews with someone who will be responsible for your money. In other words, be serious and deliberate about choosing your adviser. Never, under any circumstances, engage a faceless entity based on what they post on a website. Working with a financial advisor requires the ability to discuss sensitive and private financial data and you should be able to comfortably review the data, conditions, and goals with someone you trust and have a decent rapport with.

Remember, you don't explicitly need a financial planner or a minimum amount of money to get started with investing. You can open an online trading account with a small deposit and begin right away. This is a terrific way to learn about investing and you need to experience the process of selecting and committing trades in your stock portfolio. It is amazing how much you pay attention and learn when it's your money and your decision. This learning process can also be a lot of fun. You just need to get started yesterday, or last year. Now would be ok, I guess.

It has been my experience and observation that most self-directed investing underperforms the market to greater and lesser degrees. You should strongly consider either (a) a robo-advisor or (b) a paid financial advisor.

Taken in order, let's start with (a) robo-advisors. If you are worried about self-directed investing and don't have the minimum Assets Under Management (AUM) to qualify for a personal advisor, you still have options. One of the emerging tools for the motivated investor is something called "robo-advisors." Basically, you find a financial institution that offers this service, answer a few questions about your investment time horizon and how much risk you are willing to take, then fund the account and you are done. Complex algorithms will manage your portfolio for you.

There are multiple robo-advisor services available today and something you may want to experiment with. As of this update (Q4 2019) robo advisors have more that $2 trillion in Assets Under Management (AUM). They don't generally beat the Return On Investment (ROI) seen with human advisors from a large firm (with hundreds or thousands of analysts backing them). Robo-advisors do provide much better returns vs. self-directed investors of the amateur or the "just getting started" crowd.

Moving on to (b) human financial advisors; make sure you understand how your advisors get paid. Anyone who tells you they only charge a fee when they make money for you is probably someone you want to avoid. Be careful about those who don't have a real fee as this type of advisor tends to make money by getting get paid commission on the funds in which they invest your money. This may lead to investments that benefit them more than you. Strongly consider the flat fee compensated financial advisor, based on the size of portfolio managed. The best financial advisors have advanced software that can model up to 10 complicated scenarios factoring in how much you can contribute over time, market conditions and various market sector investments. They will also be knowledgeable on life insurance, including whole life, supplemental and term policies. They will also tend to charge a fee based on how much money they are managing for you.

There are three main categories of certifications for financial planners:

1. Certified Financial Planner
2. Chartered Life Underwriter
3. Chartered Financial Consultant

Certified Financial Planner - CFP®

The Certified Financial Planner® designation is managed by the Certified Financial Planner® Board of Standards in Washington, DC. This designation is perhaps the most widely recognized credential in the United States. This credential is the most difficult to obtain and is generally associated with fee-based financial planners. CFP holders are trained to focus on the whole picture with an exceedingly high degree of rigor, and you will find the occasional insurance agent who uses it to provide comprehensive financial plans for clients, showing them how insurance needs to be a part of their planning.

The CFP® curriculum contains five core courses that cover the following planning topics:

- Investment planning
- Insurance planning
- Estate planning
- Tax planning
- Retirement planning
- Education planning
- Ethics and the financial planning process

There are over 100 topics related to financial planning that are covered in the training materials for CFP candidates. The process to become CFP certified requires the completion of the course work followed by a ten-hour proctored board exam. After completing the course work and passing the exam, the candidate must pass a comprehensive background check before receiving their certification.

Chartered Life Underwriter® - CLU®

This designation was created in the late 1920s by the American College in Bryn Mawr, PA. It is considered to be "the" premier insurance designation in the United States insurance industry. Point of fact here is any financial plan that does not include various (yes, that specifically means more that you need more than one) types of insurance is deeply flawed. You may not want to pay for insurance, and you may not be able to pay for all the coverage you need early in your earnings career, but you should make it a priority. You also need to include it in your estate planning.

At the time of this writing the course curriculum for the CLU® had five required plus three elective courses.

The five required courses:

- Fundamentals of Insurance Planning
- Life Insurance Law
- Individual Life Insurance
- Fundamentals of Estate Planning
- Planning for Business Owners and Professionals

Candidates can select any three elective courses from this list:

- Financial Planning (Process and Environment)
- Individual Health Insurance
- Income Taxation
- Group Benefits
- Planning for Retirement Needs
- Investments
- Estate Planning Applications

Chartered Financial Consultant - ChFC®

This credential was introduced in the early 1980s and is considered both an alternative and a compliment to the CFP® credential. It has the same core curriculum as the CFP®, and requires three additional elective courses that allows a degree of specialization for the candidate.

Category	CLU®	CFP®	ChFC®
Comprehensive Board Examination Required?	No	Yes	No
Number of courses required?	8	5	8
Specialty (if any) targeted by this certification?	Life Insurance, both personal and business	Comprehensive financial planning	Comprehensive financial planning

Is there a "best" type of financial planner?

This is where expertise and results matter. You should look for the most experienced and successful planner you can realistically afford. Keep in mind that many of the most experienced planners and advisors are in high demand and will often require a minimum managed portfolio of $100,000 to $250,000. But, don't be discouraged if you don't have this type of portfolio when you are starting out. Unless you were a trust fund baby or born into wealth, we all have to work our way up. The goal of good planners and is to help people succeed, and you can sometimes convince them to take you own to help you grow your portfolio even if you don't meet their minimum requirements.

Do you have wealthy friends and successful people in your life? If so, ask them who they might recommend. Don't be shy about asking for that introduction.

Back to "best" type of planner/advisor and their qualifications. A simple way to begin is to look for someone who has all three certifications, but those individuals are not necessarily easy to find. At a minimum, find an individual that has at the very least the CFP® certification. Look an individual who will meet with you face to face on a regular basis, and who will evaluate your portfolio and overall financial health frankly without dancing around the things you could do better.

Choosing a financial planner (framework of questions to ask):

1. How do you get paid?
2. What licenses, certifications or credentials do you have?
3. How long have you been in this business?

4. How many clients do you have?

5. How many clients like me do you have?

6. How many clients do you have with a net worth of $500K or more?

7. What services do you (and your firm) provide?

8. Who will support me? You, personally or an alternate or an anonymous team?

9. What type of clients do you specialize in?

10. Can you show/share a sample financial plan?

11. How do you approach investing?

12. How will we work together (f2f, email, phone) and how often will we be in contact?

13. Why should I work with you and what makes you better than the next person on my list?

14. Have you consistently done better than the DJIA and S&P indexes?

What if I want to manage my own portfolio?

Self-directed investing can be rewarding and fun, but only if you understand how the market operates and what tools you can use to your benefit. At the beginning of this chapter, we promised not to dive into the deep end of the investment pool, but if someone is recommending something, they should at least flip on the lights by the diving board before you take your first plunge. So, here are a few recommendations on selecting an online trading service:

- Look for heavily discounted trading fees

- Identify any "extra" costs, such as calling the 800-support desk

- Stop loss/trailing stop/limit order services are a must have, deal breaker

Some tools are a "must have."

1. Real time data (many sites offer a slightly delayed data set)
2. Consistent (timely) placement of orders

3. Customization and shortcuts
4. 10 years historical data (more if possible)
5. Ability to set up and run strategy tests
6. Automation for buy/sell actions
   - Trailing stop orders
   - Conditional orders
   - Short selling
7. Integrated mobile application

To get a feel for these tools, let's review the trailing stop automation function:

This tool is basically an autopilot for your investments and should be consider a deal breaker if it is not available on your trading platform of choice. It's designed to "trail" your stock as it increases in value and protect (sell) in the case of sudden market downturn. Here is how it works; You buy a stock for $25 per share and you fully embrace the risk that the market doesn't always go up. In this case your stock climbs from your initial buy price of $25 to $63 (excellent job picking this one) over some period of time. Not being able to watch your stock and sell it when a major shift or bad news day occurs, you could literally ride the stock down below your purchase point, losing all your potential profit and more. So, to protect yourself, you pick a loss threshold that is not static, but is based on how much in percentage of the price of your stock you are prepared to lose. Let's say at a $63 price ($38 profit) you want to be protected from a sudden price drop, but don't want to sell your winning stock just because the market fluctuates a bit. So, you decide on 10% and set that as a "trailing stop." This means if your stock drops more than $6.30 in a trading session then you will automatically sell all, or a portion of that stock. This option is great for protecting yourself from sudden downturns, and what's even better about it is the fact that it will "trail" or follow the stock up, meaning if your stock moves up from $63 to $70, then the trailing stop would be invoked at 10% of $70, selling only if the stock drops to $63 or lower. If your stock continues to climb then so does your trailing stop threshold. If your $70 stock drops to $45 dollars, your stock sale triggers at $63 and you preserve most of your gain. You will be alerted to the trade, then you can decide if the stock has the potential to recover. If you think the stock will again got up, you can purchase more stock when it drops to $38 (or whatever your purchase threshold is) and the process starts all over again. Of course, this scenario shows the best-case example. So be careful about re-buying a stock that is in free fall. You need to be able to identify the difference in an events-driven downturn and company driven stock price decline.

After you've established your online trading account, here are some rules to start with:

- Don't use your portfolio as credit (margin) for trading

- Don't trade options

- Don't trade futures

- Don't commit all your disposable cash at once, opportunities come and go, and you want some flexibility

- Create an investing plan with targets, risk tolerance and investment holding period

- Minimize transaction costs and fees

- Use the internet to research your stocks, particularly the "beta" characteristic

- Mutual funds let you hold a large, diversified portfolio of stocks, so consider these as you learn the stock market

- Learn about "Blue Chip" stocks

- Learn what the Dow Jones Industrial Average and Standard & Poor's index really tell you

- Learn about Spyders, drip investing, dividend investing, mutual funds, dollar cost averaging

What's a *beta characteristic?* The beta characteristic is just one of the many factors you would need to understand and use in your evaluation and buy/sell decisions for your portfolio. I called this out in the list above as it is probably one of the most available and easiest to understand metrics. Simply put the beta characteristic is an indicator or risk and performance expectations in relation to the overall market at that point in time. Sometimes this is called volatility. A beta of more than 1 is considered to have a higher volatility than the market. Less than one, more stable. Stocks with betas of more than one tend to go up in price more than the market when it goes up, and move down more in price when the market goes down. Negative betas are possible, and would do just the opposite. Negative beta would see the price of the stock go up when the market goes down. The farther the beta is from a value of 1, the more volatility (movement) you should expect in relation to the market.

At some point in time you may be a master of the stock market. It is highly unlikely that you have that skill today. Managing your own portfolio can be exhausting and stressful. My recommendation is to create your own small online portfolio to keep a hand in, but to turn over the bulk of your investments to a full-time professional as soon as you can

Back to our core focus:

Three ideas worth repeating:

1. Live within your means
2. Maximize your primary income
3. **Create multiple streams of income**

At this point we've covered your primary income as your first stream of income, your retirement savings as your second, and we've recommended you begin investing in the stock market as your tertiary or third stream of income.

Isn't that enough? Absolutely not, you need at least one more stream of income, and more if possible to reach your goals. What you need to understand is unless you are in the business of frequently completing very large transactions (think high-end real estate sales), you need to create streams of income which consistently generate medium-to-small-to-micro transactions. In terms of generating and accumulating wealth, the most common path in the last 100 years has been via a service company. Service companies can range from low inventory and low skills required all the way up to and including those companies that find and source specific, high skill individuals to other companies.

Some of your businesses must run and conduct transactions without requiring you to generate and close each transaction, because you simply can't become wealthy if you must be present at every sale or transaction. You need a business that runs 24 X 7 X 365 with minimal interaction from you.

Today you have more options for creating your own business or generating another source of income that any other time in history. The high-speed connectivity of the internet creates a multitude of options. Hint: if you don't have the skill, certificate, or degree to follow your dreams, the internet is a huge enabler for distance learning, tips and tricks, as well as a profusion of incredible wealth of how-to videos. There is nothing standing between you and your dreams except air; the resistance is low so don't waste time, just get started.

The internet has been a real game-changer for companies, and especially for SMBs, as it provides them with the same exposure to potential customers as it gives larger companies. In fact, there is a huge group of Small to Medium Businesses (SMB's) that simply would not exist today without the advantages, markets and client exposure provided by the internet.

The game change advantage of the internet is hard to understate. For an example, let's describe the optimal 21st century SMB online business at a high level. This business has no full-time employees, it has no inventory, no storage facilities, and no expensive office space. It is open 24 X 7 with or without you looking in on it. It is instantly accessible by everyone in the world with an internet connection or smartphone. All payments, invoicing and shipping are done automatically from third party suppliers. This type of web-based business connects product and service consumers with product and service providers. You create a web storefront, you set up the business-to-business connections, some automated reporting and your job is to deal with exceptions and find a way to expand your catalog offering. Oh, and cash the checks. Take a moment to think about this. A business that runs on its own, with little to no supervision. The owner of this business only needs react to exception conditions and the detection and reporting of those can be highly automated. This was simply impossible 20 years ago.

Is there a web-based business waiting for your business idea?

Stop here and grab a pad, something to write with and start brainstorming. Is there anything, a service or product you think would be a good fit? Don't assume anything. Don't assume that there is already a better mousetrap. Think from YOUR personal perspective. Is there anything you see as a market you could sell into? If you have a skill or passion about a specific product, method, or skill, consider creating a business around it. It doesn't have to be huge, but is there any niche or specialty that you could start with? Web stores are cheap and easy to set up, all you really need is a product.

Be OPTIMISTIC. Be PROACTIVE. Be INNOVATIVE and be CREATIVE.

Is it really that easy? No. But if you fail to try, you simply fail. It's almost that easy if you can come up with something people want to buy. It certainly takes a bit of work getting your product catalog set up and the web store designed, plus arranging for payment processing, and a few dozen other details that we won't bore you with here. A simple internet search will give you everything you need. Search on "starting an online business" or something similar.

Variations of the "optimal" online business require you to directly source the product or service. At the more desirable end of this spectrum you might have to hire and schedule the service providers or create a supply chain process that builds the products you sell. The least desirable is where you personally must provide the service or create the product, but you might want to start with that and grow into a business you can sell or turn over to a competent and trusted manager. Many very wealthy individuals created their wealth by becoming "serial" entrepreneurs. They identify a market, create the initial company and find a buyer once it is profitable.

If this is not for you, or not enough for you, consider the concept of residuals. This is without a doubt one of the most intriguing forms of income. Residual income is a situation in which you continue to get paid after the work is done. This is NOT a common form of income, but is one of the most sought after and one you should try to create.

Some examples of generating residual income are:

1. Parking lots
2. Storage units
3. Laundromats
4. ATM machines
5. Multi-level marketing
6. Vending machines
7. Rental property
8. Royalties from books
9. Royalties from intellectual properties
10. Stock photography royalties
11. Blogs

12. Insurance sales

13. Credit card processing agreements

14. Alarm monitoring services

15. Oil, gas, and mineral leases

Some of those items listed may be out of reach for you. For example, most of us do not have land with gas, oil or mineral deposits that can be leased. But many of the categories listed are within your grasp depending on your experience, education, and ability to innovate along with how much sweat equity you are willing to invest. The insurance business is probably the most common way to create residuals. You sell the policy and if the insured makes the payments, you get a small residual. Life insurance generally pays much higher than auto insurance. However, this model is changing, and now you must be an active insurance agent to be compensated in this way. This means your residuals most likely won't fund your retirement.

Residuals are generally small fractional amounts of a renewal or repeating sale. Unless you have a best seller book or a patent on hardware or software, you'll need to create volume over time. The best type of residual is one where you don't have to resell, service or support the "buyer." One of the best multi-marketing opportunities is a business that goes into a deregulated energy market and sells contracts to individuals and businesses, but doesn't own the energy distribution infrastructure (wires and pipes), meters or provide emergency repair services.

Multi-level marketing is cited in the previous paragraph, and specifically the deregulated energy market because of the size of the market and the fact that it's not an "optional" service. There is huge opportunity with this, but multi-level marketing is a strange bird and may not be for you. Multi-level marketing is not a shortcut to income, it requires a specific set of skills, often demanding in-person face time and adept social skills. If this is something you are interested in, you must do the same due diligence you would for any other investment or commitment, including educating yourself on the market size and penetration, as well as the requirements to create and maintain cash flow. For some, this is a tremendous opportunity that meshes with their natural style, interests, and ambitions, while for others it may be a poor choice.

If you have some free time, lots of energy and ambition, there are many other ways to create residuals. You might consider creating a blog, writing an eBook, or maybe giving the monetization of a social media channel a shot. Forbes has a great article you might want to reference, (see the citations) covering 13 social media stars who made between $2.5MM up to $12MM in 2015. The fact that they can monetize (via advertising space and sponsors) their favorite activities with millions, yes millions of people regularly viewing their sites defines a market that did not exist 10 years ago. The top earner, PewDePie literally plays video games and has 40 million subscribers. Michelle Phan, who pulled in a cool $3MM is a self-taught make-up artist who demonstrates various techniques and methods. In 2014, the top earning YouTube star was DisneycollectorBR; this person basically buys and unwraps Disney toys and provides her loyal fan base of 6.5 million subscribers a look at the product before they buy. It is reported that she pulled down a cool $4.5 MILLION in one year. If you have a talent, hobby, or interest, you should give this type of opportunity a hard look as part of your multiple streams of income strategy. Again, like any other real opportunity, you must do your homework. Internet viewers are notorious for their short attention span, so you will have to capture and hold their interest over time.

Remember, when a social medial artist goes live for the first time, they are instantly tapping a market with over three BILLION users, where over 850 MILLION of those are English speaking natives. Just in case you were interested, in second place are the Chinese with 700 MILLION users, and in third place, Spanish speaking internet users come in at around 250 MILLION.

http://www.internetworldstats.com/stats7.htm

http://www.forbes.com/sites/maddieberg/2015/10/14/the-worlds-highest-paid-youtube-stars-2015/

So, opening an internet business gives you access to an almost unbelievable number of potential buyers and subscribers. Tiny fractional segments of these populations can be hugely profitable. Think about it.

Other Important Things to Consider

Let's wrap up this chapter by including some items you should consider when managing your money.

Do you have aging parents? Will this affect your location and or expenses? Do you need to be near them? Do they have wills? Can you take care of them if they fall ill? Is it that time of life for you sit down and talk with your parents about having access to their finances?

Does your family have specific medical needs? Does this affect location or expenses? Being close to the best care you can afford can be critical.

Do you have military term life insurance? If so, keep it in force and make your payments as they come due. If you don't have a policy, consider acquiring one before you leave the service.

Do you have kids headed to college? How are you going to pay for that? Have you researched and created a tax-free savings account? What other options do you have? This is a HUGE topic and should be discussed with a financial advisor as the variation in the creation and use of a 529 plan varies widely from state to state. The details matter with 529 plans and you need to be an expert on the plan you choose. Other options include setting up residency in states that provide lottery- funded scholarships (Arkansas, Florida, Georgia, Kentucky, New Mexico, South Carolina, West Virginia, and Tennessee). There are also large numbers of scholarships available for those who can use the internet search functions. College is expensive and can make a real dent in your retirement, so take it very seriously and plan well.

Taxes are a big part of money management. The best advice we can give is to hire a professional to help you with this element of your money management and to always pay your taxes. When you get to the point where you need to move beyond the simple 1040ez tax form, you need to start working with a professional. This generally happens when you purchase a home and want to start itemizing your tax deductions. In this case, the mortgage interest deduction is one of the best tax write-offs available. There are other deductions you may be able to leverage, and to that point there is a wealth of knowledge you can find from books, seminars and web sites that claim to help you "pay zero taxes." Beware though, most of the tips, techniques and methods are risky and presented as a broad panacea, when in fact they are only applicable in very narrow use cases. Certainly, take the time to educate yourself on taxes, but ask yourself if you shouldn't be spending your time with your family or generating income rather than learning every edge case about taxes. There are so many nuances in the IRS tax code that you will never learn them all. If you decide to aggressively manage your taxes and deductions then you should buy the services of a tax audit protection company. You should get two options at a minimum; first, an audit of your taxes before you file and second, representation during any IRS audit. Don't buy the "kinder, gentler IRS" mantra, if you get audited get immediate professional help. Under no circumstances should you respond to any calls or correspondence from the IRS without representation. In many cases, doing so will void your audit protection warranty. Let the professionals deal with the IRS and shield you from their tactics. Also, remember you are required to keep three years' worth of supporting data (receipts, notes and such). Keep your tax records for 7 years if you file a claim for a loss from worthless securities or bad debt deduction. Keep your actual return FOREVER. This will prevent an audit that requires you to prove that you filed your return in some past year.

Military discounts are everywhere, and many citizens show their appreciation by offering military discounts, including but not limited to:

Auto	Car Rental	Clothing	Computers
Education	Electronics	Entertainment	Fitness
Flowers	Food	Health & Beauty	Home & Garden
Jewelry	Restaurant	Retail	Service
Shipping & Storage	Travel	Hotel	Wireless

Major vehicle manufacturers offer discounts and incentives that can bring the cost of a new car down to significantly below invoice. Have you always wanted a Harley? They have incentives and discounts to help you make that dream come true. Big box hardware stores offer 10% off for every purchase made by those on active duty or retired. For those who didn't retire out of the service, you can still get those discounts on military-type holidays so plan your major purchases accordingly. The number and type of discounts and savings available to you as a veteran are simply mind boggling. Many of the owners and founders of these companies served or had a close family member serve, and they understand the hardships and sacrifices you made. Take full advantage of this offering as part of your money management plan and never, ever pay full price. Last note: If you are not active or retired, you may need your Veterans Administration card to get these benefits, or you DD-214 may be good enough, but don't be surprised if someone asks you to prove your service.

This chapter opened with a promise that it couldn't cover all the things you needed to know. Hopefully, it has succeeded in providing you a framework to help you understand your strengths and weaknesses when it comes to Money Management, perhaps even sparked an idea or two. Jump in and become as smart and knowledgeable as you need to support your target lifestyle. To "trust but verify" you need the ability to audit and evaluate.

Core Concepts mapping

Core Four – You are uniquely prepared to manage your own future. Your military training has prepared you to take on the challenge of "money management" for you and your family. Your training in attention to detail and "trust but verify" habits will help you tremendously here. Create goals, make a plan, and constantly measure your progress against your goals. Just like in the service, when you need to learn a new skill, go find a good mentor in addition to self-education.

Core Five – You have skills and capabilities that are marketable. Should you choose to pursue a career after the service, you will be in demand in almost any job market. With the additional income comes additional significant responsibilities. Take the money and make solid decisions on debt, savings, and investments.

Core Six – You have gaps in your skills and capabilities that you need to close. Few of us know enough about money management and all that it entails to do this on our own. This is particularly true as income goes up and retirement looms. Money management, investment, savings, and financial savvy is not a core military skill, so you are likely behind the curve compared to your non-military peer age group. Get professional support as you learn and even with a professional, don't follow their advice blindly. Learn as much as you can so that you can give informed consent and understand the implications of your decisions.

Core Seven – You now have more responsibility for your life, and much more opportunity to screw it up. You are on the clock. Depending on your time horizon and life goals, you need to make the best decisions you can. Sub-optimal decisions early in life can be overcome. Stupid financial decisions late in life can be devastating. This is an important part of your life. Read, learn, search, absorb and discuss with friends and family. Money isn't everything, but it makes the ride better. Goals, plans and execution. Get to it.

Personal perspective:

We've all been there and seen them, the military pensioners who are just getting by. Some live in nice little houses with white picket fences with perfectly manicured lawns. Vacations are taken, hobbies indulged as there is more than enough money and everyone is always happy. More often the story is different. Alcoholism is rampant in the retiree community. Money is very tight, and a single economic negative event can wipe out savings and change life dramatically for the worse.

We've seen good people hit the end stop of their careers and not really have a clue what to do next. Those that retire at twenty years have a lot of time and opportunity for creating second careers and generating wealth. Those that stay for forty years, generally have much fewer options. They aren't the most flexible thinking people in the world. They either imagine that others have been the beneficiary of some type of "luck" or other intangible benefit that accounts for their success. Nothing could be farther from the truth. They have simply lived inside the imaginary box that the military constructed that is designed to make us dependent on the military and not take responsibility for our own lives. I learned this lesson from a tough, not so old, E-9 who took me under his wing after he had to help me with a few, umm, course corrections. As he was retiring after twenty years, he took the time to show me what he was facing. It wasn't a bleak situation as he was only about forty years old. He actually shared his impressive savings with me...he had almost a hundred thousand dollars in savings. I was blown away, wow, that was a lot of money. No need to ever work again. He quickly punctured that balloon as he explained to me that he didn't think that was near enough. He had plans to get out, work the next ten years in a well-paying contractor position and then retire. His wife worked outside of the home as well. He took the time, to this day I'm not sure why, to point out all the good, bad, and indifferent aspects of the military and finance. He poured a lot of time into my mostly oblivious head and only asked in return that I pass it along to those who were receptive to the knowledge. What happened to my mentor? He was as good as his plan, he did it, retired out of the military at 42 and his second career at 53 and I have it on good authority that he spends his time with his wife, his dog and is surrounded by grandchildren that he spoils rotten and who think their grandparents hung the moon.

Chapter 16 - Education

The section of the book "**Core Five – You have skills and capabilities that are marketable**" exposed both a bias towards hiring individuals with prior service and a rationale for why they get hired. In this chapter, we'll spend some time on the what and why of continuing your education to ensure you have that marketability.

Under-employment is rampant in today's job market. You want to work at the top of the market using your skills to the best of your advantage, not at the bottom or middle. People who settle for under-employment often find that condition of employment, over time, becomes permanent. For this chapter keep your eyes wide open, even if you don't like what you hear.

You've heard this before, and I'm going to repeat it as a reminder: *competition is fierce and you are probably under-educated*. There are most likely be a few of you who are officers with bachelor's degrees, but in today's market even that provides uncertain benefits.

Having a formal degree significantly improves your odds of avoiding an under-employed condition. The recommendation for a formal degree is not absolute, but why not stack the deck in your favor? One of my mentors once said, we may all have the potential to run a six-minute mile, but until you do it, it doesn't count and you can't prove it.

Before you get defensive and start mentally listing all the formal and informal training you've achieved, you need to realize you always have room for improvement. The bottom line is for the civilian job market, you are probably under-educated. Some of you will find jobs that are directly related to your military MOS equivalent. Keep in mind every technical skill has a shelf life, and while you may have skills you can leverage. The good news is that you should be able to double your military income easily, but specific skills will certainly pay better. The bad news is that technology moves on and your skill specific job will evaporate one day. To prevent this, you need to be a lifelong learner and make plans for to keep your updated and current. You need some way to ensure you get the training you need to refresh and upgrade these skills periodically, otherwise a younger version of you, fresh from the service will be cheaper and more effective to hire.

You need to protect your marketability, and the most permanent way to accomplish this is with a degree that doesn't have an expiration date. Formal education is one of the most powerful actions you can take in your life to ensure your continued employability, and while it is not the only path to success it gives you more options and flexibility. If you're not interested in college, consider getting vocational or technical training, because having in-demand vocational and technical skills are a good thing, and being certified and licensed is even better. Education is one of those life-defining choices, and you need to make the one that is best for you and the life you want to live. Remember, some jobs just aren't available in every nook and cranny of the world.

Vocational and technical programs tend to be shorter and much more focused on preparing their students for employment, and these are considered trade or career schools. You will find technical schools teach the theory and science required for a given program, while vocational schools take a more on the job training (OJT) approach, with hands-on training to help the students acquire the skills needed to perform the job successfully.

It's not that hard to get to the $60-70K salary range in various technical/vocational type jobs, and while they require specific technical training and aptitude are listed below, they are attainable. Remember that this is a point in time list, and you should do your own research.

1. Computer Technologist – Hardware, infrastructure and managing availability
2. Computer Programmer – Object Oriented coding, User Interfaces, vendor specific applications
3. Network Specialist – The world is the network, line technicians to computerized global networks
4. Radiation Therapist – Treating cancer patients
5. Dental Hygienist – Jobs are available in almost every community
6. Nuclear Radiation Technologist – Support and maintain medical radiation systems
7. Ultrasound Technician – Emerging field, high-tech ultrasound is now replacing some radiation scans
8. Registered Nurse – Never enough to cover the demand

9. HVAC technician – Very portable and in demand

10. Paralegal – Pays well and if you're good at it, can pay very well

11. Diesel Mechanic – Always in demand if you like to lay your hands on your work

12. Electrician – Always in demand

13. Heavy Equipment Operator – The heavier the equipment, the higher the pay

14. Home Inspection – Used by private parties and financial institutions

15. Oil & Gas – Large number of specialized skills and jobs that pay well

16. Welding – Lots of flexibility for a skilled welder

17. Plumbing – Many types of plumbers, usually in demand in every community

18. Truck Drivers – Jobs, jobs, and more jobs if you have a clean driving record

19. Gunsmithing – Resurging with the recent interest in defensive and recreational shooting

This list could go on and on and will never give you all the options and opportunities that a solid internet research session will provide.

In the civilian market, having a degree is proof you can do more than most. Again, it's not an absolute requirement, but it levels the playing field and broadens your horizons, making you a much more capable employee. For those officers only with a Bachelor's degree reading this, strongly consider getting an advanced degree. Your primary competition is from other officers who have the same level of education as you.

Education allows you to have control over your life. One of life's inconvenient truths is as you age, mental and physical capabilities will decline. You want to do those things that keep as many options open as you can for as long as possible, and being a life-long-learner (with formal education) gives you more options. Can I produce a list of high income, highly employed individuals without degrees? Absolutely. However, if you were to sit down with them like I have, and ask them if they were at a disadvantage without a degree, 99% would respond "absolutely." It is often their number one regret.

Under-employment can be a real derailer of your life and the goals you've set for yourself. I've seen more than one well-educated person working for tips in the food service industry. Make no mistake, this is not taking a shot at these people because we should all do what we need to survive. However, working for tips is certainly not thriving; those jobs are hard and require long hours. You have skills and experience that can serve you and your family better, if you can find the right job.

While the food service industry is the stereotype for this analogy, consider other situations. How about the formally trained electrical engineer with years of experience who suddenly finds himself pulling wires in new construction. This guy is paying for his insurance out of pocket, with no vacation and no pay for work days cancelled due to bad weather or other factors. Other examples include the person who's been trained and worked for years in high-end military technology now finding themselves doing residential cable TV trouble calls, or the fellow who has worked on high-tech turbo-charged engines changing oil at the local strip mall's 5-minute oil change franchise? These and others work very long hours for low(er) pay and less than stellar benefits when they could likely do much better if they took the time to leverage their skills and once again turn to education to help them transition to something which is less of a dead-end.

The concept of underemployment is another data masking shell game with our government's periodic unemployment reporting statistics. If you dig into the unemployment reporting you will find a couple of interesting truths. There's a category of persons who simply stop looking for work and those that are under employed. Those are huge swaths of the population you won't hear about when some spokesperson is declaring victory for a small percentage change in the unemployment statistics. That same increase would be wiped out if the no-longer-looking-for-work numbers were added in. Of course, with statistics and data we should always fall back on the mantra that "all models are wrong, some are useful."

Absolute statistics of this type are difficult to obtain, but the current average for 2016-2017 is about 14%.

Think about a situation where 14 of 100 persons who have jobs are underemployed in our economy. That means they are also under compensated. Do you want to be part of that statistic? Obviously not. So, make an honest and deliberate assessment of where you are in terms of training, skills and education. Plan to close specific gaps to achieve your target state.

You have three types of skills at your disposal;

- The first is your general military training and bearing. This is the set of skills you have earned and honed during your career. You know how to be part of a team both as a teammate and individual. You likely have a splendid work ethic that allows you to outwork almost all your civilian competition. You have tremendous confidence and experience with learning multiple new skills and concepts from the ground up.

- The second type of skill set you have is directly related to your job. As we discussed in previous chapters, you will likely be very well educated in your specialty vs. your peer age group. You have likely completed a very intense primary training course and one or more secondary trainings. These courses are generally like drinking from a fire hose for days, weeks and months at a time.

- You may have a formal college education. Your Associate's, Bachelor's or Master's degree in any field is a huge plus.

- Some of you were fortunate enough to attend military graduate school or advance subject training equivalents

We should continuously remind ourselves of the paradigm that "blood and access beats hard work and skill every time." Translation: People do things for people. Families will choose family over the best worker time and time again. If you have access to the leadership/decision makers you will gain influence and have greater opportunities than those in satellite locations.

Let's restate for emphasis, (hey, to be fair, you are military and sometimes need to have knowledge beaten into you).

Competition for good jobs is fierce, but you can even the odds with formal and vocational or technical education. Because Military Occupation Specialty training is so specific, don't count on getting a pass here.

Speaking of competition, even the type of degree you get can make a difference in the level of success you achieve. There are two types of degrees, Bachelor of Science and Bachelor of Arts, and I believe that an "of Science" degree is ever so much more useful than an "of Arts" degree when it comes right down to it. Engineering degrees are some of the best.

If you have an Associate's degree, I congratulate you and recommend you don't stop there, because it's almost like a consolation prize and doesn't give you much advantage. If you have a bachelor's degree, you now have the beginnings of a competitive edge. For a concrete competitive edge on separating from the military, get a Master's Degree while never forgetting the best of your competition will have a PhD.

If you are attending a college while still in the service, make sure your school is accredited, ensuring your degree will meet the standards set by private agencies and it recognized by schools and employers alike. Accreditation is the keyword to help you avoid the paper-mills that take your money and print useless diplomas and certifications. If you go through a program that is not accredited you may still acquire the knowledge, but you won't get the credit for doing it. Your goal should be to get all the credit you deserve from your military service (see the DD-214 section later in this chapter) and get transferable college credits for any classes you take.

Accreditation can be confusing, particularly when it comes to taking courses online. To that end, you should learn about the two types of accreditation regional and national. Regionally accredited schools are more focused on the academic type of learning commonly associated with traditional colleges and degrees. Nationally accredited schools tend to deliver rigor around career-specific training with a focus on keeping the curriculum up to date and relevant. Nationally accredited schools will usually recognize and grant full credit transfers from regionally accredited schools. The reverse is less likely given the differences in focus.

You can't use your military education benefits at a school that is not properly accredited, so be sure to check with the Department of Education to verify accreditation:

http://ope.ed.gov/accreditation/

If you have the opportunity to choose your military education and schools, be knowledgeable and selective. Accumulate all the badges and achievements you can along the way.

You do have skills, every one of you, so let's take a walk down that path and put some things into perspective. For our first point of comparison, let's choose a veteran who has been enlisted for four-years veteran, an E-5. We'll use this rank as a starting point because you have to be pretty squared away to make E-5 in four years.

The military is literally run by E-4s and E-5s, and of all the NCO ranks (to take nothing away from the senior E-6 through E-9 ranks who usually fill a supervisory role), the E-5 has the largest impact on the lower ranking soldiers, Airmen, Marines and Sailors. This rank is responsible for the hands-on, in your face training of their individual charges on cleanliness, military bearing and daily accomplishments. The E-5 must be very capable of carrying out their assigned missions correctly.

This pressure cooker-like environment usually produces a person with outstanding capability that can be applied within their core specialty or discipline, as well as in other areas of interest. With a good set of goals sustained personal motivation, you're not likely to find a better candidate for your next job opening, and no one can match this Veteran job candidate. If our NCO has been able to acquire a bachelor's degree (and if you are still in the military, you should work diligently towards getting your degree), then that person becomes a professionally attractive hire.

After this though it gets much more complicated, as social and professional networks begin to play a factor along with skill specialization and formal education.

How about Officers? Officers are subject to higher standards of performance which results in incredible pressure because the scope of responsibility is much larger at a relatively young age. This causes lower performers to stand out like a burning building at night.

Every service member must pass through the crucible to become a productive member of the military, Officer and Enlisted alike. The salient point here is if you ask any Officer with four years of service what they think of a newly commissioned O-1 from any school or academy, the response will be something along the lines of "poorly organized potential that needs a lot of work." If you ask the same question to your Enlisted E-5 and above, the answer is always "dangerous." However, the pressurized process of weeding out the worst and building strong capable Officer Corps leaders is not pretty, but it is effective and just takes time.

The same elements of evaluation used in the previous enlisted comparison, plus more apply to the Officer Corps. After four years on active duty, similar but higher-pressure factors that shaped our NCO have been at work on our Officer. The round-the-clock schedules, even greater leadership and management responsibilities, and constant review and supervision have created a much more capable individual. At this point our outstanding Officer has hopefully received two promotions (time in service of 18 months + 24 months), positioning our Officer significantly higher on the hire list than our E-5. Remember our Officer is also generally four years older than our E-5.

Even with all that training and experience, finding a job comparable to their service responsibilities is going to be difficult. Just like our E-5, our O-3 has generally had a much higher degree of training, responsibility, and critical leadership exposure than their civilian counterpoint. The Officer will rarely find a peer position with the same managerial and supervisory control, but jobs of that type usually require very specialized experience and financial management skills not generally required or acquired in the military.

DD-214

As you prepare to separate, the second most important document you need to understand is your DD-214. This is your Certificate of Release or Discharge from Active Duty. There are two versions, "short" and "long."

You need to work with your local personnel office in *advance* to make sure everything is in your service jacket, with one of the most important items being your DD-214. In fact, you should start working months in advance and make sure everything you've done is properly included in your service record, as that's what the local personnel office will work from. If something is missing, get it updated and make sure all your award, rank, medals, and education items are included.

The military has a huge problem with accurate record keeping. In one of the most publicized cases, military historians identified a huge gap in the action reports for the Gulf War as well as the conflicts in Afghanistan and Iraq. Many military Veterans were and continue to be denied benefits due to problems with their records which indicates they were never in battle. To avoid this problem, and long before you begin the separation process, you need to constantly review your service and medical records to ensure they are up to date and accurate. Don't take someone's word for it, trust but verify.

Your experience during this last transaction with the base personnel office will vary. After you leave the service, you generally lose access to these people so any mistakes, inadvertent or otherwise, will not haunt them. It becomes your problem from the other side of the country and from off the base. Again, we aren't maligning every human resource or other personnel-related occupations, but this is NOT the time to "hope" they get it right. This is the time to dot every "i" and cross every "t," three times over. Get it right.

Here's a huge tip, if you are a high achiever or have been around for a long time, you likely have an extensive list of schools, badges, awards, and medals that MUST be added to the DD-214. You need to make a list, check it verses your service jacket.

You will often be presented with the "short" form of the DD-214, but do not settle for that.

Be sure you know everything that should be on your DD-214. Anything not on the form, simply evaporates as if it didn't happen. While there are processes and procedures to get the form amended, it's not something you want to experience from outside of the service.

Let's say that again; If it ain't on the DD-214 form it didn't happen. If you don't get it fixed before you separate or retire, it's almost impossible to get it amended later.

Make sure you aren't negotiating what is on your DD-214 on your last day on base. I learned this from the school of hard knocks because that's what happened to me!

Become an expert on the DD-214 form. Here's an overview:

A DD-214 form is prepared in eight copies and distributed as follows:

- Copy 1 – Service Member

- Copy 2 – Service Personnel File

- Copy 3 – United States Department of Veterans Affairs

- Copy 4 – Member (if initialed in Block 30)

- Copy 5 – United States Department of Labor

- Copy 6 – State Director of Veteran Affairs

- Copy 7 & 8 – Distributed in accordance with Military Service Department directions (shredded and retain)

If you need to update your DD-214, then it is done with a DD-215 form using the same copy (8) format.

If you are already out of the service, the link below is the place to get your data. You can submit a request online, but must mail or fax in a signature accompanying the request for it to be processed.

http://www.archives.gov/st-louis/military-personnel/public/awards-and-decorations.html

Why the emphasis on the DD-214 in this chapter focused on Education? The answer is simple; many schools and institutions of higher learning will grant you real college credit based on what's on the DD-214 form. Some employers (the smart ones) will ask you to provide your DD-214 as proof that you've been trained on the systems you claim.

Our military veterans, Officer or Enlisted, are generally a cut above the same-aged candidates in the job market. The more their experience maps directly to a specialized and in-demand skill set, the more likely they are to get hired. Having a degree makes a tremendous difference.

Don't forget to take advantage of the training and education programs from the Department of Veteran Affairs which can be found at:
http://www.benefits.va.gov/gibill/

These programs include:

1. Post-9/11 GI Bill
2. Montgomery GI Bill
3. Reserve Educational Assistance Program (REAP)
4. Veterans Educational Assistance Program (VEAP)
5. Survivors and Dependent Assistance
6. Accelerated Payments
7. Co-Op training
8. Correspondence Training

9. Entrepreneurship Training

10. Flight Training

11. Institutions of Higher Learning

12. National Call to Service Program

13. Licensing and Certification

14. National Testing Program

15. Non-College Degree Programs

16. On-The-Job and Apprenticeship

17. Tuition Assistance

18. Tutorial Assistance

19. Work-study.

Do your homework in advance, make choices that move you in the direction that you want to go, and don't just get carried along with the current.

Core Concepts mapping

Core Eight - Life is still hard – No level of education guarantees you a job or a career. No job gives you a guarantee of permanent employment. Acquiring education, training and experience stacks the odds in your favor, but doesn't ever add up to certainty. Keep your options open and always have a plan (multiple streams of income) to support yourself and your family.

Personal perspective:

I have the honor of knowing several educators and was once responsible for a military technical training element with 20 instructors and over 500 students in the pipeline at any given point. My time as a teacher and supervisor of instructors gave me a tremendous appreciation for anyone in the teaching profession. One of the interesting things with the recent economic downturn is there is now a glut of potential teachers in the candidate pool, raising the bar for teaching experience and education. Today a master's degree is a big advantage to an age twenty-something teacher. For an age forty-something educator, a master's degree is expected, so to create the same competitive advantage the educator needs a Ph.D.

Chapter 17 – Insurance

Here is one thought before we dive in; if you are married and/or have children, it is your obligation to provide for the financial well-being of your family. This means you should provide enough insurance benefit to see your children through college and your spouse through the rest of their life. You can be more generous, but this should be the minimum.

In a way, not paying for insurance is like gambling in Vegas and life is the house. There are no winning strategies or ways to really beat the house over the long term. At some point in your life, you are going to get sick and die. It will happen to every single one of you, and for those of you who think that you are wasting your money on insurance, it's only a matter of time.

Do you really need insurance? Yes, you do. Insurance must be a well-managed component of your financial plan. What type and how much varies, and unless you are independently wealthy, you should have insurance to cover the major components of your life. Insurance coverage can get complicated and because no licensed insurance agent was involved with creating the detail provided in this chapter, so consider it to be just an overview or primer. You are responsible for learning this in greater detail and making the decisions that are right for your life.

What types of insurance should you have?

1. **Life Insurance**. You should have enough to pay off your debts, replace your earning potential after your death regardless of age. Done properly this will see your spouse with a comfortable income and a home that is paid off. There's a specific formulaic approach for determining how much insurance coverage you should buy which translates to determining a lump sum payout amount that can be invested to provide an annual income from the interest (rate of return on investment) which will cover your lost income.

    Debt Amount + (Income Desired divided by Expected Rate of Return) = Death Benefit needed

    Note, you should be very conservative estimating the Expected Rate of Return (ERR) you use. Don't fool yourself hoping for huge returns on this investment, because neither the economy nor investments follow anyone's projections. I would recommend you do not use any value higher than 4% for ERR.

If you don't have a specific set of debts you want to pay off, then remove that part of the formula. This will reduce the total amount of coverage you need while still providing sufficient monies to provide for your family's current and future expenses.

Don't forget about taxes when you use this formula! This income will be taxable and will reduce the actual annual benefit by some factor, depending on your family's tax situation.

For higher levels of insurance, you generally have to take a medical exam as you age. This exam is fairly invasive as you are measured, weighed, and have your blood sampled. Additionally, it is likely your doctor will be required to provide your medical records and you will also be asked to provide a comprehensive family medical history. All of this information is necessary for the insurance company to properly gauge their risk of insuring you. If you are not truthful through any part of this process, the policy can be declared null and void regardless of how much you've paid in. Let me put this another way, getting insurance coverage is like dealing with taxes, so don't cheat.

There are two categories of life insurance: Term, Whole and AD&D.

    a. **Term Life Insurance** – This is the insurance that pays out when you die. It comes in various forms and packages, and is the most ordinary form of life insurance.

        i. Level Term Insurance – Benefits stay the same, but the cost of the policy increases as you age.

        ii. Decreasing Term Insurance – Death benefits drop (sometimes as frequent as every year) as you age, with some reduction or stabilization of cost.

    b. **Whole Life Insurance** – Also provides a death benefit, but this type of life insurance is one that charges more in the early years of an insured's policy, allowing older persons to stay insured. The interesting thing about whole life insurance is that, by law, the "over payments" accumulated from the earliest years are available as a cash-out option if the policy is terminated.

c. **Accidental Death and Dismemberment** – Also known as AD&D and unlike the various term and whole life options, this one does not require a medical exam or detail about your family's medical history. AD&D is often described as a supplemental policy which pays out only for covered accidents (the list is long and very comprehensive). If someone has both life and AD&D insurance and dies of old age or of a medical condition, the AD&D policy does not pay. If that same person were to die due to a slip and fall, a car accident or by some other accidental method, both the Life and AD&D policies would pay out. In some cases, if a person is not able to secure enough life insurance coverage due to health issues, a good AD&D policy can be used as a mitigating strategy.

d. **Veterans Group Life Insurance** – Hopefully you have been buying more than the minimum of Servicemembers Group Life Insurance (SGLI). This policy terminates when you leave the service and should be converted to Veterans Group Life Insurance at that point.

VGLI is a life insurance program which allows you to convert your SGLI coverage to renewable term insurance, and members with SGLI coverage are eligible for VGLI upon release from service. VGLI, is overseen by the Department of Veterans Affairs, but is administered by the Office of Servicemembers' Group Life Insurance.

Upon release from active duty, active duty for training, initial active duty for training or upon separation from the Ready Reserve, SGLI coverage may be converted to VGLI or, if desired, to a commercial life insurance policy effective at the end of the 120-day SGLI extension period.

It is important you maximize your SGLI coverage to the $400K limit before you separate, because you will be able to convert over to the maximum VGLI coverage of $400K immediately. You can only convert SGLI to VGLI for the coverage in force at your separation date, so if you don't maximize your coverage before you separate, you can only increase your VGLI by $25k *every five years*!

Within approximately 45 to 60 days following your separation from service, you should receive an application from OSGLI. You have up to 485 days (15 months) from your date of separation from the service to apply for VGLI, and if you don't meet the deadline, you will lose your eligibility for VGLI. If you do not receive an application from OSGLI in the mail, you may apply for VGLI using a form SGLV 8714, *Application for VGLI*. Submit the form along with your DD-214 or other proof of service.

There are some other types of service-related insurance you should know about:

i. FSGLI or Family Servicemembers' Group Life Insurance. Provides for spouses and children.

ii. SGLI or Servicemembers Group Life Insurance. SGLI is a program that provides low-cost term life insurance coverage to eligible Servicemembers. If eligible, you are automatically enrolled (you need not apply for coverage) and issued the maximum SGLI coverage.

iii. SDVI or The Servicemembers Disabled Veterans Insurance. This program was established in 1951 to meet the insurance needs of certain veterans with service-connected disabilities. S-DVI is available in a variety of permanent plans as well as term insurance. Policies are issued for a maximum face amount of $10,000.

iv. SGLI-DE or Servicemembers Group Life Insurance Disability Extension. Veterans are eligible for SGLI-DE if they are totally disabled at discharge. You can apply for SGLI-DE within two years of separation, and you will receive two years of coverage free from date of separation, not application.

v. VMLI or Veterans Mortgage Life Insurance. Insurance that pays up to $200,000 towards your mortgage upon your death. VMLI is only available to Servicemembers and veterans with severe service-connected disabilities who received a Specially Adapted Housing (SAH) grant to help build, remodel, or purchase a home. They must also hold title and have a mortgage on the home. Veterans must apply for VMLI before their 70th birthday.

vi. **VGLI or Veterans Group Life Insurance.** Veterans Group Life Insurance (VGLI) is a program that allows you to continue life insurance coverage after you separate from service. VGLI provides lifetime coverage as long as you pay the premiums. You may enroll for a maximum amount of coverage that is equal to the amount of Servicemembers Group Life Insurance (SGLI) coverage you had when you separated from service

vii. **TSGLI or Servicemembers Group Life Insurance Traumatic Injury Protection.** Provides automatic traumatic injury coverage to all service members covered under the SGLI program. It provides short-term financial assistance to severely injured Servicemembers and Veterans to assist them in their recovery from traumatic injuries. TSGLI is not only for combat injuries, but provides insurance coverage for injuries incurred on or off duty.

2. **Property Insurance.** You should maintain enough insurance on your properties (residence, other properties, vehicles, and major recreational purchases) to repair if damaged and cover replacement costs if destroyed. You need to structure your policy leveraging replacement cost, because otherwise you may not be able to rebuild your house for its assessed value. So, with property insurance, go a little large. The other aspect of property ownership and insurance is the concept of liability. This legal term and the responsibilities that go with it can be widely interpreted. Any event that results in injury or death to a loved one will often result in a lawsuit from the injured party or deceased's family. As a homeowner, a lawsuit like this can drive you straight into financial ruin. All states have financial responsibility laws pertaining to automobiles and you should have some coverage from personal liability via your renters or homeowner's policy. Lastly, you need to choose and manage your deductible, which is the amount of money you will pay out of pocket (up front) for an incident. The higher the deductible, the less your policy costs. It's almost impossible to

buy a policy with $500 deductible for a house or car these days, so most people settle for a $1,000 deductible. For any damage above the deductible, be smart about filing a claim because your insurance will go up. If you have a $1,000 deductible and the cost of repair is $1,500 or less, consider paying it out of your pocket.

    a. Homeowner's Insurance – Includes structures (you can't insure land) and possessions. If you suffer a catastrophic loss (fire, flood, earthquake or storm) that destroys your structure, it is unlikely you will have a comprehensive list of your possessions and the receipts showing what you paid. It is therefore imperative that you create just such a list for all the major and minor possessions in your house. If you make a major purchase, update your insurance. At a minimum, take a walk-through video of every room in your house and save it somewhere (safety deposit box or cloud backup). This will help you reconstruct your home after a major event. Do not expect the insurance company to just pay you face value on the policy.

    b. Renter's Insurance – If you rent, you should have this coverage. The same rule applies as with homeowner's insurance, make sure you have a way to demonstrate or reconstruct the contents of your rental. Do not expect the insurance company to just pay you face value on the policy.

    c. Automobile and other Vehicle Insurance – Cars, boats, motorcycles, jet skis, airplanes and even snow mobiles should be insured. This provides you replacement and repair remuneration and protection from any liability while you or someone else is operating your machine. Liability lawsuits and financial obligations can destroy you financially. Don't settle for the minimum state required liability coverage, talk to your insurance agent and make sure that you have proper coverage.

3. **Short and Long-Term Disability insurance.** Even though these are different policy types, (LTD generally picks up when STD runs out), we'll lump them together for the sake of focus. This type of insurance is designed to replace part, or all your income should you become hurt or sick and can't work. While in the service, if you were injured or sick you would still receive your full pay while recuperating, but this is not true for the civilian world. If you

don't go to work, you don't get paid. Most employers offer this type of insurance for a relatively low cost, and you should pay for it with no regrets. This should not be confused with AD&D insurance which is designed to pay out death benefits or other major injury benefits due to an accident. With disability insurance, you don't have to die or lose a finger (or more) to receive benefits from your policy. Also, if you are hurt on the job, you should be covered by your employer's workman's compensation insurance. What are the odds that you will need this type of insurance? The Social Security Administration uses a statistical rate of 1 out of 3 (33%) twenty-year-olds will need this benefit before they retire. The insurance industry often uses a lower statistic of 1 out of 4 (25%) for the same age group and period. The average disability period experience is roughly cited at about three years. That's three years without income.

    a. Short Term Disability or STD – Despite the unfortunate acronym, this is an important policy to have, as it will generally replace 60% of your income for up to two years. The average annual policy cost is less than $300.

    b. Long Term Disability or LTD – Picks up when STD benefits end. Benefits can run until retirement age (65) with some policies. Usually replaces 50-60% of income. Average

4. **Civilian Healthcare Insurance.** If you don't qualify for any of the Veterans healthcare programs, you need to buy healthcare insurance available to civilians. The best way to do this is through an employer because pricing will reflect the benefit of volume discounts. If your employer does not offer healthcare coverage, you can acquire it through an insurance agent or on the open market. Don't make the mistake of thinking you can beat the odds and avoid purchasing healthcare insurance. Did you know that 80% of an individual's lifetime healthcare expenses occur in the last decade of life? Think about that. If you are under age 65 (which is when you become eligible for Medicare), then you need to be under the best healthcare plan that meets your requirements. Remember you can't switch plans in the middle of an illness so it's kind of a "go to war with the military that you've got" situation. Choosing a healthcare plan is complicated, so you need to review and compare the types of coverage, maximum benefits and out of pocket expenses you are willing to live with. If you are lucky enough to have employer-offered insurance coverage, your employer will usually offer you a choice of various plans and options with side-by-side

comparisons. If you can't get insurance through work, the Healthcare Exchange offers comparisons of various insurance plans on its websites. There are three types of healthcare categories:

   a. Medical – Covers office, wellness care, hospital visits and prescription drugs. The lower your out-of-pocket expenses are, the higher the cost will be for your premiums. There are simply too many medical coverage options to list here. You should take the time to really learn about the various options, benefits, and costs before you make your final choice.

   b. Dental – Covers preventative care, cleaning, and some major dental work. Like medical coverage, there are numerous offerings and options, so you need to take the time to understand the implications of your choices. If you have children, remember most teenagers will need braces.

   c. Vision – Covers exams, lenses, and frames, as well as contacts (to some extent). If no one in your family wears glasses or contacts, then this is less of an issue until you reach age 40. After that, all bets on having good vision are off and you are strongly encouraged to buy vision insurance. There are some medical conditions, such as diabetes, which require an annual eye exam and will therefore be covered under your medical insurance.

5. **What is Obamacare?** The actual name of the program is the Affordable Care Act (ACA). This government-regulated program requires all citizens to acquire and maintain healthcare coverage of some type or pay a penalty. The law eliminates pre-existing conditions, stops insurance companies from dropping you when you are sick, protects against gender discrimination, expands free preventative services and health benefits, expands Medicaid and CHIP, improves Medicare, requires larger employers to insure their employees, creates a marketplace for subsidized insurance providing tens of millions individuals, families, and small businesses with free or low-cost health insurance, and decreases healthcare spending and the deficit.

The key for most of us is the "marketplace" or "exchange" that is created by the Affordable Care Act. This is a state by state construct where those persons not covered under an employer-offered healthcare plan can supposedly buy equivalently priced coverage. Unfortunately, sticker shock occurs when someone who was previously insured as part of a company plan tries to by the same in the marketplace. Most people don't realize just how much the employer pays as part of the group coverage policies they offer. The actual out-of-pocket cost to an individual can easily be 3-times the amount they were paying as part of the employer's group policy.

Another wrinkle in the Affordable Care Act marketplace is the period during which you can enroll, which is generally, the three-month period between November 15th through February 15th. However, if you experience a "qualifying" event such as a job change, loss of job or one of several other conditions, you can enroll at any time during the year.

There is some variability when you look at the state-by-state adoption of the ACA. The insurance marketplace continues to evolve as Insurance providers make year-by-year decisions on whether they will participate in a given state and what plans they will offer at what rate.

6. **Veteran Affairs (VA) Healthcare.** Generally, if you served at least 24 months continuous duty, you qualify for VA benefits and healthcare via Tricare (see next section). However, you are subject to income limits., which means if you make too much money, you won't be granted VA benefits or healthcare coverage. The income limits are modified each year, have geographic location and number of dependents restrictions, so check the VA website for the most current data. As of the writing of this book, the limit ranged from $18K to $70K for a Veteran with two dependents. Where you live is a key factor in this calculation.

    There are exceptions to the income rule. You must first have been discharged under Honorable Conditions. After that, if you meet one or more of the following criteria, you will qualify for VA benefits and Tricare healthcare (from the official VA website):

    a. Medal of Honor recipient

    b. Purple Heart Medal recipient

    c. VA certified service-connected disability of at least 10%

    d. Discharged from service because of a disability that was not a preexisting condition

- e. Discharged from the service as part of an "early out" program (10 USC 1171 and 1173)
- f. Discharged from the service for hardship reasons (10 USC 1173)
- g. Former prisoner of war
- h. Receiving a VA pension
- i. Served in a Theater of Operations for 5 years post discharge
- j. Vietnam service between January 9, 1962 - May 7, 1975
- k. Persian Gulf service between August 2, 1990 -November 11, 1998
- l. Stationed or resided at Camp Lejeune for 30 days or more between August 1, 1953 and December 31, 1987
- m. Classified as Catastrophically Disabled by the Veteran's Affairs administration
- n. Previous years' household income is below VA's national income or geographically adjusted thresholds

7. **Tricare coverage for Veterans.** Tricare covers Department of Defense active duty and retired uniformed service members and families. If you are or were active, this is probably one of the most undervalued benefits of your service. Here are four things you need to know about Tricare options:

   - a. **Tricare Prime** – This offering acts like a Health Maintenance Org (HMO) offering, as you will be assigned to a Primary Care Provider (PCP) through whom you must coordinate any specialist referrals. You will likely have to live close to a military facility which has healthcare infrastructure to take advantage of this option. This is the lowest cost option, with an annual enrollment fee and fee (shared-cost or co-pay) for each time you receive medical care.

   - b. **Tricare Extra** – This option is more flexible and more expensive than Prime. You can use any Tricare Network Provider (TNP), and like most civilian plans, you will pay an annual deductible and after that deductible is met, the plan will pay 80% of covered medical expenses.

c. **Tricare Standard** – Provides the most flexibility at the highest cost, but it allows you to obtain healthcare services from virtually any provider. Similar to Tricare Extra, you still pay the annual deductible, and in addition you must pay 25% of what the Tricare System says the medical service should cost. For further information, there's a well-designed web site you can use for reference:

www.tricare.mil

Before you obtain medical services from a provider, you should know if they are "participating" or "non-participating," because the amount of coverage your policy provides is different for each. A participating provider is one who has an agreement with your insurer, whereas a non-participating provider does not have an agreement with your insurer. Unfortunately, there is no national list of participating providers, so you should ask the medical provider yourself. For non-participating providers, beware, as they are under no obligation to meet the fee limits under Tricare and can charge up to 15% more for any service. If that is the case (and it usually will be), you are responsible for this overage, not Tricare. Additionally, you may have to pay a non-participating provider all costs up front and then file a DD 2642 form for reimbursement.

d. **Tricare for Life** – This coverage automatically kicks in when you reach the age (65) and qualify for Medicare. You must enroll in Medicare Part B at age 65 which will require you to pay monthly premiums. In return, Medicare Part B will cover services and supplies that are medically necessary to treat any health conditions you have, including outpatient care, preventive services, ambulance services and durable medical equipment.

To remain covered by Tricare for Life, you MUST be enrolled continuously in Medicare Part B.

Under Tricare for Life, you will receive your medical care from Medicare providers. Initial costs will be covered by Medicare and Tricare for Life will cover anything not paid by Medicare. The good news is you will no longer have to pay an annual deductible or shared cost for visits under this program.

8. **Medicare.** Most US taxpayers and citizens will qualify for Medicare coverage. The length of time you've paid Social Security and Medicare payroll taxes will affect the cost of Medicare benefits. You need to earn 40 hours of Social Security "credits" to maximize your benefits and minimize your costs.

As of 2016, you receive one credit for each $1,260 of earnings, up to the maximum of four credits per year. The earnings required per credit increases slightly each year, and the credits you earn remain on your Social Security record when you change jobs or stop working.

Even if you don't have the requisite credits, an occurrence which rarely happens as service members pay Social Security just like everyone else, all is not lost. Not having enough credits just means that you may not qualify for premium-free coverage of Medicare Part A. You can also qualify based on your spouse's Social Security credits.

Do you qualify for Medicare? Generally, as stated above, the answer is yes, but you must meet some general requirements:

- Must be a U.S. citizen or legal resident
- Must have resided in the United States for a minimum of five years
- Must have at least 10 years (40 credit rule) in Medicare-covered employment

If you meet the first condition above, then you will qualify for benefits if any of the following apply to you;

- Are 65 years of age or older?
- Are you under age 65, but receiving disability benefits from the Social Security Administration (SSA) or the Railroad Retirement Board (RRB)?
- Do you have amyotrophic lateral sclerosis (ALS, or Lou Gehrig's disease)?

- Do you have end-stage renal disease (ESRD), which is permanent kidney failure that requires a transplant or dialysis?

Medicare coverage:

a. **Medicare Part A:** Covers inpatient care in facilities such as hospitals and skilled nursing facilities. Medicare Part A also covers hospice care and limited home health care. Note that nursing home expenses are limited under Part A.
b. **Medicare Part B:** Covers the costs of health care that occur outside of actual medical facilities, such as doctors' visits, outpatient procedures and lab tests. Part B will help but not completely cover the cost of services related to health care, such as mobility devices (scooters and wheelchairs) oxygen tanks and ambulance expenses. In addition to providing coverage for health care needs that qualify as medically necessary, Part B also covers certain preventive-care services such as screening for heart conditions, diabetes, and certain types of cancer.
c. **Medicare Part C:** Allows you to buy insurance from certain private healthcare insurers to cover medical costs not paid by Parts A and B. You will have to pay for this insurance just like any other private provider, but generally at a reduced cost. You will need to educate yourself on this option and its costs to determine if you need it. Generally, you should be adequately covered under Tricare for Life if you are a retiree.
d. **Medicare Part D:** Provides prescription drug coverage from private insurance companies. You will want to compare coverage and prices. In some cases, this is included when you buy Part C coverage.

Medicare has a variety of rules which determine the type of coverage you get. For example, if you enroll in Part A, you must enroll in Part B, but you can get Part B without having Part A. To enroll in Part D (prescription drug coverage) you must be enrolled in either Part A *or* Part B. You must have Part A and Part B to enroll in the private Medicare Advantage plan or to buy Medigap supplemental insurance.

There's a quirky enrollment issue with Part B. If you don't sign up when you reach age 65, you can incur a permanent penalty. This is not a typo so please make note, if you don't enroll in Part B when you are first eligible, you will likely pay a penalty forever. The actual law states that a 10% penalty is imposed "for each full 12-month period" delay when enrolling in

Part B. There are some mitigating circumstances like when you have group health insurance from your or your spouse's employer. The good news is that partial 12-month periods don't count against you at all. The bad news, for example, is that if you are 25 months late, you will be assessed a 12 month (10%) + 12 month (10%) + 1 month (0%) = 20% penalty in perpetuity. Note there is no penalty for the 25th month because for a delay of less than 12 full months, the penalty does not apply.

It's important to know that Medicare enrollment is broken down into four types, periods, conditions, and coverage types:

e. **Initial Enrollment Period (IEP)** – Seven-month period starting three months before the month you turn 65 and extending three months beyond.
f. **Special Enrollment Period (SEP)** – Occurs when you are older than 65 but have had insurance coverage via a group health insurance plan from you or your spouse' employer. There is an eight-month grace period after you stop working and lose your employer-provided coverage.
g. **Automatic Enrollment** – This occurs when you start receiving Social Security or Railroad Retirement benefits. You are automatically enrolled in Medicare Part A and Part B at age 65 (or later if you defer your benefits). You don't have to accept Part B if you are still covered by an employer group healthcare plan.
h. **General Enrollment** – Each year January 1st through March 31st you can sign up if you didn't do it properly during IEP or SEP periods. Your coverage won't start until July 1st, so you could have a gap in coverage, and remember if you are late by any single or multiple of 12 months, expect the permanent penalty for Part B.

To sum it up, you need insurance for your life, health and property to l give your survivors replacement income, help you repair or replace your material possessions and help keep you as healthy as you can be as you continue on your journey through life. Plan well and live well. Don't skimp, avoid, or ignore this crucial element of your financial and wellness planning.

Core Concepts mapping

Core Six – You have gaps in your skills and capabilities that you need to close. You need to learn all the topics covered in this chapter. Even if you rely upon professional advice, you still need to participate and make the final, educated decision about your options.

Core Seven – You now have more responsibility for your life and much more opportunity to screw it up. It's simple, ignore these aspects at your own peril. You will continue to age and with the passing of time, you will see unexpected and unwelcome changes to your life and health. Be smart, responsible, and realistic. You need insurance and the more you can afford, the better you and your family will weather the challenges that life puts in your path.

Personal perspective:

You need life insurance, healthcare insurance and renters or homeowner's insurance. I once watched a friend of mine decline slowly and painfully from economic prosperity into financial ruin all because he decided to self-insure for healthcare. A family member became fell terribly ill requiring a significant amount of expensive healthcare before passing away. This was not a happy ending, as this family lost their business, home, and savings.

Chapter 18 – Hiring Advantages

As a percentage of the population, Veterans are a small minority. Your service should mean something to your fellow Americans, and it does. Most of our citizens have some type of connection to friends or family who've served, or just they appreciate your service in general. As covered in Chapter 15, some businesses just like the quality of person who has served that they offer incentives to win your loyalty and business.

Veterans as a % of the population US 2012 Census

State	%	State	%	State	%	State	%
Alabama	10.4	Illinois	7.5	Montana	12.7	Puerto Rico	3.8
Alaska	13.6	Indiana	9.2	Nebraska	10.4	Rhode Island	8.5
Arizona	10.7	Iowa	9.7	Nevada	11	South Carolina	10.9
Arkansas	10.4	Kansa	10	New Hampshire	10.6	South Dakota	11
California	6.5	Kentucky	9.4	New Jersey	6.4	Tennessee	9.6
Colorado	10.4	Louisiana	8.9	New Mexico	11.4	Texas	8.5
Connecticut	7.7	Maine	11.6	New York	5.8	Utah	7.4
Delaware	10.8	Maryland	9.7	North Carolina	9.8	Vermont	9.6
District of Columbia	6.0	Massachusetts	7.3	North Dakota	10.5	Virginia	11.7
Florida	10.2	Michigan	8.7	Ohio	9.6	Washington	11.2
Georgia	9.5	Minnesota	9.0	Oklahoma	11.2	West Virginia	11.1
Hawaii	11.1	Mississippi	9.1	Oregon	10.7	Wisconsin	9.2
Idaho	10.6	Missouri	10.4	Pennsylvania	9.3	Wyoming	11.1

From http://factfinder2.census.gov which is the US Department of Commerce US Census website

This can manifest in many ways, but one of the most important advantages is preferential treatment. Depending on how you represent yourself, you can almost be guaranteed a positive bias. You may also qualify for a formal hiring advantage with the Federal government. You absolutely are entitled to Veterans Affairs benefits at both the State and Federal level. Lastly and certainly not least, there are an incredible number of companies, from local Mom and Pop businesses to Mega Corporations that offer discounts on goods and services to Veterans.

You have absolutely earned these benefits and advantages, but to take advantage of them, you must first know they are available and second, make use of them. As you walk around town or poke around on the internet, there is no way to identify you as a veteran automatically triggering these benefits and discounts. You must learn about them and, for lack of a better term "activate" them in various ways.

Take the time to learn and stay on top of the various programs, initiatives, and discounts you've earned.

In Chapter 15 we provided some information about military discounts available to you. Here, we will cover some of the legal constructs that you can benefit from.

Veterans have several advantages in the job marketplace, many which are tied to the government or to government contractors. For most of these jobs, the first tollgate is your discharge type, so if you were discharged under Honorable or General conditions, you should be fine, but anything else will be problematic.

Jobs for Veterans Act of 2002, 38 U.S.C. 4212(VEVRAA)

This act requires government contractors to take affirmative action by employing and advancing in employment certain Veterans in recognition of their service. Companies who contract with the government will usually ask you to self-identify as a Veteran during the application process. It is important that you know beforehand if you are entitled to claim this protected Veteran status. The categories details are provided below and are broken out into four distinct qualifications; (1) disabled veterans; (2) recently separated veterans; (3) active duty wartime or campaign badge veterans; and (4) Armed Forces service medal veterans.

1. **Disabled Veteran:** Military entitled to compensation (or who but for the receipt of military retired pay would be entitled to compensation) under laws administered by the Secretary of Veterans Affairs or discharged/released from active duty because of a service-connected disability.
2. **Recently Separated Veteran:** Discharged or released from active duty within the last 36 months.
3. **Campaign Badge Veteran:** Meets one of two conditions:
    a. Served on active duty during one or more of the periods of war outlined in 38U.S.C. § 101.
        i. Indian Wars: January 1, 1817, through December 31, 1898. The veteran must have served thirty days or more, or for the duration of such Indian War. Service must have been with the U.S. forces against Indian tribes or nations.
        ii. Spanish-American War: April 21, 1898, through July 4, 1902, including the Philippine Insurrection and the Boxer Rebellion. Also included are those individuals engaged in the Moro Province hostilities through July 15, 1903.

      iii. Mexican Border War: May 9, 1916, through April 5, 1917. The veteran must have served for one day or more in Mexico, on the borders thereof, or in the waters adjacent thereto.

      iv. World War I: April 6, 1917, through November 11, 1918, extended to April 1, 1920, for those who served in the Soviet Union. Service after November 11, 1918, through July 2, 1921, qualifies for benefits purposes if active duty was performed for any period during the basic World War I period.

      v. World War II: December 7, 1941, through December 31, 1946, extended to July 25, 1947, where continuous with active duty on or before December 31, 1946.

      vi. Korean Conflict: June 27, 1950, through January 31, 1955.

      vii. Vietnam Era: August 5, 1964, through May 7, 1975. February 28, 1961 through May 7, 1975, for a veteran who served in the Republic of Vietnam during that period.

      viii. Persian Gulf War: August 2, 1990, through a date to be prescribed by Presidential proclamation or law.

      ix. Served on active duty in any campaign or expedition for which a campaign badge has been authorized under the laws administered by the Department of Defense. This is generally associated with the Armed Forces Expeditionary Medal cared by President John F. Kennedy in 1961.

4. **Armed Forces service medal Veteran:** There are two requirements:
   a. Served on active duty in a U.S. military operation for which an Armed Forces Service Medal was awarded pursuant to Executive Order 12985 (61 FR1209) and awarded the Armed Forces Service Medal, created by President Bill Clinton in 1996.
   b. Armed Forces Service Medal, which must be listed on your DD Form 214

Veterans Unemployment Compensation (UCX)

At separation or retirement, you are eligible for unemployment compensation, but this only applies if you don't transition directly into a job.

The US Department of Labor's "Unemployment Compensation for Ex-Servicemembers" program (UCX) provides benefits for eligible ex-military personnel as well as for former members of the National Oceanographic and Atmospheric Administration (NOAA. The program is administered by the states as agents of the Federal government.

https://workforcesecurity.doleta.gov/unemploy/ucx.asp

- If you were on active duty with a branch of the U.S. military, you may be entitled to benefits based on that service
- You must have been separated under honorable conditions
- There is no payroll deduction from service members' wages for unemployment insurance protection, and benefits are paid for by the various branches of the military or NOAA

State law under which the claim is filed determines benefit amounts, number of weeks benefits can be paid and other eligibility conditions.

You should file a claim as soon as possible after discharge, and to do so you'll need your SSN, DD-214 and separation orders.

You may be able to draw as many as 30 weeks (varies by state) of benefits. The rate of compensation depends on your last pay rate in the service. While this benefit is something you should investigate, you should not expect to be able to survive on it alone.

As of this writing (in 2017), the state rates can be found in a table listed in the References and Links section of this book. Most of the state unemployment agency links are provided there.

The highest weekly state rate:	Massachusetts	$742 + $25 per child
The lowest weekly state rate:	Mississippi	$235
Territory:	Puerto Rico	$133

Average: $358 for 20 weeks

*Guam does not technically have unemployment compensation, but you may be covered under UCX. There is some information available about filing for UCX in CONUS, but the author was unable to track down the specifics.

Veteran Hiring Preference

Let's start with the federal hiring "Veteran Preference." Depending on your circumstances, you will receive between 5 and 10 points which are added to your score on a civil service examination. for the specific language and details on this federal regulation, please reference the addendum "Veteran Preference Federal Code." You must provide your DD-214 to qualify for these additional points, and if you are requesting the 10-point benefit you must submit standard form SF-15 "Application for 10 Point Veteran Preference."

You are eligible for a **5-point** preference if you:

1. Served on active duty for more than 180 consecutive days, other than for training, any part of which occurred during the period beginning September 11, 2001 and ending on August 31, 2010, which was the last day of Operation Iraqi Freedom

2. Served on active duty between August 2, 1990 and January 2, 1992

3. Served on active duty for more than 180 consecutive days, other than for training, any part of which occurred after January 31, 1955 and before October 15, 1976

4. Served in a war, campaign, or expedition for which a campaign badge has been authorized or between April 28, 1952 and July 1, 1955

You are eligible for a **10-point** preference if you:

1. Have a service-connected disability

2. Received a Purple Heart

Under certain conditions your spouse, widower or mother may also qualify for the 10-point preference. The following is taken verbatim from the Office of Personnel Management (OPM) website.

Spouse Hiring Preference

Ten points are added to the passing examination score or rating of the spouse of a disabled Veteran who is disqualified for a Federal position along the general lines of his or her usual occupation because of a service-connected disability. Such a disqualification may be presumed when the Veteran is unemployed and;

- is rated by appropriate military or Department of Veterans Affairs authorities to be 100 percent disabled and/or unemployable; or
- has retired, been separated, or resigned from a civil service position on the basis of a disability that is service connected in origin; **or**
- has attempted to obtain a civil service position or other position along the lines of his or her usual occupation and has failed to qualify because of a service-connected disability.

Preference may be allowed in other circumstances but anything less than the above warrants a more careful analysis.

Note: Veterans' preference for spouses is different than the preference the Department of Defense is required by law to extend to spouses of active duty members in filling its civilian positions. For more information on that program, contact the Department of Defense.

Widow/Widower Hiring Preference

Ten points are added to the passing examination score or rating of the widow or widower of a Veteran who was not divorced from the Veteran, has not remarried, or the remarriage was annulled, and the Veteran either:

- served during a war or during the period April 28, 1952, through July 1, 1955, or in a campaign or expedition for which a campaign medal has been authorized; **or**
- died while on active duty that included service described immediately above under conditions that would not have been the basis for other than an honorable or general discharge.

Mother of a deceased Veteran Hiring Preference

Ten points are added to the passing examination score or rating of the mother of a Veteran who died under honorable conditions while on active duty during a war or during the period April 28, 1952, through July 1, 1955, or in a campaign or expedition for which a campaign medal has been authorized; and

- she is or was married to the father of the Veteran; and

- she lives with her totally and permanently disabled husband (either the Veteran's father or her husband through remarriage); or

- she is widowed, divorced, or separated from the Veteran's father and has not remarried; or

- she remarried but is widowed, divorced, or legally separated from her husband when she claims preference.

Mother of a disabled Veteran hiring preference

Ten points are added to the passing examination score or rating of a mother of a living disabled Veteran if the Veteran was separated with an honorable or general discharge from active duty, including training service in the Reserves or National Guard, performed at any time and is permanently and totally disabled from a service-connected injury or illness; and the mother:

- is or was married to the father of the Veteran; and

- lives with her totally and permanently disabled husband (either the Veteran's father or her husband through remarriage); or

- is widowed, divorced, or separated from the Veteran's father and has not remarried; **or**

- remarried but is widowed, divorced, or legally separated from her husband when she claims preference.

Note: Preference is not given to widows or mothers of deceased Veterans who qualify for preference under 5 U.S.C. 2108 (1) (B), (C) or (2). Thus, the widow or mother of a deceased disabled Veteran who served after 1955, but did not serve in a war, campaign, or expedition, would not be entitled to preference. Reference 5 U.S.C. 2108, 3309; 38 U.S.C. 5303A

Core Concepts mapping

Core One – You are NOT like the others. You have earned your benefits the hard way. There was a period of time that covered a span of *years* when your life was not your own, because you were at the beck and call of our republic in large and small ways. You were underpaid, over-worked and subject to some of the most challenging and frustrating aspects of life. At all times and at any point, you were expected to put your life on the line. That may sound trite, but stop and think about it. Deployed or not, active or reserve, you could be called up, had orders cut and sent into a place where life and limb were at risk daily. Those who were deployed were always at risk whether from aging equipment, incorrect maintenance, direct or indirect fire and several other situations; the risk was always there.

Core Nine – The Republic is powered by the engine of Capitalism. For all the time you were in the military, you were under-compensated. No matter what your financial situation after your departure from service, why would you leave money on the table or not take advantage of the benefits offered? You need to be very smart about your money, and even more smart as your income and wealth increase. One of life's most important truisms is you should take advantage of every moral, legal and ethical advantage made available to you.

Personal perspective:

I admit it, I'm a proud guy. I like to make my own way through life without depending on others. My wife has commented on more than one occasion that I'll go out of my way to help people who don't have the best track record of stepping up to help us. Asking for a discount or worse, expecting one just isn't in my DNA. But years ago, that perspective changed for me in a radical way. I was out with some ex- service friends for dinner and we were sharing experiences. Our server couldn't help but notice us as we might have been a little loud, and she asked us if we were military saying they gave a 10% discount to military personnel. For some reason, we all looked a little sheepish about taking advantage of the offer. After a minute, she walked away, and we went back to sharing experiences. A little later this older guy walked up and told us he was the manager. He was very nice and friendly and again extended the offer of the discount if we could show him any ID. When we didn't take him up on his offer, he smiled and gave us a little lecture on economics, saying he wasn't going to lose any money on the situation. His philosophy was that tapping into former military was a win-win in the community. By offering the discount, the reputation of the businesses in the area would go up and attract other prior military, their family, friends, and others. So, the discount wasn't completely about the money, and it didn't hurt that the overall effect was a benefit to customer traffic and cash flow.

Chapter 19 – Veterans Affairs

The United States **Department of Veterans Affairs** (VA or DVA) is a government-run military **Veteran** benefit system with cabinet-level status. The VA provides patient care and federal benefits to veterans and their dependents. The VA can be one of the greatest advantages you have in your post-service life, but only if you know how to leverage the multitude of programs it is responsible for.

Most people after familiar with the VA for two reasons, Healthcare and VA loans. However, the VA has many more programs and offerings for Veterans you need to know about.

We covered healthcare in the previous chapter and as recommended earlier, you *should* buy your own home, but before doing so, you should learn about VA loan guarantees as this is one of the biggest benefits you will receive from your service.

Here is the link to all the VA-sponsored offerings http://www.va.gov/

Just like any government-run program, there is a mountain of information and even more bureaucratic process you'll need to understand to take advantage of most VA programs. Some of them won't apply to you, but you should investigate each and every one to see if you can benefit from them.

The right place to get started with a publication called *"Federal Benefits for Veterans, Dependents and Survivors."* At the time of this writing, publication number 978-0-16-092508-5 was dated 2014 and contained 145 pages of salient information. For goodness sake, take the time to read this thing BEFORE you separate or now because you are aware of its existence!

You can view it online or download a PDF file for local use and/or printing from this link: http://www.va.gov/opa/publications/benefits_book.asp

As repeatedly stated through the body of this book, you need to get to the most accurate and up-to-date information available. If a source seems dated, look for the most up-to-date information on the website or call the help desk. If it's an option, drive to a local office and make new friends.

Here are some key points taken from the publication:

Veterans of the United States armed forces may be eligible for a broad range of benefits and services provided by the U.S. Department of Veterans Affairs (VA). Some of these benefits may be utilized while on active duty. These benefits are codified in Title 38 of the United States Code.

General Eligibility: Eligibility for most VA benefits is based upon discharge from active military service under other than dishonorable conditions. Active service means full-time service, other than active duty for training, as a member of the Army, Navy, Air Force, Marine Corps, Coast Guard, or as a commissioned officer of the Public Health Service, Environmental Science Services Administration or National Oceanic and Atmospheric Administration, or its predecessor, the Coast and Geodetic Survey.

Dishonorable and bad conduct discharges issued by general courts-martial may bar VA benefits. Veterans in prison must contact the VA to determine eligibility. VA benefits will not be provided to any Veteran or dependent wanted for an outstanding felony warrant.

Discharge Requirements for Compensation Benefits
To receive VA compensation benefits and services, the Veteran's character of discharge or service must be under other than dishonorable conditions (e.g., honorable, under honorable conditions, general).

Discharge Requirements for Pension Benefits
To receive VA pension benefits and services, the Veteran's character of discharge or service must be under other than dishonorable conditions (e.g., honorable, under honorable conditions, general).

Discharge Requirements for Education Benefits
To receive VA education benefits and services through the Montgomery GI Bill program or Post-9/11 GI Bill program, the Veteran's character of discharge or service must be honorable.

To receive VA education benefits and services through any other VA educational benefits program, including the Survivors' and Dependents' Educational Assistance (DEA) program, the Veteran's character of discharge or service must be under other than dishonorable conditions (e.g., honorable, under honorable conditions, general).

Discharge Requirements for Home Loan Benefits
To receive VA home loan benefits and services, the Veteran's character of discharge

or service must be under other than dishonorable conditions (e.g., honorable, under honorable conditions, general).

Discharge Requirements for Insurance Benefits
Generally, there is no character of discharge bar to benefits to Veterans' Group Life Insurance. However, for Service Disabled Veterans Insurance and Veterans' Mortgage Life Insurance benefits, the Veteran's character of discharge must be other than dishonorable.

Certain VA Benefits Require Wartime Service: under the law, VA recognizes these periods of war:

Mexican Border Period: May 9, 1916 through April 5, 1917, for Veterans who served in Mexico, on its borders or in adjacent waters.

World War I: April 6, 1917 through Nov. 11, 1918; for Veterans who served in Russia, April 6, 1917 through April 1, 1920; extended through July 1, 1921, for Veterans who had at least one day of service between April 6, 1917 and Nov. 11, 1918.

World War II: Dec. 7, 1941 through Dec. 31, 1946.

Korean War: June 27, 1950 through Jan. 31, 1955.

Vietnam War: Aug. 5, 1964 (Feb. 28, 1961, for Veterans who served "in country" before Aug. 5, 1964) through May 7, 1975.

Gulf War: Aug. 2, 1990, - (through a future date to be set by law or Presidential Proclamation)

Important Documents

To expedite benefits delivery, Veterans seeking a VA benefit for the first time must submit a copy of their service discharge form (DD-214, DD-215, or for World War II Veterans, a WD form), which documents service dates and type of discharge, or provides full name, military service number, and branch and dates of service. The Veteran's service discharge form should be kept in a safe location accessible to the Veteran and next of kin or designated representative.

The following documents will be needed for claims processing related to a Veteran's death:

1. Veteran's marriage certificate for claims of a surviving spouse or children.

2. Veteran's death certificate if the Veteran did not die in a VA health care facility.

3. Children's birth certificates or adoption papers to determine children's benefits.

4. Veteran's birth certificate to determine parents' benefits.

eBenefits

eBenefits is a joint VA/Department of Defense (DoD) Web portal that provides resources and self-service capabilities to Servicemembers, Veterans, and their families to apply, research, access, and manage their VA and military benefits and personal information through a secure Internet connection.

Through eBenefits Veterans can: apply for benefits, view their disability compensation claim status, access official military personnel documents (e.g., DD Form 214, Certificate of Release or Discharge from Active Duty), transfer entitlement of Post-9/11 GI Bill to eligible dependents (Servicemembers only), obtain a VA-guaranteed home loan Certificate of Eligibility, and register for and update direct deposit information for certain benefits. New features are added regularly.

Accessing eBenefits:

The portal is located at www.ebenefitsva.gov

Servicemembers or Veterans must register for an eBenefits account at one of two levels: Basic or Premium. A Premium account allows the user to access personal data in VA and DoD systems, as well as apply for benefits online, check the status of claims, update address records, and more.

The Basic account allows access to information entered into eBenefits by the Servicemember or Veteran only. Basic accounts limit the self-service features that can be accessed in eBenefits.

To register for an eBenefits account, Veterans must be listed in the Defense Enrollment Eligibility Reporting System (DEERS) and first obtain a DoD Self Service (DS) Logon.

Servicemembers can access eBenefits with a DS Logon or Common Access Card (CAC).

They can choose from two levels of registration: DS Logon Level 1 (Basic) and DS Logon Level 2 (Premium).

If Veterans attempt to register and are informed they have no DEERS record, VA will first need to verify their military service and add them to DEERS. All VA regional offices have staff familiar with the procedures for adding a Veteran to DEERS.

A DS Logon is an identity (user name and password) that is used by various DoD and VA Websites, including eBenefits. Those registered in DEERS are eligible for a DS Logon. A DS Logon is valid for the rest of your life.

Many people will be able to verify their identity online by answering a few security questions. A few may need to visit a VA regional office or TRICARE Service Center to have their identities verified. Servicemembers may verify their identity online by using their CAC.

Military retirees may verify their identity online using their Defense Finance and Accounting Service (DFAS) Logon.

Veterans in receipt of VA benefits via direct deposit may have their identity verified by calling 1-800-827-1000 and selecting option 7.

Others may need to visit a VA regional office or TRICARE Service Center to have their identities verified in person.

Let's be honest, you likely won't read *"Federal Benefits for Veterans, Dependents and Survivors"* from cover to cover. Even if you do, it probably won't stick with you. In our information overloaded and attention-deficit world, you need a way to quickly find the information you need. The best way to do this is to read that publication, but if you choose not to or just don't have the time, here's a cheat sheet of top level programs which may offer several sub-programs that would benefit you, that can be found on the VA website:

> **Pre-Discharge:** It is to your advantage to submit your disability compensation claim prior to separation, retirement or release from active duty or demobilization. Processing times tend to be much shorter for claims submitted pre-discharge than after discharge. Pre-discharge programs provide Servicemembers with the opportunity to file claims for disability compensation up to 180 days prior to separation or retirement from active duty or full-time National Guard or Reserve duty (Titles 10 and 32).

Compensation: Disability Compensation is a tax-free monetary benefit paid to Veterans with disabilities that are the result of a disease or injury incurred or aggravated during active military service. Compensation may also be paid for post-service disabilities that are considered related or secondary to disabilities occurring in service and for disabilities presumed to be related to circumstances of military service, even though they may arise after service. Generally, the degrees of disability specified are also designed to compensate for considerable loss of working time from exacerbations or illnesses

Education: This is an excellent resource for all types of training and programs. Topics include Post-9/11 GI Bill, Montgomery GI Bill, REAP, VEAP, Survivors and Dependent Assistance, Accelerated Payments, Co-Op training, Correspondence Training, Entrepreneurship Training, Flight Training, Institutions of Higher Learning, National Call to Service Program, Licensing and Certification, National Testing Program, Non-College Degree Programs, On-The-Job and Apprenticeship, Tuition Assistance, Tutorial Assistance and Work study.

Vocational Rehabilitation & Employment: You may receive Vocational Rehabilitation and Employment (VR&E) services to help with job training, employment accommodations, resume development and job seeking skills coaching. Other services may be provided to assist Veterans in starting their own businesses or independent living services for those who are severely disabled and unable to work in traditional employment.

Home Loans: VA helps Servicemembers, Veterans, and eligible surviving spouses become homeowners. As part of our mission to serve you, we provide a home loan guaranty benefits and other housing-related programs to help you buy, build, repair, retain or adapt a home for your own personal occupancy. VA Home Loans are provided by private lenders such as banks and mortgage companies. VA guarantees a portion of the loan, enabling the lender to provide you with more favorable terms.

Life Insurance: VA provides valuable life insurance benefits to give you the peace of mind that comes with knowing your family is protected. VA's life insurance programs were developed to provide financial security for your family given the extraordinary risks involved in military service.

Pension: VA helps Veterans and their families cope with financial challenges by providing supplemental income through the Veterans Pension and Survivors Pension benefit programs.

Transition, Employment and Economic Impact: The VA's Office of Transition, Employment and Economic Impact (TEEI) is dedicated to helping our transitioning service members, Veterans and their families use the benefits they've earned to achieve long-term economic success.

Special Groups: The VA has developed programs that are designed to help target Veteran demographics. These include Elderly Veterans, Gulf War Veterans, Homeless Veterans, Incarcerated Veterans, Korean War Veterans, Lesbian, Gay & Bisexual Veterans, Minority Veterans, Native American Veterans, Former Prisoners of War, Veterans Living Abroad, Women Veterans and World War II Veterans.

Services: Services offered include Beneficiary Financial Counseling, Career Center, Educational and Vocational Counseling, Fiduciary Program, Independent Living, Mortgage Delinquency Assistance and VetSuccess on Campus

Applying for Benefits: This is a well-designed section of the VA web site that includes a list of benefit types and the method and specific form required to apply for the same.

Locations: Includes a comprehensive list of Regional Benefits Offices for the North Atlantic District, Southeast District, Midwest District, Continental District, Pacific District, and an interactive map to help you find the closest Benefit Office. It also includes a list of Regional Loan Centers located in Atlanta GA, Cleveland OH, Denver CO, Houston TX, Phoenix AZ, Roanoke VA, St. Paul MN, and St. Petersburg FL.

VBA Claims Transformation: In the face of dramatically increasing workloads, a growing inventory and a backlog that affects Veterans of all eras – and both first-time filers and Veterans coming back to the VA for a supplementary claim – the Veterans Benefits Administration must deliver first-rate, timely benefits and services, faster and more effectively than ever before.

From the VBA website: To achieve our goals for improving the delivery of benefits to Veterans, we have built an aggressive Transformation Plan that includes initiatives to re-train and reorganize our people, streamline our business processes, and build and implement new technology solutions to eliminate the claims backlog and process all claims faster and at a higher quality.

Customer Service Standards: In an effort to measure, track and improve the Veteran experience as a customer, the VA has implemented a comprehensive set of standards.

VBA Performance: The Veterans Benefits Administration (VBA) Office of Performance Analysis and Integrity provides real-time status updates and other information on the claims and backlog inventory so you can track our performance in serving those who've served our nation.

Media and Publications: Provides quick links to publications, videos, and fact sheets for VA programs.

Summary

When dealing with the VA you need to embrace the idea that mediocrity is the norm, not the edge case. Be prepared to settle for average to poor service and be delighted by anything better than that. The folks who work at the VA aren't getting rich and they are understaffed and over-tasked.

Remember that "people do things for people" and if you are a demanding PITA (which stands for Pain-In-The-Ass as I was informed by a teenager) you will likely see the response time and level of service you receive as a reflection of how you treat the VA employees.

Learn about and take full advantage of all your VA benefits. If you do nothing else, learn about the VA Home Loan program which is not an actual loan, but a guarantee of repayment. It will help you avoid paying Private Mortgage Insurance, (PMI), which is an insurance premium you have to pay in a traditional mortgage if you don't have a minimum of 20% for a down payment. The PMI payment stays in place until you have paid down the loan to 80% of the original appraised value. There's a little ambiguity on this, because regulations say that the mortgage servicer must remove the PMI when the balance drops to 78%. Best to avoid this altogether. Your VA mortgage isn't completely free as it requires a "funding fee" up front when you acquire your mortgage. The fee does vary based on the amount of down payment you provide. For a zero-down payment loan you will pay a 2.15% non-refundable fee. If you provide a 5-10% down payment, you pay 1.5% and any down payment over 10% will reduce the fee to 1.25%. Even with the funding fee, this is a huge win for you.

These benefits level the field for you to some degree, but they don't necessarily provide a competitive advantage if you are seeking civilian employment. These programs can help you transition to civilian life and assist you in applying your training, education, and work experience in securing the best job and quality of life possible.

The key word is "assist" which means you still have a lot of heavy lifting to do, so get to it.

Core Concepts mapping

Core One – You are NOT like the others. Exploit your differences as advantages. Many employers want to hire former military of varying ranks and skill levels. But they want to hire professionals who can integrate into their culture and leadership styles, so if you don't fit into the culture, move on.

Core Five – You have skills and capabilities that are marketable. With the help of the VA you may find placement or bridge training programs to transform your military skill set into a more widely marketable set of skills. Your military service will also directly translate into credits at vocational and accredited Colleges. Taking advantage of this education credit conversion will help you save money and reduce the overall time required and cost of most programs. The VA can help guide you through this process.

Core Seven– You now have more responsibility for your life and much more opportunity to screw it up. Learning about your benefits and entitlements AFTER you leave this service is sub-optimal. There are some timeframes and deadlines you need to be aware of, so start learning your earned VA benefits as early as you can. The clock may not start until you are out, but you can directly impact your options and goals by preparing beforehand and being an expert on VA programs that will help you.

Core Eight – Life is still hard. The VA does not offer a guaranteed path to success, but it is designed to help and assist. Transitioning from military to civilian life can be complicated and confusing. It is up to you to apply yourself, learn the various systems and options and make things happen. Your life is your responsibility, take it seriously and leverage all the advantages that you've earned.

Personal perspective:

The VA can be hit and miss. You should never settle for less than excellent support. You may receive mediocre support, but always push back and request to be treated as you deserve. While things are changing under the Trump administration, there are still more than a few individuals working in the VA who should have been fired or retired long ago. When you encounter one of those persons, escalate. I needed a referral to a specialist for a serious condition which I was told would be reviewed and I would have a response within thirty days. Thirty days was just not acceptable as I needed to see a physician immediately! I tried to walk the request through, a process with which I believe all Vets are probably familiar. That effort didn't work, 30 days passed and still I got no response. I went back and found out the supervisor who was reviewing my request had left the VA, and worse yet I was told I had to start all over and wait another 30 days before I got a response. I have no idea if this was a real guideline or something made up, but I realized I wasn't going to get this resolved in a timely manner. So, I took a chance and decided to fight city hall. I escalated all the way to my state Senator to resolve the issue. Of course, this didn't happen overnight, but it was worth it. I don't believe this red tape horror story is consistent with the goals of the VA, and I'm glad I didn't just sit back and hope my request would eventually be processed. Stay the course and expect that same experience that you would get from an equivalent civilian service. Remember, the VA is supposed to be your advocate, but you need to participate, provide feedback, and have a voice.

Chapter 20 – Aging and staying healthy

One day you will look in the mirror and think we were all so young, healthy, and fit, what happened?

You are getting older, and if you could test yourself against your 18-year-old body, you would find every year has taken a toll. While your 25-year-old self may only lose a half a step, your thirty-year-old self will have lost more. As we age we take hits on our mental abilities, our endurance, our strength, our flexibility, and our mobility. Ultimately, we fall into physical and possibly mental decline and then we're gone.

Of course, we all understand these ultimate truths. We may not like knowing about them, but we understand and yet often, we ignore them. Remember it's not just you that is aging and dealing with these issues, but your spouse, parents, grandparents, friends, and others. Some of the people in your life will live their lives to the fullest, right up to the last minute maintaining their mental acuity and physical capabilities, but some will not. We will all see loved ones impacted by disease, accidents and other issues that will impact their capabilities and quality of life. It is imperative you face these challenges with patience, fortitude and understanding.

We are certainly living longer, in fact the average life expectancy for a male (this number is hard to pin down, by the way) is about 76, and the average life expectancy for a female is 81. If nothing else, you should be taking steps to ensure you live at least this long.

If you are curious about how long you might live (on average), you should check out the "Retirement & Survivors Benefits: Life Expectancy Calculator" provided on the Social Security website. You can get a rough idea how long you should plan for based on your current age, and provides interesting data:

https://www.ssa.gov/OACT/population/longevity.html

You've heard an older friend or relative say that "getting old isn't for the weak" and unfortunately, there isn't a truer bit of wisdom. Knowledge is power, so prepare yourself for what is going to happen. Understand the challenges facing most seniors and plan to live the best life you can.

What challenges do seniors commonly face? Of course, it is impossible to list them all, but consider these as a start:

1. **Weight Gain:** Avoid packing on those pounds, because as you age, your body's ability to maintain a healthy weight decreases. You need to adjust your food intake and exercise properly. Lean about the body mass index (BMI) and make it a goal to stay in the normal weight bracket. Doing this will help you avoid or reduce the impact of so many weight-related problems that it is probably the single biggest factor you can control about your health.

2. **Failure to Exercise:** If you leave the service and take a civilian job, the frequency and level of your exercise will likely take a nose-dive if you don't build it into your schedule. As you get older, exercising will take significantly more effort and your recovery period will be more painful and lengthy.

3. **Failure to Eat Properly:** Seniors often fall into a vicious cycle where they are constantly focused on their next meal. There are many reasons for this including loneliness and boredom, and falling into the practice of eating out constantly results in over-eating which is devastating to maintaining their health and target weight. To avoid this, you need to start building and reinforcing good eating habits right now. Learn how to eat healthy, eat the best fresh, low fat, low sugar foods you can afford. Occasionally you might try to follow a vegetarian diet, particularly if you are overweight.

4. **Money**: You need enough money to live comfortably, which means having the funds to cover base expenses with enough money left over for discretionary spending and unexpected expenses. You should plan for significant increases in the cost of drug prescriptions and healthcare, even with various healthcare insurance programs. Your 70-year-old self needs more maintenance and upkeep than your earlier versions. Many experts believe that seniors need at least $25K per year per person for normal living expenses.

5. **Depression**: Everyone gets discouraged at times, for any number of reasons. Depression is different, as it describes the prolonged, medically recognized condition that can seriously and detrimentally affect you and your quality of life. There are real health risks associated with depression. Learn to recognize the signs and talk to your doctor, because as a member

of the Armed Services, you are statistically more susceptible to this condition. For more detail, please read the chapter "The (potential) downside of your military service." To help you maintain balance in your life get out, be active and spend time with your family and friends.

6. **Falling:** As you get older, your risk of being seriously injured in a fall skyrockets. Statistically, this is especially true of women. Consider eliminating area rugs and mitigating slippery bathroom floors.

7. **Substance Abuse:** Approximately twenty percent (20%) of seniors have had an issue in their lives with substance abuse, increasing their vulnerability to further substance abuse later in life. Substances abused include alcohol and tobacco as well as illegal and prescribed drugs. You are a grown up, so make good decisions here. If you have an addiction, you can get help from many sources and the VA is a good place to start.

8. **Oral Health:** At the time of this writing it is estimated that a quarter of adults over the age of 65 have *no teeth*! Some of these numbers can be attributed to treatments that promoted full dentures, but not all. As you age, proper tooth and gum care becomes more problematic. Be proactive about your health and take care of your teeth and gums.

9. **The Flu:** As a younger person, you likely avoided getting a flu shot. Most of us have had the flu at one point or another and it was debilitating. As a senior, influenza and pneumonia can literally kill you. Get your flu shot every year, regardless of your current age. Visit your doctor immediately if you suspect you have either the flu or pneumonia.

10. **Common Medical Conditions:** Some of the more common conditions and detail on each is provided for you below. This list is not intended to provide medical advice nor should it be used as an absolute reference. As always, do your own homework:

    a. *Heart disease is the leading cause of death in the over-65 population.* Statistically speaking, if we don't die before our sixties, Cardiovascular Disease (CVD) is what will probably end us. This disease comes in many different forms, and regular checkups, proper treatment, diet, and exercise are your best defense.

    b. Cancer is the second leading cause of death in the over-65 population. Regular checkups and screenings will increase the odds of early detection and treatment. Take this very seriously and see your doctor regularly. If you are diagnosed with cancer, then do your research to find the doctor and treatment program you in which you have the most confidence.

c. *Respiratory diseases are the third most common cause of death in the* over-65 population. This category of diseases includes pneumonia, chronic bronchitis, COPD, asthma, and others. If you have a chronic condition, or even a temporary respiratory condition, seek expert medical advice and follow the treatment plan. Respiratory diseases can rapidly lead to complications in other areas of your health.

d. *Arthritis is the most common denominator for the older populations.* For those who suffer from the most severe manifestations, it will mean significant loss of mobility and constant, debilitating pain. In most cases, however it will simply mean reduced range of motion and some painful movement, but it is manageable.

e. *Dementia comes in many forms, all of which are devastating.* Some types of dementia are treatable, caused by medical conditions such as hormone imbalances, metabolic disorders, and infections. Unfortunately, the more common types, such as Alzheimer's and Vascular dementia have degenerative impact on the brain and are not reversible. The social (family) and financial impacts to a person suffering from this disease are significant

f. *Diabetes is another condition that impacts many people, later in life.* The good news is it is usually treatable, with treatment varying by type. Type II is treated with oral medication, Type I is treated with injections. Both types require close monitoring and management of food intake and blood sugar levels. Diabetes and extra weight often go hand in hand, so, manage your weight.

g. *High blood pressure is a real threat.*

h. *Tobacco use is something to avoid in all forms.* While smoking is absolutely the worst form of Tobacco consumption, all use in any form is hard on your body. If you smoke, you should spend an hour or so surfing the web looking for images for "smoker's lung." Smoking and other tobacco use have so many detrimental impacts that it would take over this book.

    i. *Avoid the triple threat of heart disease, high blood pressure and diabetes.* This combination will kill you. If you wait until you are fat, old, and out of shape, you may not be able to come back from this.

You need to get to your fit weight now, as you won't always have the capacity to do so.

Understand the science behind being fit and follow it. As you age, your capacity for doing work and your rate of healing will decline. Your capacity for doing work is a well-known and measurable concept called VO_2max, and the concept for this measurement of capability was developed in the early 1920s by Nobel Prize winner AV Hill. Simply put it is V (volume) X O_2 (oxygen) and max (the maximum measured use), so your ability to generate force and your endurance is governed by your body's ability to move air and use the oxygen provided. There are multiple methods and formulas designed to measure an individual's capability for VO_2max.

While there are other methods and derivatives of getting to this data, unless you are a professional athlete or training for very high-level competition you don't need to understand or be tested for it. What you should understand is the study of the body's capability to do work as represented in the VO_2max measurement has led us to a deeper understanding of what happens to our aerobic capability as we age.

For many years it was accepted that the body' aerobic capacity declined in a straight line at 10% per decade, becoming most noticeable around age 50. Today, it is more widely accepted that beginning in our 30s and 40s we see between 5-10% decline in aerobic capacity every 10 years and around 20% decline per decade after age 60. Some studies show that the "per decade" decline goes vertical in our mid to late 60s.

So, we're all going to get older and have less capacity to do work. Some long-term studies have shown you can reduce the rate of decline if you maintain the intensity of your physical training. Translated, while you may enjoy and benefit from doing Tai Chi in the park, you really need to pump up the volume and intensity of your exercise to stay fit and healthy as long as you can. Medical studies, and other serious fitness experts use a concept called Metabolic Equivalent of Task (MET), sometimes shortened to just metabolic equivalent, to measure the amount of exercise for a given task. The baseline is 1 MET, or how much energy you burn sitting at a desk or on a couch. Everything is compared to that. For example:

Task – moderate pace walking = 6 METs

Duration – 30 minutes

6 METs X 30 minutes = 180 MET minutes

You would then go on to calculate your total MET minutes for a week. Moderate exercise levels require a *minimum* of 3,000 MET minutes per week. How well do you stack up? See the table below for some sample activities and MET ratings.

Activity	METs per Minute
Walking at 2 mph	2.5
Household chores	2.8
Tai Chi	3.0
Walking at 3 mph	3.5
Calisthenics (moderate effort)	4.5
Weight Training (muscle building)	5.0
Elliptical trainer	5.0
Calisthenics (vigorous effort)	8.0
Mountain biking (uphill)	14.0

A simple search on the internet for "MET table" will give you a comprehensive list (pages and pages) for MET values for all sorts of chores, tasks, and exercises. This will give you a valuable tool set to track your activity levels and compare to your goals. You could also buy a "Fitbit" or other type of wearable device and let it track your actual movement and heart rate. There is a tremendous amount of hype around these devices including class-action lawsuits about their accuracy. In other cases, these devices, and the records they produce are being used for and against users in legal cases. There's a bottom line to this topic. You need to track your activity levels with what works best for you, but you need to track, evaluate, and adjust to ensure you meet your goals.

Please note that as you age, you should understand your health and your true capabilities for strenuous physical exercise. Male readers who are already resistant to doctor visits, pay attention here. You need to exercise, but you need to get a comprehensive physical first. Your separation physical (required by the military) will do just fine. If you haven't had a physical in a while, go get one before you start on any serious exercise regime. As you age, do not skip your checkups! Talk to your doctor, tell him or her what your exercise and/or recreational plans are and LISTEN to the feedback, advice, or instructions they provide.

Get your sleep. Even though you've proven repeatedly you can function for extended periods with little or no sleep, your aging body needs regular, restful sleep. Medical knowledge about sleep requirements and sleep deprivation has advanced tremendously in the last twenty years. Sleep deprivation studies have definitively proven that your physical and mental performance is significantly degraded when you don't get enough rest. How much is enough? Adults should get a minimum of seven hours of sleep each night. Teens and children should get a minimum of nine hours. Accumulating a debt of sleep deprivation during the week can leave you functioning at the level equivalent to someone who is mildly intoxicated. More severe sleep deprivation can affect you emotionally, increase blood pressure and even cause hallucinations in extreme conditions.

Your time in service has taken its toll on your body and your health. It doesn't really matter how long you served; you were impacted. Some issues won't show up until later in age, some may be plaguing you now. I once met a Colonel of Infantry in his 50s who had to sell his house because his knees were just not able to handle the stairs. Your vision may not have been impacted, but almost every job in the service will have left you with some type of hearing damage. If you are still in, wear that eye and ear protection folks, and double up if you can!

You'll need to pay attention to your health and get screened for a plethora of issues throughout your life. Don't turn your back on medicine, it is a wonderful by-product of our technology, science, and very bright minds.

One of the best screening checklists available is maintained by the U.S. Preventive Services Task Force. This group of volunteers has been working diligently since its formation in 1984 to help bring "evidence-based" recommendations to the medical practice.

You can find their website at: http://www.uspreventiveservicestaskforce.org/

Their screening list can be found here:
http://www.uspreventiveservicestaskforce.org/BrowseRec/Index

They list 95 types of health screenings you should be offered by your medical provider in general, as well as by age, gender, and specific health risk factors.

Of course, this isn't going to be a definitive list of screenings simply because medical science continues to progress. As stated multiple times before, the Internet is a great resource, use it to search for variations on these phrases and learn more:

- Preventative health screening
- Health screening
- Age specific health screening
- Health screening for men
- Health screening for women

As we age, the world becomes more dangerous to us. Our bodies are more susceptible to certain age-related conditions. We begin to pay the full price of our younger self's habits and decisions.

Staying fit and active is easier to say than do, but is critical to longevity and good health. You need to eat well, exercise, maintain your optimal body weight and use your brain. Failure to focus on any of these will shorten your life and will negatively impact on the quality of life you have left.

Core Concepts mapping

Core One – You are NOT like the others. Your body has been affected by your service, and the wear and tear can be tremendous. Be aware, and be prepared.

Core Seven– You now have more responsibility for your life and much more opportunity to screw it up. Maintaining your health is your responsibility. If you have a service-related injury, make sure you get it documented so you can get the necessary long-term treatment and benefits after you leave. Don't skimp on medical insurance embrace it as part of your new life. Stay fit, keep active and manage all the factors of your life you can.

Core Eight – Life is still hard. Getting old(er) isn't for the weak. Exercise, eat properly and manage your health. Recognize that your mental and physical capacities will diminish with time. Recognize that everything will hurt more and healing will take longer. Make the most of every minute of your life.

Personal perspective:

I separated from the Service and started working overseas with various military contractors. I'll spare you the reasons that I let myself go, gaining over forty pounds. I wasn't exercising, didn't eat right and skipped medical checkups. Then, in my forties, I tripped and fell off the ramp of an MRAP vehicle and damaged my hip. Because I didn't get it treated properly, and was unable to do sustained, calorie-burning physical activities my weight gain increased, leading to other complications including surgery to fix my hip. It took over five years to get myself back to some semblance of health. The moral of the story here is you will likely leave the service in good physical shape for your age, keep it up because your older self will thank you for it.

Chapter 21 – The potential downside of your military service

You need to read this. Even if you are fine today, you may have challenges later in life. Statistically speaking, you probably joined the military right out of high school or college. In either case, you were dropped into the most stressful job in the world at a relatively youthful age. You have been repeatedly (ad nauseum) counseled and educated on the dangers of addiction as part of your mandatory service training.

What you haven't been educated or trained on is the true impact of your time in the service, so let's get very real for a bit. You have been stressed beyond belief, and you shouldn't downplay this or shrug it off. While others were living in a stable family environment, and flirting with the idea of going to college or learning the bottom rungs of the corporate ladder, you were living in a pressure cooker where there were no do overs. If you screwed up, people got hurt or worse yet killed. Regardless of whether you were in a support role, fighting a war on the front-line or doing something in between, you worked without proper kit, with people who didn't get it and under ridiculous timelines. And in all situations, it had to be done right, everyone had to do their job or people got hurt.

Add to the fact that likely saw someone in your extended military family get hurt. It could have happened to you personally, and it could have been a training accident, vehicle crash, allergic reaction, actual battle, or some stupid mistake, but the odds are you lived through one or more life-changing events.

You've likely seen things your family and friends' simple can't comprehend.

The stress of military life, plus the risk of life and limb are compounded by another factor; you were likely isolated and distant from your normal support system of friends and family. Those to whom you would normally turn were located thousands of miles away, and far too distant to make a meaningful connection and get the support you needed.

What does this mean to you? Are we saying that you are a ticking time bomb? The answer is no because most of us are all right. But in addition to the physical impact to your body, you have accumulated what we call "mental scar tissue." Just like a physical scar, it may never impede your movement through life, however, some of us need and deserve some extra support. Adding to this combustive mixture is the fact you are planning for or embarking on another huge, stressful change as you move back to civilian life.

Anger can be a good thing when it motivates you to achieve your goals and overcome obstacles. However, many Veterans allow themselves to maintain a slow, simmering anger at that world when things don't go their way. This can be toxic to every aspect of your life, don't let yourself fall into this situation. Don't give in to the path of flashpoint anger, be slow to anger and quick to forgive.

People make better decisions when they are informed and have a working knowledge of what they are getting into. You are statistically at risk for several things including higher incidence of problem drinking, prescription drug abuse, depression, and PTSD. Learn to recognize the symptoms and stay in control of your life if you are affected.

Here are a few general statistics put together by the National Institute on Drug Abuse:

- Less than 3 percent of active military use illegal drugs vs. 12 percent of civilians
- More than 11 percent of active military misuse legal drugs
- There is lots of binge drinking going on, almost half of the military says they've done this at one time or another
- About 20 percent of the military report that they binge drink every week and 27 percent of Combat Veterans binge drink weekly
- Tobacco use, primarily smoking is about equal to civilian use, reported at about 30 percent, but for combat Veterans the number is much higher

You are less likely to use illegal drugs thanks to the zero-tolerance drug policy put into place in 1982. Some of you likely drink too much, and any binge drinking is too much. Any illegal drug use or prescription drug abuse is too much, and if you are a smoker you just need to stop.

You may find the transition out of the military extremely stressful, and you may be tempted to turn to your favorite substance to help smooth things over. Don't do it.

All things should be taken in moderation except for drugs and tobacco. Just don't do it.

If you can manage a moderate intake of alcohol and avoid being an ass by putting yourself and others at risk, then society will tolerate your drinking. Get a DUI and everything changes, even with the first conviction. You lose your driving privileges, may see mandatory jail time, and will certainly pay thousands of dollars in legal fees, penalties, and other expenses. If you are reckless and stupid enough to be charged with a DUI, hire a lawyer.

What about depression? Everyone gets discouraged from time to time, but what you need to be concerned about is an extended period of depression. This is not a medical reference text not meant to replace the advice and diagnosis from a doctor or therapist. If you start to have difficulties, see a professional!! Some behaviors which may indicate you are depressed are (this should not be considered a comprehensive list):

- Unexplained mood swings
- Constantly irritable
- Changes in energy level and appetite
- Having a tough time focusing your thoughts, experiencing memory issues, or having difficulty concentrating
- Loss of interest in things that previously were enjoyable to you
- Feeling empty, hopeless, or guilty
- Physical manifestations such as constant pain, headaches and digestive issues that don't respond to common treatment

Resource: http://www.mentalhealth.va.gov/depression.asp

If you know or suspect you have a problem, talk to your doctor immediately. He or she will be able to point you to the correct care provider. Additionally, there are many resources that will help. We've provided a few here, and keep in mind most employers provide access to counseling and treatment via their health care plans.

There are some very wild and inaccurate suicide "facts" being touted across the internet. One study most often cited was conducted by the VA. In that study is stated that there are a ludicrously high number Veteran suicides per day. This is NOT factual. The study was deeply flawed and based on statistical sampling. I make this point because you need to know that your brothers and sisters in arms are not killing themselves at this ridiculous rate. The real number is still too high with the most reliable statistics placing the total number of suicides at 265 for 2015. Despite multiple attempts to link the recent conflicts in Afghanistan and Iraq to higher suicide rates among those Veterans, the actual data does not support that claim. What does all this mean to you? It means that you are at a higher risk of suicide than your civilian counterparts, regardless of what, where, when or how you served. Take this very seriously, as Service members are at double the risk of suicide compared to civilians. The comparative numbers are hard to pin down, but as of 2016 the number of military suicides were plotted at about 30 per 100,000 individuals compared to the civilian statistic of about 12.5 per 100,000. There are so many contributing factors to any suicide that a single root cause is rarely identified.

Fill your life with family, friends, adventure, and laughter. Create a bucket list and start checking items off as you fulfill your dreams. Even though the years of military service have taken both a physical and mental toll, be optimistic and joyful, it really is the best preventative medicine.

Core Concepts mapping

Core One – You are NOT like the others. You can be both mission and goal oriented. If you lose your way with the small bits of life that don't always go as planned, adjust your focus. You have skills that will help you stay on track, so use them.

Core Two – You have been forged in fires your peers can't understand. The world is a dangerous, confusing place that most Americans can't comprehend. You once had a place in the world that made a difference; you were part of the (forgive the dramatic language) team that brought the light that holds back the darkness. Always remember that as your experiences will define you forever.

Core Four – You are uniquely prepared to manage your own future. Be responsible and every day take those actions that move you toward your goals. Be disciplined and be honest with yourself. Get help if you need it by finding a confidante with whom you can talk and who can understand your experience.

Core Eight – Life is still hard. Life is waiting just around the next corner to try to kick your ass over and over. Come up swinging when you get knocked down, and keep getting up as many times as it takes.

Personal perspective:

Without getting into the stories about what happened during times of conflict, I've seen a guy's hand blown apart by a faulty air tool, a shipmate drown when he slipped between the pier and the ship, and a good friend so severely injured when he was hit by a drunk driver that he lost his military eligibility due to the number of bones that were shattered. I've seen drug addiction and alcoholism destroy careers and ruin families. I've lost friends both in service and out to suicides. I don't think I'm special or alone in these experiences. Some of these people were in the wrong place at the wrong time while some made a single bad decision. Others saw a series of sub-optimal choices lead them to the path of self-destruction. Regardless, I believe there is always hope, and there is always help for those who are brave enough to ask for it. It is my closely held belief that if some of these people had asked for help, they would still be with us.

Chapter 22 – Simple timelines and Checklists

Separation comes with various timelines and perspectives. You have a lot to do and not enough time to get it all done. The first thing we need to do is sensitize you to the time you don't have. If you have decided to separate/retire then you have a formal time horizon you can see from the exact point in time your decision was made. In this chapter, we're going to do our best to help you think and structure a checklist for your separation/retirement.

The clock is ticking, and you should feel the pressure to prepare properly as immediate and urgent. Even the DoD thinks you should start planning 12 months prior to separation and at least 24 months before you retire. More realistically, you should start planning for retirement five years in advance, giving you the ability to influence your last tour of duty so you end up near or at the location you've chosen to retire. Yes, at the same time you still have a life and duty to deal with, and you should expect life will throw up obstacles and impediments at the absolute worst time. The core message here is get started right now. The more time you have, the more things you can get done, resulting in a better outcome. Don't procrastinate, you don't have enough time to start with so don't waste any of it.

When the author left the service, there was no such program as the DoD's Transition Assistance Program (TAP or sometimes known as DoDTAP) to help make the switch. In fact, there was a huge negative stigma associated with any decision to anything other than committing to a full career with the military. That pressure is "officially" gone now, but be aware it continues to lurk in the shadows. All who served should be proud of their service, but those who stay for the full ride are a different breed and sometimes have a tough time watching top talent walk out the door. Expect that you'll be heavily pressured to stay, depending on your capabilities, reputation, and expertise. Take full advantage of the TAP program with the realization you may have to drive the process if you have a lackluster TAP representative. If you are fortunate to have a strong coordinator, then count your blessings and ask that person if, based on their experience, there are any additional actions, steps, processes that could help you.

TAP isn't perfect and your mileage will vary. The data available at the time of this writing indicates only about 50% of those who utilized TAP were satisfied with the program. Remember you and you alone are responsible for your future. Do more than just work the TAP program, build your own checklists (see more below), be a voracious learner and drive towards your goal. You will only get out of this process what you put into it. Garbage in...well, you get it.

Think of it this way, you should be well prepared with many of the checklist items completed and important decisions made by the time you reach the twelve-month mark prior to separation. For retirees, five years of preparation is highly recommended but, once you've made the decision to stay in the service for the full ride, you should start planning for your endgame. So, shoot for having your plan ready for flawless execution at separation +24 months. This means learning about your options, making decisions, and following up on dozens of issues that will take you to that point in your future when your last day, hour, minute and second of service is behind you.

When you leave the service, you become somewhat of a non-entity to those you leave behind. Squad mates, friends, casual and close acquaintances will be 100% more focused on their service life and duty than on you. In a relatively short period of time, they will disperse from the last place you saw them; they will move on to new duty stations and their associated adventures or they may separate just like you and drop out of sight.

There will come a point where you will no longer have access people, places, tools, and processes that have always been there for you. You used to know who to call on, and what that you might have to negotiate to solve problems and get things done. But this is no longer your world, now you've walked away from that social and professional network of support. No matter how well you prepare for that point, it will be a shock to your system when you leave your duty station for the last time.

If you are a pilot, then you know the value of working a checklist. Wash, rinse, repeat; a checklist takes out almost all the human error of omission (did I check that) of the process. Unfortunately, nothing can eliminate the human error of commission (I did it wrong) out of the equation. To help mitigate errors of commission, check your list multiple times, and ask for help from a second set of Mark I, Mod 0 eyeballs when possible.

Now that you understand how important it is to use checklists, let's get started. Keep in mind these are examples, so modify these templates to meet your goals. If you come up with a better mousetrap here, please let me know as I would love to see your checklist. Check our website "GetOutandThrive.com" for other checklists from our community.

Let's start with a period beginning two years before your last day in the service. If you plan to take terminal leave, then make sure you move the timelines back to the point where your last day on the checklist coincides with your last day on base.

TWO Years in Advance

Like compound interest, taking action at this point in time can make an enormous difference in the quality of your separation from the service. There will be a mind-numbing amount of paperwork, separation briefings, document signing and tedious details you must work through. The more you research and make progress on the must-do and nice-to-have items, the better your options and outcomes will be, so get started now. One of the first decisions you must make is to decide whether you will telegraph to your command your intent to separate. Be forewarned, if you decide to do so, you may experience significant negative bias from the command. On the other hand, you may also get tremendous support, coaching and have additional opportunities open up for you within the service. Make sure you know what you are getting into with this particular leadership culture, observe the reaction and support, or lack thereof, of those who have gone before you. You can't access the Transition Assistance Program (TAP) without communicating and engaging the command, so typically two years in advance is the right time to start. However, if you need to hold off for any reason, don't wait any longer than 12 months before separation to start TAP. At a minimum, get your hands on the Pre-separation Counseling Checklist (DD Form 2648 or its current equivalent) for an item by item review and explanation of the benefits, services, programs, and resources available to you.

You should also be aware that most military bases will have a resident office for Transition Assistance Program.

Whether or not you start your engagement with the Transition Assistance Program at the 24-month mark, you should still get started on your own at that point on the timeline.

START HERE: (no later than 24 months in advance)

1. Read this book (plus others from the suggested reading list as well as any you have on your own personal list) from cover to cover and take notes.

2. Get Transition Assistance Program (TAP) checklist (DD Form 2648)

3. Are your financial affairs in order?

    a. Are you contributing to the military Thrift Savings Plan? If not, start now! This is free money, so take advantage of it because you get a 100% pre-tax match for the first 3% of your pay and a 50%

match for the next 2% of your pay. If you maximize your contribution at 5%, then the government will match 90% of that amount (3% contribution match + 1% if you max out at 5% = 4% overall match or 90%). There are two types:

   i. Basic TSP is pre-tax deduction, which means you will pay taxes on withdrawal of any contributions and gains

   ii. TSP Roth is after tax, but all withdrawals are tax free after you meet the Roth requirements for age and account maturity.

b. Are you actively managing your investments?

   i. Diversify your financial investments, don't put all your money in a single financial instrument or other investments.

   ii. Track the performance of your investments in TSP or other accounts on a monthly basis, and make changes when required.

c. Get your savings in order!

   i. Can you live for 6 months with no income without tapping your retirement funds?

   ii. Are you saving 30% of your paycheck each month (your 5% TSP contribution counts towards this)?

d. If retiring, have you determined how much retirement pay you will be receiving? You may not be able to get down to the last penny of accuracy, but you should be able to get close.

e. Keep enough ready cash in your checking account. You should have at least 1-3 months cash supply readily accessible.

f. Clean up your debt profile and structure.

   i. Do you have any type of loan that will expire or see an interest rate increase upon separation?

ii. Consolidate your finances and take any steps available to reduce your total interest rate burden.

   iii. Shed those credit cards, you should keep one (1) card that has the most advantageous features and interest rate. Plan to pay it off, and going forward use it only as a personal emergency fund.

   iv. Eliminate any debt that you can.

   g. Start tracking your net worth.

   i. Be very real, don't fool yourself.

   ii. Create a baseline and evaluate your progress every month.

   iii. Make adjustments as required.

   h. Verify your annual Social Security contributions and wage detail to ensure you have received full credit for both.

4. Have you planned for the worst?

   a. Create a last will for yourself and (if married) your spouse, name an executor and make sure you give notarized copies to all persons impacted.

   b. Make provisions for the long-term care of your children if both parents are lost.

   c. Create a living will if necessary.

   d. Create an "Advance Medical Directive" and make sure the right parties have notarized copies.

5. Life Insurance.

   a. Check your enrollment in Servicemans Group Life Insurance which is needed to convert to VGLI at separation

  b. Review your life insurance coverage. Get coverage if you don't have it. Make sure you have enough coverage to take care of your family after you are gone.

  c. Review your accidental death and dismemberment insurance policy. Get coverage if you don't have it, and if you do have coverage, buy more if you don't have enough to take care of your family after you are gone.

  d. Start learning about the coverage and cost of civilian life insurance options.

6. Networking is critical to your successful transition, so make friends and develop allies. Remember people do things for people, not demanding strangers, so move beyond casual contact. You need to work at this by keeping track of the people with whom you come into contact, and making the effort to stay in touch. This may be awkward at first, but is an essential life skill.

  a. Social Networking will help you succeed in your personal life, so if you don't have a group of extended friends, get to work creating one.

    i. Get involved in your local community.

    ii. Get involved in your local church.

    iii. Greet people and make an effort to remember something about each one.

    iv. If you know where you are going to land when you get out, start working that location to create social contacts.

  b. Professional Networking will help you succeed in your career.

    i. At a minimum, create a LinkedIn profile or use whatever professional network(s) with which you feel comfortable.

    ii. Work to build your contact list to over 500 people.

    iii. Seek out local professionals (in and out of your field) and find ways to interact with them.

- iv. Join local and online forums and groups of professionals, and get engaged.
- v. Find a way to get face time, in person or on a video chat with other professionals.

c. Build a contact list, but for future reference, do NOT expect to extract the information you need from social media or your smartphone. You don't need to open an inquisition, simply gather the data that comes up as a part of your interactions. If you think an individual is particularly interesting, cultivate that relationship.

- i. Gather basic data about name, rank, job specialty, age, contact Information
- ii. Gather extended data about spouse, children, hobbies, personal preferences, birthday, hometown.
- iii. Gather stable contact information. Younger contacts will move around a lot, so consider asking for their parents' contact information as a way to stay in touch.
- iv. Write down as much unique or memorable information as you can about each individual, something that will help bring this individual into clear focus years later.
- v. Take a picture with the individual.
- vi. Create a hardcopy of this information on a regular schedule (every 3 months)
- vii. Keep multiple copies.

7. Find a Mentor! Seek out one, possibly two individuals willing to invest in you on a weekly basis. This is explained in more detail in the chapter on Goal Setting.

   a. Meet weekly.
   b. Be open to feedback.
   c. Create goals specific to your mentor's experience.

      d.   Track your progress.

      e.   Join an online group like LinkedIn's *Veteran Mentor Network*.

8. Back up your data, remember 1 is NONE and 2 is ONE and that's not enough to protect your data!

      a.   Back up your contacts.

      b.   Back up your computer.

9. Military Records are your responsibility to maintain, and you should assume no one really has time to assist every service member who wants to review their records. Make friends in the personnel and medical departments on your base.

      a.   Personnel record.

            i.   Review at least once per year.

            ii.   Review every time you transfer duty stations.

            iii.   Is the record complete?

                  1.   Does it have all of your training documents?

                  2.   Does it have all of your awards and medals?

                  3.   Does it have all of your duty stations?

                  4.   Does it have all of your performance evaluations?

      b.   Medical record.

            i.   Review for military member, spouse, and dependents if applicable.

            ii.   Review at least once per year.

            iii.   Review every time you transfer.

            iv.   Is the record complete?

1. Does it have the full list of your illnesses and treatments?
2. Are your prescriptions current?

10. Education will help ensure your success in the civilian world, so take advantage of all the training opportunities you can while still in uniform. Get credit for your military service, education, and training.

    a. College education.
        i. Some of your military service will translate directly into college credits. You should get that done before you separate.
        ii. Have you taken actual college courses? Do you have a transcript?
        iii. Can you leverage any on-base or military college offerings before you get out?
        iv. Consider taking CLEP exams for credit in your specialty or for something you're willing to study.
    b. Licenses and Certifications.
        i. Does any of your military training or experience entitle you to a license or certification?
        ii. Does any of your military training or experience enable you to sit for a license or certification exam?
    c. Start learning about the GI Bill (Montgomery and/or Post 9/11), and make sure you are doing everything necessary to protect your benefits.
    d. Take advantage of military tuition assistance available to you while you are on active duty.

This is a sample of what your checklist might look like after you finish the first pass. You don't have to stop with the list provided, you can add more items and remove those that don't apply. Being the overachiever that you are, feel absolutely free to work ahead on completing future checklist items!

Example of spreadsheet checklist - 1st pass at 24 months

No.	Description	24 M	12 M	6 M	3 M	30 D	5 D	Update	Notes
01.00.00	Read this book from cover to cover	X						01MAY18	Complete
02.00.00	Financial health check	X						04APR18	Complete
02.01.00	Maximize TSP contributions	X						21APR18	Moved from 3% to 5%
02.02.00	Actively managing your investments?	X						21APR18	Initial review complete. Will review on 2nd Monday
02.02.01	6 months of living expenses saved?	X						21APR18	Only have 45 days in savings, will add $X per paycheck
02.02.02	Saving 30% of income every month?	X						25APR18	See above, $X per month will take me to 30%
02.03.00	Retirement/Separation income review	X						22MAY18	Complete
02.03.01	Military retirement income?	X						09MAR18	I should see $X per month after taxes
02.03.02	Social Security income?	X						15APR18	Not eligible at retirement but on track for $X/month
02.03.03	IRA/Roth distributions?	X						15MAY18	Not old enough at retirement, must take $X/month at age 72
02.03.04	Other income?	X						02MAY18	Stock portfolio, should generate about $X/month at age XX
02.03.05	Other income?	X						03MAY18	Net rental income from property is $X/month
03.00.00	Life Insurance	X						21APR18	Complete
03.01.00	Check/Enroll in SGLI	X						21APR18	Already enrolled
03.02.00	Review Life Insurance coverage, is it enough?	X						21APR18	Adequate coverage
03.02.01	Add additional whole life as required	X						21APR18	NA
03.03.00	Review AD&D, is it enough	X						21APR18	Coverage is $X, I think I need to double it
03.03.01	Add additional AD&D as required	X						01JUN18	Added additional policy through credit union

##M = Months, ##D = Days

ONE Year in Advance

By now, you should have completed 12 months of focused effort into learning about the separation process, your finances, and goals. At this point in time, a second, slow crawl through your checklist is so important that it's hard to overstate. Pay attention to every single detail, customizing the list by adding and refining it based on your experience and needs. Now is also the time to learn as much as you can about the Transition Assistance Program (TAP) and the Veterans Administration. You are getting ready to get out, make sure you learn all you can and work on getting your checklist items completed as far ahead of schedule as possible. If you haven't already done so, start with the 24-month checklist, and if you have, do it again please. These checklists are complementary and not duplicative, so work them in sequence over and over.

11. Start taking advantage of the Transition Assistance Program.

    a. Learn about and take advantage of the Transition Assistance Program (TAP) or Disabled Transition Assistance Program (DTAP).

    b. Get a copy of the DD 2648 or DD 2648-1 pre-separation checklist. Work ahead, don't count on your counsellor to get it all right.

    c. Attend a TAP workshop.

12. Check your Verification of Military Education and Training (DD 2586) form which is accessible via the DOD TAP website. If something is missing, get it resolved!

13. Become an expert on your Veteran's Administration benefits and entitlements. Invest significant time in the Department of Veterans Affairs website. There is an incredible amount of information that you need to master, so get started now.

    a. Compensation.

    b. Benefits.

    c. Education.

    d. Home Loan.

    e. Vocational Rehabilitation.

      f.   Life Insurance.

      g.   Medical (Tricare).

14. Start researching where you are going to settle after separation. It is critical that you understand the cost of living at your target location.

15. Start building your resume.

      a.   Look up examples on the internet, you don't have to reinvent the wheel here, but you should create something that is not a boilerplate copy.

      b.   Draft, read and edit. Wash, rinse and repeat.

      c.   Learn to translate your skills and experience into civilian language.

      d.   Shed cryptic military designations unless looking for contractor-equivalent position.

      e.   Create more than one resume.

            i.   Each version should be specific to skill, specialty, and experience.

            ii.   Include generalized details about your overall experience.

      f.   Look at military translators (Military.com has a great app).

16. Learn about your options for the transportation of your household goods (HHG) to your separation location.

17. Healthcare.

      a.   Get a checkup for you and your family!

            i.   Make sure there are no lingering effects of your service that haven't been diagnosed and/or treated.

      b.   Schedule a visit with the local base dental facility, and talk to your dentist or specialist about your options and the state of your dental care.

- i. Schedule and get any serious issues addressed immediately.

c. If you are voluntarily separating, not retiring, don't have a disability and make more money than the VA limit, you will not receive access to Veterans Administration healthcare.

- i. Learn about civilian healthcare options for medical, dental and vision.
- ii. Determine your budget requirements for the level of care for which you need to pay.
- iii. Include the cost of healthcare in your prospective employer "total compensation" comparison.

d. If you are involuntarily separating, learn about Transition Assistance Management Program (TAMP) for healthcare options and your eligibility period.

e. If you are retiring, you are automatically entitled to VA healthcare (TRICARE), so learn about it, enroll, and take advantage of the benefits you will receive.

Example of spreadsheet checklist – 2nd pass at 12 months

No.	Description	24 M	12 M	6 M	3 M	30 D	5 D	Update	Notes
01.00.00	Read this book from cover to cover	X	X					01MAY19	Complete
02.00.00	Financial health check	X	X					04APR19	Complete
02.01.00	Maximize TSP contributions	X	X					22MAY19	Moved out last year
02.02.00	Actively managing your investments?	X	X					23MAY19	Yes, each month
02.02.01	6 months of living expenses saved?	X	X					24MAY19	Have 5 months saved
02.02.02	Saving 30% of income every month?	X	X					24MAY19	25% now, move up to 30% on x date
02.03.00	Retirement/Separation income review	X	X					23MAY19	2nd review complete
02.03.01	Military retirement income?	X	X					24MAY19	I should see $X per month after taxes
02.03.02	Social Security income?	X	X					25MAY19	On track for $X/month
02.03.03	IRA/Roth distributions?	X	X					25MAY19	Not old enough at retirement
02.03.04	Other income?	X	X					25MAY19	Stock portfolio, should generate about $X/month at age XX
02.03.05	Other income?	X	X					25MAY19	Net rental income from property is $X/month
03.00.00	Life Insurance	X	X					25MAY19	Complete
03.01.00	Check/Enroll in SGLI	X	X					25MAY19	Max coverage now
03.02.00	Review Life Insurance coverage, is it enough?	X	X					25MAY19	Adequate coverage
03.02.01	Add additional whole life as required	X	X					25MAY19	NA
03.03.00	Review AD&D, is it enough	X	X					25MAY19	Still need to double
03.03.01	Add additional AD&D as required	X	X					25MAY19	Need more coverage
04.00.00	Learn about TAMP		X					06JUN19	Lots to learn, working through website
05.00.00	Learn about VA benefits		X					06JUN19	Wills set aside 4 hours per week
06.00.00	Build your resume		X					08JUN19	2 resumes created
07.00.00	Healthcare		X					09JUN19	Dental for Daughter

Six Months to Go – What to Do

If you haven't taken this seriously yet, now is the time, and you must be profoundly serious and meticulously focused from here on in. Failure to launch and learn now means you will be making critical life decisions without the information you need. This should be (at a minimum) your third run through your checklist. There are literally dozens of things you must do in the next 90 days, and you must not put them off. Start now, become a voracious learner, take notes and begin making those life-impacting decisions. If you haven't started networking, do that now as part of you daily grind. Update your contact list with as much information as you can get about your personal, social, and professional connections. If you are not retiring, you should have an awesome resume by now and it's time to put it into play. The next 3 months will buzz by before you know it, so work this list every day until you've nailed down each and every item. Re-read this book and any others you've selected to help you in your transition.

18. Get copies of your Medical Records (including spouse and dependents).

19. Get copies of your Dental Records (including spouse and dependents).

20. Get a hard copy of your Social Security card (for spouse and dependents also),

21. Become familiar with *Federal Benefits for Veterans, Dependents and Survivors VA Pamphlet 80-16-01P94663* (2016 version). This is probably one of the best summaries of benefits that you will find in one place, as it includes phone numbers and websites for reference.

22. Identify your HOR or SLR for separation purposes.

    a. HOR - Home of Record (can only be changed to correct an error).

    b. SLR - State of Legal Residence is where you intend to live after you leave the service.

        i. Submit form DD 2058 to your finance officer.

23. Start planning your move in earnest to your HOM/SLR.

    a. Request "house hunting" orders if you are retiring.

    b. List your current home with a realtor if applicable.

      c. Start your search for a new home via the internet.

      d. Do NOT make an offer on any property until you've visited the area.

24. Start your job search (if applicable).

    a. Work your social and professional contact lists for opportunities.

    b. Target work in your State of Legal Residence if appropriate.

    c. Target online job listing sites, forums, groups.

    d. Put your resume into play and start applying for jobs.

    e. Look for industry-specific companies and apply directly to them through their websites.

    f. Attend career fairs.

    g. Review your HOM/SLR state for unemployment benefits.

25. Start applying for college or other training.

    a. Online courses.

    b. At your HOM/SLR location.

26. Increase your SGLI to the maximum rate to allow for maximizing your VGLI when you separate.

27. Security Clearance if applicable (terminology may not be precise for all services).

    a. Establish your current level of clearance.

    b. Determine how much time you have on your security clearance "clock."

        i. When was your last Single Scope Background (SSBI) investigation?

        ii. When was your last Periodic Reinvestigation (PRI)?

iii. General rule for currency is 5 years for Top Secret, if downgraded to Secret add 5 more.

28. Officers only, are you restricted in your options because of your previous military experience and security clearance?

    a. Go to the TAP website and search for "restrictions" to get the most current information

29. Visit your Finance Office and identify any separation pay to which you may be entitled.

30. Review your healthcare options (this may influence some of your other decisions, so pay attention to every detail).

31. Take advantage of all legal services for your family.

    a. Advanced Healthcare Directive

    b. Create or update your Will.

    c. Create or update you Power of Attorney.

    d. Make notarized copies of all documents and distribute to your beneficiaries and executor.

    e. Make sure someone in addition to your spouse has copies.

32. Start working with the transition office on your DD 214. You should be able to review a draft of yours at this point, and it must have no errors. Check it and check it again because any issues with your DD 214 could prevent employment with the government and/or getting your VA home loan guarantee.

33. Wardrobe considerations.

    a. You need a set of professional attire appropriate for your target job space.

    b. Start buying now.

    c. Be sure you have enough clothing to for two weeks without reusing anything but shoes, belt, and jewelry.

34. Have you considered transferring part or all your Post 9/11 GI bill benefits to your spouse or children? Multiple criteria must be met, and it cannot be done after you separate.

35. Make a decision to take or sell back terminal leave.

36. Engage the Relocation Assistance Program for your branch and base.

37. Household planning.

    a. If on base, get detailed clearing information and get started, be sure to triple check the details.

    b. If off base, check with your landlord for move out requirements.

    c. What will be shipped where and when?

        i. Ship or store?

        ii. To what location?

        iii. Set up appointments and schedules.

Example of spreadsheet checklist – 3rd pass at 6 months

No.	Description	24 M	12 M	6 M	3 M	30 D	5 D	Update	Notes
01.00.00	Read this book from cover to cover	X	X	X				01DEC19	Complete
02.00.00	Financial health check	X	X	X				04DEC19	Complete
02.01.00	Maximize TSP contributions	X	X	X				20DEC19	Moved out last year
02.02.00	Actively managing your investments?	X	X	X				23DEC19	Yes, each month
02.02.01	6 months of living expenses saved?	X	X	X				21DEC19	Have 5 months saved
02.02.02	Saving 30% of income every month?	X	X	X				24DEC19	25% now, move up to 30% on x date
02.03.00	Retirement/Separation income review	X	X	X				23DEC19	2nd review complete
02.03.01	Military retirement income?	X	X	X				24DEC19	I should see $X per month after taxes
02.03.02	Social Security income?	X	X	X				25DEV19	On track for $X/month
02.03.03	IRA/Roth distributions?	X	X	X				25DEC19	Not old enough at retirement
02.03.04	Other income?	X	X	X				25DEC19	$X/month at age XX
02.03.05	Other income?	X	X	X				25DEC19	$X/month
03.00.00	Life Insurance	X	X	X				20DEC19	Complete
03.01.00	Check/Enroll in SGLI	X	X	X				21DEC19	Max coverage now
03.02.00	Review Life Insurance coverage, is it enough?	X	X	X				19DEC19	Adequate coverage
03.02.01	Add additional whole life as required	X	X	X				19DEC19	NA
03.03.00	Review AD&D, is it enough	X	X	X				19DEC19	Still need to double
03.03.01	Add additional AD&D as required	X	X	X				19DEC19	Need more coverage
04.00.00	Learn about TAMP		X	X				19DEC19	Working the process
05.00.00	Learn about VA benefits		X	X				19DEC19	4 hours per week
06.00.00	Build your resume		X	X				19DEC19	2 resumes created
07.00.00	Healthcare		X	X				19DEC19	Wife outpatient in JAN
08.00.00	Get copies of medical records			X				19DEC19	Took three weeks
09.00.00	Get copies of dental records			X				19DEC19	Need daughter records
10.00.00	Start job search			X				19DEC19	Targeting various websites
11.00.00	Set Home of Record (HOM) or SLR			X				19DEC19	Identified and completed

3 Months Out – What to Do

You should be feeling footsteps behind you about now, because this is really happening and at this point you are committed to your decision there is no turning back. You need to check, double-check and triple-check your lists to make sure everything you can do is done. If you need to get some part of your record (service or medical) updated or corrected, you should focus on that task along with any other long lead time issues you've uncovered. But don't neglect the easier items, knock them out also. Re-read this book and any other source material you have selected to use as a reference. What have you missed? This is your last chance to sort out any gaps, so go through this whole checklist again.

- Re-read this book.
- Re-visit your checklist, customizing and updating as needed.
- If you aren't retiring, you should be hitting the job market, contacting recruiters, and visiting online boards and company sites daily.
- Remember the internet is one of your biggest advantages, so leverage it to help with all your action items.
- If you are just getting started with the Transition Assistance Program (TAP), you should expect to perform some additional scrutiny, as there are checklists and milestones for the Veteran's Opportunity to Work (VOW) and Veterans Employment Initiative Task Force (VEI TF) that TAP will want to make sure you understand.

38. Read the *Federal Benefits for Veterans, Dependents and Survivors* 2014 publication 978-0-16-092508-5.

39. Convert SGLI to VGLI.

40. Do you have all of your important documents stored and copied?

    a. Electronic copies.

    b. Paper copies.

    c. Copies distributed to the correct persons.

41. Complete a detailed plan and timeline for your move.

    a. Review your Relocation Assistance Program information developed at the 12-month point.

b. Double-check all of your base exit requirements.

   i. What is complete?

   ii. What is left to do?

c. Double-check all of your service exit requirements.

   i. What is complete?

   ii. What is left to do?

d. Double-check Home of Record (HOM, SLR) detail.

e. Review the schedule for your household goods shipment.

   i. Dates.

   ii. What are you keeping with you (assumes HHG will happen before you leave the command)?

   iii. Where will you stay?

   iv. Do you really understand your base housing/rental/lease termination requirements?

      1. Document anything left to do.

      2. Plan for and set target completion dates for the remaining items.

f. Is your family/spouse staying with you until the last day or will you send some or all of them ahead?

g. Will you drive or fly to your HOM/SLR?

   i. Driving.

      1. Complete all maintenance items.

      2. Complete route mapping and identify places to stay.

3. Create a "check in" method to let friends and family know you are all right while driving.

 ii. Flying.

1. Get your tickets.

2. How will you get to and from the airport?

42. Double-check your leave planning.

 a. When will your terminal leave start?

 b. Will you sell back any excess?

43. Are you still looking for a job? Make this a priority.

44. Start familiarizing yourself with your HOM/SLR.

45. Check that your financial institutions are accessible at your HOM/SLR.

 a. Address change notifications.

 b. Order new checks.

46. Research the Veteran's unemployment compensation for your target discharge state/territory, collect the specific documents and be sure you understand the steps required to file for UCX.

30 Days Left – What to Do

Thirty days are left before you separate, and if you've been doing your due diligence, this run through your checklist should be simple. You should only have a few items left to be completed, and if you prepared well and worked your checklists, you'll cruise through this period with little to no stress. Hopefully by now you have job options if you're not retiring. If not, double-down on the job hunting effort. You've also got separation physicals to get gone, and you need to get any outstanding medical and dental work finished. Is there anything you need to buy from the PX/Exchange? How about your vehicles and insurance? Is your forwarding address established? Are you ready for your household move? Are you prepared for those few days after everything is packed up and you have to live out of a suitcase? Do you need to get any work done on your vehicles? what about the transfer of school credits?

- Re-read this book, you need to refresh your knowledge to ensure you don't miss anything.
- Re-visit your checklist. Remember, customize it as needed and make sure you have done, or know every remaining item that needs to be done before your last day.
- If you aren't retiring, you should be hitting the job market, contacting recruiters, and visiting, online boards and company websites daily.
- Remember the internet is one of your biggest advantages, so leverage it to help with all your action items.

47. Household goods shipment will be completed during this period. Are you ready?

48. Do you have a copy of all of your Records? Double and Triple-check.

    a. Medical care.

    b. DD 214.

    c. DD 2586 (VMET Verification of Military Education and Training).

    d. Copy of awards and medals.

    e. Copy of medical records.

      f.   Electronic copy in addition to paper, if possible.

49. Check your records again, particularly your DD 214, and if something is missing, you must get is resolved.

50. Schedule and complete your separation physical.

51. Schedule and complete any remaining debriefs.

52. Review the Veterans Unemployment Compensation Program and documents necessary to file for your target state/territory.

One Week to Go (Before You Leave Base)

Your life is going to be complicated this week. Expect to exchange emotional goodbyes, and to feel melancholy and perhaps even anxious about what comes next. Spend time with your friends and feel confident you'll thrive in your post-separation world. Celebrate your transition, but don't let your guard down. Check and recheck your list(s), make sure you have everything you need. If you plan to go on terminal leave, you must make sure you are set up to complete/receive the final paperwork at the end of your leave period.

The absolute worst case here is to miss something that would require your return to your last duty station at your expense (round trip) to clear up a paperwork issue. Be extremely diligent in checking and confirming you've met all the requirements to exit the base and the service.

You must have the following:

1. Copy of Military records before you leave the base.
2. DD-214 before you leave the base.
3. Logins to various systems (Healthcare, DoDTAP...).
4. Copy of Medical records before you leave the base.
5. Copy of leave and/or separation orders before you leave the base.
6. Names and phone numbers of contacts in your last command and/or service who could help if you hit some type of issue.

Double and triple-check: Do you have everything you need to file for Veterans Unemployment Compensation (UCX) for your discharge state/territory?

Visit mentors and others who have been instrumental in your career to say thank you and express your appreciation. If offered, be sure to participate in any going away or retirement activities.

Core Concepts mapping

Core One – You are NOT like the others. Leverage your differences to provide you and your family the desired economic stability, peace of mind and quality of life. Don't let anything or anyone hold you back.

Core Two – You have been forged in fires your peers can't understand. Your civilian peers have followed a certain career track of which they are proud. They have their own circles of influence which they jealously guard. If you want to be accepted, you'll have to earn their respect by demonstrating patience, influence, expertise, and good decision-making skills. Telling sea/war stories won't gain you admittance.

Core Three – There are less of us than you may realize. At only about 8% of the population, you can't always count on finding a Veteran in every walk of life, particularly when you need a little help. Network and learn who the vets are in your personal and professional circles.

Core Four – You are uniquely prepared to manage your own future. You can do this, but you need to check, validate, and recheck your plans to separate. Your checklist must be a dynamic piece of work which is constantly revised and updated.

Core Five – You have skills and capabilities that are marketable. Yes, you are marketable, and the more skills, education and experience you bring, the better you will land.

Core Six – You have gaps in your skills and capabilities you need to close. At this point in time working through this book, you should have both a healthy respect for the value you bring to the civilian workplace as a Veteran, and a bit of concern about what you don't know. Close the gaps you're aware of and work on any new ones you discover.

Core Seven – You now have more responsibility for your life and much more opportunity to screw it up. Unless you are retiring, the safety net provided by the Service is gone, and you are in sink or swim mode. The sooner you start preparing for your transition, the more you will know and the better you will land.

Core Eight – Life is still hard. After you leave, life will be hard in different ways than you are accustomed to. Study, network and develop social, familial, and professional networks of people you respect who can help you through the hard spots.

Core Nine – The Republic is powered by the engine of Capitalism. If you can't live on your retirement and savings, you'll need a job. Work as far ahead as you can to secure your job as part of your exit strategy from the service. Believe it or not, some jobs will give you an offer in writing, so shoot for that if it's an option.

Personal perspective:

While still on active duty, I saw various methods used to display the "shortness" of time fellow service members had before their date of separation. One individual, with a high degree of ego made it a point make sure everyone was aware of how many days he had left. His specific method was to use a small chain attached to a "wheel book" (this was a small green 3X5 memorandum pad that was once so hard to obtain you had to be a "big wheel" to get one) with one link for each of the twenty- something days of his service remaining. His big production after the morning's formation was to count them out and then clip the previous day's link. It was funny and entertaining for the first few days, but after twenty days passing, and with more than twenty to go it became tiresome, but no one wanted to rain on his parade. Finally, one day our NCOIC asked him to do something and he made another tired joke that he was too "short" to complete the task. The old NCO grinned back at him and said *"Son, you ain't short. You'll be short when you can light a cigarette on Uncle Sam's time, and put it out on yours. Stop this noise and get your damn job done."* The older NCO then asked the guy if he had a job lined up. He shrugged and answered, "just going home on leave and I'll see what happens when I get there." If you are short and haven't prepared, then you have no one to blame but yourself.

Chapter 23 - Books to Read

The internet is a great tool for researching and looking up all kinds of information, some which is useful and some which can be a total waste of time. Finding information on how to fix something like replacing a part in a car or in an appliance is an example of how the internet can be used to solve problems. But it really isn't the tool of choice when it comes to gaining the broad-based understanding of people, processes, and situations with which you will be challenged in your new world. While you can gain some insight from various videos and other materials, it won't be enough. For that, you must expand the breadth and depth of your knowledge to which will allow you to reach to situations with an understanding of the outcomes you want to influence.

To obtain deep insight and knowledge, you are going to need to read. It's also a critical process and activity that you need to master and integrate into your best practices. You need to develop the ability to absorb, assimilate and integrate the information found in well written books. It is a rewarding and fundamental practice required for any concrete knowledge transfer of complex subjects.

Reading at your own, deliberate pace requires time and focus. There are so many terrific books to read, you simply don't have enough of either to cover every topic, so make a short list of books you want to read now, read your way through your first list, and then make another.

Some very wealthy families require that their children read two non-fiction books, or more, each month, on top of any scholastic assignments. If you are already a big fiction reader, try to balance your reading, for every fiction title, read a non-fiction book.

Where, you may ask, should you start? There are literally hundreds, if not thousands of books written on so many topics from which you can choose.

For starters, here is a list of books which may help you get started on your reading journey. The top of the list is **The Art of War** by Sun Tzu. Even though scholars now doubt the existence of a single person known as the famous Chinese General "Sun Tzu," you should still read a good summary of the collective wisdom attributed to him. There is much to be gleaned from this book as it will give you a broader perspective that will apply during your remaining military tour as well as your civilian life afterwards.

Other books to read (in no particular order)

- *Your Best Life Now* by Joel Osteen
- *The New One Minute Manager* by Ken Blanchard Ph.D. and Spencer Johnson M.D.
- *The Millionaire Next Door* by Thomas J. Stanley Ph.D. and William D. Danko Ph.D.
- *The Millionaire Mind* by Thomas J. Stanley Ph.D. and William D. Danko Ph.D.
- *The Secrets of Closing the Sale* Zig Ziglar
- *How to Win Friends & Influence People* by Dale Carnegie
- *The 7 Habits of Highly Effective People* by Stephen R. Covey
- *The Invisible Wounds of War, Coming home from Iraq and Afghanistan* by Marguerite Guzman Bouvard

Core Concepts mapping

Core One – You are NOT like the others. You will be a bit of a fish out of water and you need every advantage so read, read, read!

Core Two – You have been forged in fires your peers can't understand. Finding context and meaning in your post-military life will be important. Learn as much as you can before your last day in uniform.

Core Three – There are less of us than you may realize. And even fewer of us in positions of authority and/or earning six or seven-figure incomes.

Core Four – You are uniquely prepared to manage your own future. You've been forced to be a voracious learner while in the military, apply those skills here!

Core Five – You have skills and capabilities that are marketable. Can you create a focused resume and nail the interview for your ideal job? Read, learn, network and be ready when opportunity knocks.

Core Six – You have gaps in your skills and capabilities you need to close. Read, read, read, and network.

Core Seven– You now have more responsibility for your life and much more opportunity to screw it up. Sometimes you only get one shot, will you be ready?

Core Eight – Life is still hard. Jobs don't care about you. Corporations don't care about you. Your family cares about you every second of every day, so never lose that focus.

Core Nine – The Republic is powered by the engine of Capitalism. Pick your economic bracket and income goals, and work towards those goals every day.

Personal perspective:

Standing on the tarmac before my very first flight lesson, I was excited and more than a bit nervous. Learning to fly was one of my long-standing dreams, and today was the day it all started. My instructor was patient and kind. He didn't waste an extra syllable as we performed the pre-flight check of our airplane. After we climbed aboard and taxied to the edge of the runway and finished the last of checklist, he put his hand over mine on the throttle to get my attention. There we were, paused just before we were about to tear down the runway and leap into the blue sky. I glanced over at him, his voice coming over my head set quietly saying "the worst place to have a problem is when your runway is behind you and the sky is above you." As that sunk in, I felt like I had been punched in the gut. This was suddenly very real, and I was literally responsible for what happened next, there was no chance for do overs if I made a mistake. I nodded, rechecked everything and confirmed there were no issues, nor anything missed. He watched me like a hawk through the entire process and gave me a small smile, nodding as I finished. Then we tore down the runway and flew into the sky. What a day, and what a lesson from just one, soft-spoken sentence.

Chapter 24 – Retirement financials

The quality of your life in retirement will mostly be determined by your health and income. Your health and aging was covered in Chapter 20. For this chapter, let's focus on retirement income.

You should have at least two sources of income in your retirement. The minimum set looks like this;

1. **Military Retiree** - This person will retire directly from the service (congrats!) and will be able to count on these forms of income;
    a. Military Pension
    b. Social Security
    c. Personal (after tax) savings

2. **Military Retiree + Civilian Retiree** - This person will have completed the requisite time in the military to retire and worked in the civilian sector long enough to generate some retirement type savings. They should be able to count on these forms of income;
    a. Military Pension
    b. Social Security
    c. 401K/IRA type savings
    d. Personal (after tax) savings

3. **Veteran + Civilian Retiree** - This person will retire directly from the service (congrats!) and will be able to count on Social Security for retirement income and should have another form of retirement income;
    a. Social Security
    b. 401k/IRA type retirement savings
    c. Personal (after tax) savings

How much retirement income should I have?

This is a complex subject, but we can use a few simple rules to help plan.

1. Get a financial planner/advisor. They aren't free and can charge you up to 2% annually of your assets under management (AUM). Don't let that scare you off as a good advisor will make you more money than that in good economic times and will limit your losses in a downturn.

2. Assume you need at least as much income as you have while working. No one wants to hear this. For some reason there's this mythology out there that you can live on less in retirement. That may be true if you have paid off your home, have decent vehicles without a note and are in great health and don't have unexpected expenses. This is not reality. In addition, your healthcare costs will likely double then triple as you age.
3. Set up multiple streams of income (see Chapter 15 on Money Management). No matter your military retiree status, you will receive Social Security benefits and Medicare. While both will help, they will not be enough to live comfortably unless you are debt free and own your own home. Even then, you'll still have out of pocket expenses for property taxes, income tax, healthcare and other sundry items that will burn down your discretionary income.
4. If you have an employer match 401k plan, maximize your deductions to ensure that you get the full employer match. Otherwise, you are leaving money on the table.
5. Save, save, save. Make sure you have savings of your own outside of any retirement plan (government or private). Plan for at least two years' worth of expenses at a minimum, five years' worth would be better. This saved money should be invested in a Roth or IRA or 401k.
6. Are you contributing to the military Thrift Savings Plan? If not, start now! You can take it with you when you leave. This is free money, so take advantage of it because you get a 100% pre-tax match for the first 3% of your pay and a 50% match for the next 2% of your pay. If you maximize your contribution at 5%, then the government will match 90% of that amount (3% contribution match + 1% if you max out at 5% = 4% overall match or 90%). There are two types:
    a. Basic TSP is pre-tax deduction, which means you will pay taxes on withdrawal of any contributions and gains
    b. TSP Roth is after tax, but all withdrawals are tax free after you meet the Roth requirements for age and account maturity.
7. The militaries Savings Deposit Program (SDP) is a short-term savings program that is only available to service members who are deployed in combat zones or other operations and are receiving Hostile Fire Pay/Imminent Danger Pay (HFP/IDP). You can only set up an SDP account after you've been deployed for 30 consecutive days or for at least one day in three consecutive months. You can build your financial savings by reaping the benefits of SDP's guaranteed high 10% annual return

compounded quarterly. The only downside is that you have to withdraw your money when your tour ends.

Let's talk about Social Security

Special Social Security credits for Veterans

If you served between 1978 – 2001 you have accrued additional Social Security credits because of the low pay to service members. When veterans apply for retirement or disability benefits, Social Security checks their records. If they have qualifying military service, they get credit for additional wages for their military service. These credits are added to the veteran's lifetime earnings record — not to the veteran's monthly benefit check. But because Social Security uses lifetime earnings as the basis for figuring out a person's retirement benefits, the credits can ultimately raise the monthly payment.

For this period of service, every $300 in active duty basic pay, veterans are credited with an extra $100 in Social Security earnings, up to a maximum of $1,200 a year. But if you enlisted after Sept. 7, 1980, and didn't complete at least 24 months of active duty or a full tour, you may not be able to receive these added credits.
In 2001, Congress eliminated the program. Thus, military service in calendar year 2002 and later years no longer qualifies for the special credits.

Can I draw both Social Security and my military pension?

The answer is absolutely and unequivocally yes.

Will my military pension decrease my Social Security benefits?

No. However, there certain government jobs (working for the US Postal Service as an example) pay into a different system than Social Security and that might reduce your Social Security benefit payment.

Until 1984, employment by the federal government was covered under the Civil Service Retirement System (CSRS) and not by Social Security. If you worked for a federal agency during those years, you did not pay Social Security taxes on your earnings and those earnings are not shown on your record.

In 1984, a second retirement system—the Federal Employees Retirement System, or FERS—was introduced. People who began working for the Federal government in 1984 or later are covered by FERS instead of CSRS. Also, some workers who had been covered by the CSRS program chose to switch to the FERS program when it became available.

Are there situations where my Social Security Benefit can be reduced?

Yes. If you take your benefit before reaching your full retirement age (FRA) then your SS benefit will be reduced by $1 for every $2 you make in excess of $18,240.

In the year you reach full retirement age, your benefits will be reduced by $1 for every $3 you earn above $48,600 (for 2020). Starting with the month you attain full retirement age; your benefits will no longer be reduced.

This is important: *These dollars are not lost forever; instead, your Social Security benefit will be increased to account for them after you reach full retirement age.*

After you reach FRA, you will not see a reduction in your SS benefit no matter how much you earn.

If you make more than a certain amount of "combined" income, then part of SS benefits will be taxed as income. This happens when you cross the $32,000 line of income and which triggers income tax of up to 50% on your Social Security benefit. If you have more than $44,000 income, then up to 85% of your benefits may be taxable.

Yes, it is crazy that you can be taxed twice on this income and this is another place were a good financial advisor can help. Regulations and laws are constantly being modified by lawmakers and agencies. You need an advocate who understands the current environment and coming changes.

Can my Spouse draw Social Security based on my earnings?

Spouses are entitled to the higher of (a) their own retirement benefit or (b) spousal benefit.

Spouses can only earn the full 50% spousal benefit if they and the earning spouse wait to receive benefits at full retirement age (FRA). Otherwise, the benefit they receive is based on 50% - the penalty applied at the time of the higher earning spouse's benefit activation.

If you qualify and apply for your own retirement benefits and for benefits as a spouse, Social Security always pays your own benefits first. If your benefits as a spouse are higher than your own retirement benefits, you will get a combination of benefits equaling the higher spouse benefit.

Your benefits as a spouse do not include any delayed retirement credits your spouse may receive.

If you begin receiving benefits: between age 62 and your full retirement age (FRA), the amount will be permanently reduced by a percentage based on the number of months up to your full retirement age.

If you are under full retirement age and continue to work while receiving benefits, your benefits may be affected by the retirement earnings test.

At your full retirement age, your benefit as a spouse cannot exceed one-half of your spouse's full retirement amount.

For a spouse who is not entitled to benefits on his or her own earnings record, this reduction factor is applied to the base spousal benefit, which is 50 percent of the worker's primary insurance amount. For example, if the worker's primary insurance amount is $1,600 and the worker's spouse chooses to begin receiving benefits 36 months before his or her normal retirement age, we first take 50 percent of $1,600 to get an $800 base spousal benefit. Then we compute the reduction factor, which is 36 times 25/36 of one percent, or 25 percent. Applying a 25 percent reduction to the $800 amount gives a spousal benefit of $600. Thus, in this case, the final spousal benefit is 37.5 percent of the primary insurance amount.

When should I start receiving my Social Security benefits?

This is a common question. It boils down to how long you expect to live and what other sources of income you may have vs. your expected expenses.

The current "full" or "normal" retirement age (FRA) is 67 years, assuming you were born after 1960.

Taking Social Security benefits before you reach full retirement age may not be in your best interest.

Social Security payouts are designed to be actuarially equivalent for someone with average mortality, theoretically it shouldn't make a difference when an individual starts collecting. External factors may affect the actual worth of benefits received. These include inflation as measured by annual cost-of-living increases, the time value of money, probable investment returns, and marginal tax rates.

An absolute truth you need to lock down:

No do overs, no forgiveness. Whenever you start taking your Social Security benefit, that's the number you have to live with for the rest of your life (except for very small cost of living adjustments).

Give me the Social Security numbers, how much at what age?

Assuming your full retirement (FRA) age is 67

- You will take a 30% penalty at age 62
- You will take a 25% penalty at age 63
- You will take a 20% penalty at age 64
- You will take a 13% penalty at age 65
- You will take a 7% penalty at age 67

Deferring taking your Social Security income until after full retirement age are given a delayed retirement credit each year past that age until age 70, equivalent to an 8% increase for those born in 1943 or later. This creates the fewest number of checks received but results in a much higher monthly benefit. To determine the most appropriate age for a retiree to begin receiving income, calculating Social Security break-even age is beneficial.

Note: You do not accrue delayed retirement benefits after age 70.

Use the Social Security calculator to do you own "what-if's" and see what your benefit will be before and after full retirement age (FRA).

https://www.ssa.gov/OACT/quickcalc/early_late.html

Choosing a retirement savings vehicle

If you work for a large employer after your service, you may be able to contribute to either a traditional 401(k) or 403(b), a Roth 401(k) or 403(b), or both. If you're self-employed, or if a 401(k) or 403(b) isn't offered where you work, you may need to choose between a traditional or Roth IRA, or both.

To get started you need to consider these factors;

- Choose between paying taxes now or in retirement. Opting for a tax benefit when your marginal rate is the highest generally makes sense.
- How good you are about saving is also something to keep in mind.
- Having both a traditional and a Roth account (if you can) may be appropriate.

Most employers have eliminated old style pensions and replaced them with 401k style investments. These usually come with a matching provision. For example, you might need to contribute 6% of your pre-tax income to earn a 4% match of your total salary. This is a fantastic deal as you get 10% for the price of 6%.

You can usually contribute more than the match requirement, but there is a limit and it differs by employer.

You can put all your savings into an employer's plan, but it is not recommended due to the limited number of investment vehicles offered by the company plan.

A **Roth IRA** is an individual retirement plan you can open directly with a bank or investment firm. It is not employer-sponsored, so anyone can open a Roth IRA, regardless of your employer. You also might have even more control and flexibility over the types of investments you make with a Roth IRA since you'll be working directly with an investment firm

A **401(k)** is an employer-sponsored plan that is often included in the benefits package of a full-time job. If you elect to use a 401(k), you can sign up through your employer, but the account is usually managed by an investment bank like Fidelity or Vanguard. When you enroll, you can choose how much of each paycheck you'd like to contribute toward your account. Many employers will match some or all of your contributions with money of their own, so if you don't take advantage of a 401(k), you're literally leaving money on the table. Most 401(k) plans allow you some control over how your cash is invested — you can either use a hands-off approach and let the bank make all investment decisions, or you can play a more active role.

Note: 401(k) matches usually required a 36-month vesting period. If you leave before that time, you won't get all your matched dollars.

Stepwise formula for successful retirement investing

If your employer offers a 401(k) match -while still active, the TSP qualifies, use it!

1. Contribute enough to earn the full match. Check your employee benefits handbook. If you see that your employer matches any portion of the money you contribute to the company 401(k) plan, do not bypass this opportunity to collect your free money.

2. Next, contribute as much as you're allowed to an IRA. Depending on which type of IRA you choose — Roth or traditional — you can get your tax break now or down the road when you start withdrawing funds for retirement.

3. After maxing out a traditional IRA or Roth IRA, revisit your 401(k). Even after you've gotten the employer match — and even if your investment choices are limited, which is one of the main drawbacks of workplace retirement plans — a 401(k) is still beneficial because of the tax deduction.

    a. The money you contribute to a 401(k) will lower your taxable income for the year dollar for dollar. And don't forget about the added benefit of tax-deferred growth on investment gains.

If your employer doesn't offer a 401(k) match

1. Contribute to a traditional or Roth IRA first. Not all companies match their employees' retirement account contributions. When that's the case, choosing an IRA — and contributing up to the max — is generally a better first option.

2. After maxing out IRA benefits, contribute to your 401(k). Here again, the tax deferral benefit of a company-sponsored plan is a good reason to direct dollars into a 401(k) after you've funded a traditional or Roth IRA.

Other stepwise actions in common

1. When you've maxed out 401(k) and IRA's, keep saving.
2. Consider investing in other income producing vehicles (Bonds and real estate come immediately to mind)
3. Ensure your savings is drawing the highest interest possible (consider a bank with no physical branches, they tend to much higher returns). Internet banks are still covered by the Federal Deposit Insurance Corporation (FDIC) and you will be covered for up to $250,000, so don't worry.

What is this "Minimum Required Distribution" for IRA's I keep hearing about?

Your required minimum distribution (RMD) is the minimum amount you must withdraw from your account each year. You generally have to start taking withdrawals from your IRA, SEP IRA, SIMPLE IRA, or retirement plan account when

you reach age 70½. Roth IRAs do not require withdrawals until after the death of the owner.
- You can withdraw more than the minimum required amount.
- Your withdrawals will be included in your taxable income except for any part that was taxed before (your basis) or that can be received tax-free (such as qualified distributions from designated Roth accounts).

What types of retirement plans require minimum distributions?

The RMD rules apply to all employer sponsored retirement plans, including profit-sharing plans, 401(k) plans, 403(b) plans, and 457(b) plans. The RMD rules also apply to traditional IRAs and IRA-based plans such as SEPs, SARSEPs, and SIMPLE IRAs.

The RMD rules also apply to Roth 401(k) accounts. However, the RMD rules do not apply to Roth IRAs while the owner is alive

How much must I withdraw to meet the require minimum distribution?

From the IRS website; Generally, a RMD is calculated for each account by dividing the prior December 31 balance of that IRA or retirement plan account by a life expectancy factor that IRS publishes in Tables in IRS Publication 590-B, Distributions from Individual Retirement Arrangements (IRAs). Choose the life expectancy table to use based on your situation.
- Joint and Last Survivor Table - use this if the sole beneficiary of the account is your spouse and your spouse is more than 10 years younger than you
- Uniform Lifetime Table - use this if your spouse is not your sole beneficiary or your spouse is not more than 10 years younger
- Single Life Expectancy Table - use this if you are a beneficiary of an account (an inherited IRA)

Other relevant notes on IRA's

A traditional IRA is ideal for those who favor an immediate tax break. Contributions may be deductible — that means your taxable income for the year will be reduced by the amount of your contribution. But, if you're also covered by a 401(k), your deduction may be reduced or eliminated based on income. If you (or your spouse) has a workplace retirement plan, check out the IRA limits.

A Roth IRA is an excellent choice if you're not eligible to deduct traditional IRA contributions, or if you don't mind giving up the IRA's immediate tax deduction in exchange for tax-free growth on your investments and tax-free withdrawals in retirement.

Roth IRA eligibility is not affected by participation in a 401(k), but there are income limits.

Other benefits of an IRA? They offer access to a virtually unlimited number and type of investments, giving much more control over your investment options: You can bargain-shop for low-cost index mutual funds and ETFs vs. being restricted to the offerings in a workplace retirement account, and you can avoid paying the administrative fees that many 401(k) plans charge.

Can I take my 401(k) with me when I change employers?

Yes, you can, with a few caveats. There are three ways to take your retirement savings with you when you leave a company. The first is to transfer the funds from your old plan to one offered by your new employer, assuming it offers a 401(k). Another option is to complete a tax-free transfer or rollover of the money into an Individual Retirement Account (IRA). And finally, you may elect to cash out your 401(k) balance and get a check directly.

1. Move your 401(k) savings into the new plan offered by your new employer. No penalty, no problem.
2. Move your 401(k) saving out of the old employer's plan and into an IRA (usually a ROTH). It's important that you do this at arm's length. If you don't have the money moved from one plan to the other without touching it, your previous plan administrator will automatically withhold 20% for taxes purpose AND a 10% early withdrawal penalty. They will not bend on this or make an exception for you.
3. Take the money directly (least recommended). If you do this before you are 59.5 years old, you see your savings reduced by;
    a. 20% Federal Income Tax
    b. 10% early withdrawal penalty
    c. X% State Income Tax

Core Concepts mapping

Core One – You are NOT like the others. Your skillsets have been focused on the business of war and logistics. You may not have the innate understanding of retirement finances, but you have the training and determination to learn, make that *master*, the information you need.

Core Six – You have gaps in your skills and capabilities. Planning for retirement is complicated and you may not be able to go it alone. Learn what you can, determine the amount of time you have until your full retirement (assuming that retiring from the service means that you will work in the civilian economy). Once you are familiar with the terminology and concepts, try to make a realistic plan. Then, find a financial advisor and discuss your plan. Listen to what they say. It is much better to learn that your "plan" won't work when you still have a decade or more to adjust.

Personal perspective:

I've watched too many of my peers, who didn't come from a wealthy background, screw up their retirement. I should probably use a stronger word, but screw up will work. If they had just saved a little more, or avoided some of their extravagant purchases of stupid crap, they would have been worlds ahead of where they ended up. People just don't understand that time is both their biggest advantage and worst enemy. My brother, the Marine, always says that he can do anything with time and money. The less you have of one, the more you need of another. That is such a basic truth, that I wish I could pour it into the brains of the young men and women serving at this moment. I wish someone would have done that for me! While serving, we rationalize pushing out preparing for the to a later date, if we get that far. Start planning for tomorrow right (expletive deleted) now.

Chapter 25 – Plan Now for Later

As you settle into civilian life, you'll find you're busier than ever and time will pass quickly. At some point in your life, you'll look back and wonder when you got old. The bottom line is we all age, and death has a way of sneaking up on us whether or not we're ready, so for the sake of you and your family you should be as prepared as possible for the end of your life.

No matter how well we eat and exercise…everyone dies. There's only one way out of this life. Some lives will be tragically short or have an unexpected and abrupt end. Those who live out their natural span will ultimately fall into physical and possibly mental decline. Hopefully, along the way you'll have lived a long life full of love and triumph and surrounded by family.

Often, by the time some of these types of conditions are detected, the person is in rapid decline and may not be able to make important decisions that they should have taken care of long before. The various symptoms of aging can gang up on you and your clear thoughts. It is imperative that you lay a framework for your later years while you are still at peak mental acuity.

Don't put this off, and regardless of your age, you should get started now. There are many things to consider, decisions to be made and documented. Having clear documentation is critical. Make sure you keep your life insurance policies current and in good standing. Make sure you and your loved ones have a last will and an advance medical directive. Make sure that all your important paperwork in stored in a safe, secure place and is accessible. Cloud backup, thumb drive and hardcopy copies should be used. If you or your spouse survive the death of the other, these documents are critical, and not having them can compromise the surviving spouse's economic well-being. Additionally, these same issues can be doubly difficult for your children if both parents pass at the same time, or in any order before the children reach the age of majority.

If possible, you should engage a professional estate planner, a lawyer, and an accountant to ensure you've properly protected all your assets. Ask your friends and others you respect for referrals, and if you find someone via the internet, be sure to thoroughly check their references and credentials. Are you not convinced you need professional support? Here's a *short* list of things to do to make sure you have given your beneficiaries to the ability to deal with the passing of a loved one.

This list should not be considered all-inclusive. Find a good lawyer, accountant and estate planner and follow their advice!

1) **Gather your important documents:** These will vary, depending on your situation but will likely include the following information:

    a) Full legal name

    b) Social Security number

    c) Legal residence

    d) Date and place of birth

    e) Names and addresses of your spouse and children

    f) Location of birth and death certificates and certificates of marriage, divorce, citizenship, and adoption

    g) Employers and dates of employment

    h) Education and military records

    i) Names and phone numbers of religious contacts

    j) Membership in groups and awards received

    k) Names and phone numbers of close friends, relatives, and lawyer or financial advisor

    l) Names and phone numbers of doctors

    m) Medications taken regularly

    n) Location of living will and other legal documents

    o) Sources of income and assets (pension from your employer, IRAs, 401(k)s, bank accounts, etc.)

    p) Social Security and Medicare information

    q) Insurance information (life, health, long-term care, home, and car) with policy numbers and agents' names and phone numbers

r) Names of your banks and account numbers (checking, savings, credit union)

s) Copy of most recent income tax return

t) Location of most up-to-date will with an original signature

u) Liabilities, including property tax—what is owed to whom and when payments are due

v) Mortgages and debts—how and when paid

w) Location of original deed of trust for home and car title and registration

x) Credit and debit card names and numbers

y) Location of safe deposit box and key

2) **Securely store your important documents**: The list of "important" documents can be quite lengthy and bulky. Provide original documents when possible and certified copies with an actual imprint of the stamp if your state uses that type of notary device (as opposed to ink-only). A best practice is storing your papers in a bank safety deposit box, but this may limit access during off-hours. Another option is to buy a fire-proof safe so you can store your documents locally. Do your research here as the definition of fire-proof is based on the amount of time a given safe can withstand the temperature for which it has been certified. Reviews by fire-fighting professionals about how fire-proof safes really perform shows your mileage will vary. True fire-proof safes with 120 minutes of protection can be expensive, so consider a two-part strategy which uses both a safety deposit box and a safe for local storage. Some documents, such as an advanced medical directive and durable power of attorney should be given to the persons to whom you are entrusting that responsibility.

3) **Advance medical directive:** Sometimes called a living will or medical power of attorney. This is an incredibly important document so if you don't already have one, get it executed as soon as possible. Naming your healthcare agent gives that person broad powers to make healthcare decisions for you when you cannot make them yourself or you cannot communicate your decision. You should discuss your wishes concerning life-prolonging measures, mental health treatment and other health care decisions with your health care agent. Be specific and thorough, because except for specific limitations or restrictions

identified in the document, your health care agent is legally authorized to make any health care decision for you while you are incapacitated.

4) **Current medical condition:** This information can be critical for medical care you may need in an emergency and when your doctor's office is closed. Someone should have access to a list of medications you're taking, any known allergies and the names of all your doctors. Take pictures of all your medications and keep them on your phone, send to a trusted friend or relative.

5) **Add your spouse as co-owner to all properties and financial accounts**: This ensures those assets are protected from going through probate in the event of your death. Instead, they immediately go directly to your spouse avoiding delays which can occur when trying to access or use resources. If you don't have a spouse, is there a trusted individual in your life that you can add? The best case would be someone you trust and who has a vested interest in not paying estate taxes on what they would inherit anyway.

6) **Update beneficiary information on insurance policies:** Insurance payouts do not pass through probate, nor are they subject to income taxes for the recipient. Make sure you have this set up exactly the way you want it.

7) **Grant access to safety deposit boxes:** Many people have valuable assets stored in bank safety deposit boxes, and if you're one of those individuals, be sure you have provided authorized access to the right person(s).

8) **Durable power of attorney:** A durable power of attorney is designed to allow someone to make legal and financial decisions for you when you are incapacitated. This is not to be confused with the advance medical directive" document which only provides authority for medical decisions. You should set up your power of attorney to be invoked only if you are incapacitated. Any condition triggering such an event should require your medical situation to be certified, in writing, by a competent medical authority. Granting others control over your financial resources is always risky, even when dealing with family members. If you pick the wrong person, you could wake up one day finding your assets depleted and having no clear legal recourse to recover what has been taken. Also, in the event you do not recover, your estate could have been significantly diminished before your passing. If you have these or other concerns, speak with a lawyer about creating a joint configuration where two parties are named and both must act in concert on any decisions made. In any

case, be sure you have designated an additional successor in the event one of your designees is unavailable or unwilling to serve.

9) **Plan for increasing healthcare costs:** Perhaps this should be reworded as plan for your healthcare costs to be the largest expense of your later years. The two best ways to fight increasing healthcare costs are by staying fit and eating right, but those behaviors most likely won't succeed in completely protecting many of us. Having enough money is the key to staying independent, so plan for that.

10) **Create the structure to carry out your wishes:** This will always be a mixture of people and legal documents. Get your trusts, wills and directives set up in advance and review them annually. Some decisions must be made and documented immediately, with the most significant one being who will care for your children if you die before they reach adulthood. Hopefully you live long enough to be blessed with children and grandchildren, but in the meantime you need to think about what can and will happen in the future if you're not around.

11) **Talk to your friends and family about your wishes:** While this may make others uncomfortable, you share your wishes with those people in your life who will be supporting you as you grow older, infirm, and face the end of your life. Those supporting you will be faced with tough decisions and regardless what's laid out in some document, they need to hear from you what you really want. This will give them the confidence that they are acting according to your wishes. They most assuredly need, and deserve to hear this directly from you so they don't end up trying to interpret something written in a document or worse yet guessing about what to do in a time of crisis and mourning.

12) **No checklist is all encompassing:** All models are wrong, even though some are useful. Tailor this list to all the unique facets in your life, then check it again and revisit it annually.

Core Concepts mapping

Core One – You are NOT like the others. For those who avoided experiencing debilitating or crippling conditions, your time in the military has without a doubt still affected you. Remember, it's not just the mileage, it's the condition of the road you've traveled. The longer your time in the service, the more the damage you'll see, much like what happens to a professional athlete. Your eyesight may or may not have been impacted, but it is more than likely your hearing has been degraded. Depending on the circumstances in which you served, you may experience even more challenges as you age. Be smart, plan for these things and live the best quality of life you can, no matter what.

Core Two – You have been forged in fires your peers can't understand. Getting older can be painful and frustrating. So what? It's not like you have an alternative. Dig deep, remember your training and other sub-optimal situations you've endured and put a big smile on your face as you start every day.

Core Three – There are less of us than you may realize. Pay attention to and get involved with the Veterans in your community. These are some of the best people in the world who can and will provide support for you as you age.

Core Four – You are uniquely prepared to manage your own future. It's your job. Ignore planning for your later years at your own peril.

Core Five – You have skills and capabilities that are marketable. Consider volunteering so you can help others less fortunate than you. Find a way to contribute to those in need and give back to your community at the same time.

Core Six – You have gaps in your skills and capabilities you need to close. Get professional help and finish strong. Start planning now for the best life you can have during your remaining years on this earth.

Core Seven– You now have more responsibility for your life and much more opportunity to screw it up. Thinking about your own decline is troubling, but it is your responsibility. Don't shirk, delay, or turn away from this must do chore. Embrace the challenge, plan accordingly and be prepared.

Core Eight – Life is still hard. There is only one way out. Some will go early, some will linger and suffer and a few will live a long, healthy life. You have some ability to affect the factors that influence what happens to you. Stay fit, don't get fat, and eat healthy. These are some of the hardest things in life to accomplish.

Core Nine – The Republic is powered by the engine of Capitalism. You will need more money to support your health and active lifestyle as you age. Some studies cite that 90% of healthcare expenses occur in the last twenty years of life, so plan accordingly and make sure you have the resources to care for yourself and your spouse.

Personal perspective:

The phone rang about 11:00 in the morning. I was working from home. My wife was out doing something fun with our preschool daughter. I answered and found it was our neighbor, distraught and calling from a downtown hospital. She told me earlier that morning she had been driving her husband to the airport for business travel when he said he didn't feel well. Her husband is a Marine who is many years distant from active duty, and when she glanced over at him she saw he was literally grey in color. Knowing he was in serious trouble; she drove past the airport and to a nearby hospital which was known for the quality of its doctors and its emergency care. Her husband was undergoing surgery when she called me. He had a heart condition which is often described as a widow-maker, which occurs when the left anterior descending artery becomes blocked. Under a normal course of care, he would probably have been told to take some aspirin and make an appointment for a cardio stress test in a few days. Had that happened, in all likelihood he would have stepped onto a treadmill and dropped dead before the test was completed. Fortunately, our neighbor is a highly intelligent woman and got him to the best place in time for proper treatment. This guy was very fit and healthy for his age when this happened. So, take note and prepare for what can happen regardless of how well you take of yourself. I'm glad to say that he came through the surgery just fine and is still doing well.

Chapter 26 – Being Thankful

How often do you take the time to count the ways in which your life is going well? Shall we play a game?

Stop right now and make a list of all the things in your life you are thankful for, and then make a list of all the things you would like to improve. I'll wager there are some things that are on both lists and there fewer items on the improve side.

Even when we are challenged with the obstacles life and fate have so much fun putting in our way, there is so much to be thankful about. Life seems linear, but is in fact, multi-dimensional, and it is rare that every aspect in our lives is bad.

We all have special people in our lives for which we should be thankful. In varying combinations and quantities, we have parents, spouses, children, friends, coaches, and mentors all who invested in us. Take the time to stop every now and then to count all the good things in your life. Don't ignore the opportunities for improvement, but stop and be thankful for those things that have gone your way.

Take the time to call that old friend you were just thinking about. Pick the phone and randomly call your parents if you can. If they aren't around anymore, take the time to honor their memory by doing something that would make them proud of you.

Show those persons in your life you appreciate them, and please do this as often as you can.

Hold your family close and forgive them for being imperfect humans, after all, they forgive you for the same.

Be thankful you have the opportunity to be you, in this wonderful place and time.

Chapter 27 – RaNdOm thoUghtS

Remember, everyone's got an opinion and those proffered without invitation are usually worth what you pay for them, maybe less. Keep in mind if anyone tries to tell you the transition back to civilian life is easy, walk away as fast as you can and clear your mind. That snake oil is for slackers and underperformers.

Avoid shortcuts like the plague.

Make plans.

Execute those plans and adjust when needed.

Put your family first.

Enjoy the ride into the next great adventure of your life. You've done your part protecting and serving, and for that you deserve unflagging respect. Your brothers and sisters in arms salute and thank you for your service.

Hopefully, you have gotten to this point and have found some value for your hard-earned dollars. The author and contributors to this book wish you the very best in your new life.

I certainly welcome feedback and hope to keep this book in print and electronic formats for a long time to come. If you think I have gotten something right or wrong, need an update or maybe even a new section, please let me know. I would love to hear from you.

If you are willing to share, I'll be building up a knowledge base of jobs, useful links, checklists and whatever else I can post to the website:

www.olanprentice.com

Respectfully,

Olan Prentice

References and Links

Military Oaths
Only one Oath originally

During the Revolutionary War, the Continental Congress established different oaths for the enlisted men of the Continental Army.

The first oath, voted on 14 June 1775 as part of the act creating the Continental Army, read:

I _____ have, this day, voluntarily enlisted myself, as a soldier, in the American continental army, for one year, unless sooner discharged: And I do bind myself to conform, in all instances, to such rules and regulations, as are, or shall be, established for the government of the said Army.

The original wording was effectively replaced by Section 3, Article 1, of the Articles of War approved by Congress on 20 September 1776, which specified that the oath of enlistment read:

I _____ swear (or affirm as the case may be) to be trued to the United States of America, and to serve them honestly and faithfully against all their enemies opposers whatsoever; and to observe and obey the orders of the Continental Congress, and the orders of the Generals and officers set over me by them.

The first oath under the Constitution was approved by Act of Congress 29 September 1789 (Sec. 3, Ch. 25, 1st Congress). It applied to all commissioned officers, noncommissioned officers, and privates in the service of the United States. It came in two parts, the first of which read: "I, A.B., do solemnly swear or affirm (as the case may be) that I will support the constitution of the United States." The second part read: "I, A.B., do solemnly swear or affirm (as the case may be) to bear true allegiance to the United States of America, and to serve them honestly and faithfully, against all their enemies or opposers whatsoever, and to observe and obey the orders of the President of the United States of America, and the orders of the officers appointed over me." The next section of that chapter specified that "the said troops shall be governed by the rules and articles of war, which have been established by the United States in Congress assembled, or by such rules and articles of war as may hereafter by law be established."

The 1789 enlistment oath was changed in 1960 by amendment to Title 10, with the amendment (and current wording) becoming effective in 1962.

Enlisted Oath

I, (NAME), do solemnly swear (or affirm) that I will support and defend the Constitution of the United States against all enemies, foreign and domestic; that I will bear true faith and allegiance to the same; and that I will obey the orders of the President of the United States and the orders of the officers appointed over me, according to regulations and the Uniform Code of Military Justice. So help me God.

Enlisted Oath for the National Guard (Army or Air)

I, (NAME), do solemnly swear (or affirm) that I will support and defend the Constitution of the United States and the State of (state name) against all enemies, foreign and domestic; that I will bear true faith and allegiance to the same; and that I will obey the orders of the President of the United States and the Governor of (state name) and the orders of the officers appointed over me, according to law and regulations. So help me God.

Officer Oath

"I, (NAME), having been appointed a (rank) in the United States (branch of service), do solemnly swear (or affirm) that I will support and defend the Constitution of the United States against all enemies, foreign and domestic; that I will bear true faith and allegiance to the same; that I take this obligation freely, without any mental reservation or purpose of evasion; and that I will well and faithfully discharge the office upon which I am about to enter. So help me God."

Crucial difference between Officer and Enlisted Oath

All officers of the Uniformed services of the United States must swear or affirm an oath of office upon commissioning that differs slightly from that of the oath of enlistment that enlisted members recite. It is required by statute, the oath being prescribed by Section 3331, Title 5, United States Code. The most notable difference between the officer and enlisted oaths is that the oath taken by officers does not include any provision to obey the orders of anyone appointed above them. Whereas, enlisted personnel are bound by the Uniform Code of Military Justice to obey lawful orders, commissioned officers in the service of the United States are bound by this oath to disobey any order that violates the Constitution of the United States.

Presidential Oath of Office

I do solemnly swear that I will faithfully execute the office of the President of the United States, and will to the best of my ability, **preserve, protect, and defend the Constitution of the United States.**

http://en.wikipedia.org/wiki/United_States_Uniformed_Services_Oath_of_Office

http://usmilitary.about.com/od/joiningthemilitary/a/oathofenlist.htm

Military Holidays and other important dates

Stay connected to your legacy. Celebrate your military holidays and share knowledge of the how and why with your family and friends.

January

January 16, 2017 - Martin Luther King Jr. Day: This holiday is core to what you sacrificed for. Equality and Freedom and the loss of a great man. A day set aside to celebrate the life and achievements of Martin Luther King Jr., an influential American civil rights leader.

February

February 3, 2017 - Four Chaplains Day: A day set aside to honor the four U.S. Army chaplains who gave their lives to save others when the troop ship USAT Dorchester sank during World War II.

February 20, 2017 - President's Day: Honor the leader of our military. A day originally set aside to honor George Washington.

February 19, 2017 - Coast Guard Reserve Birthday

March

Month of the Military Caregiver: During the Month of the Military Caregiver, Americans recognize and honor military caregivers' sacrifices and successes.

March 3, 2017 - Navy Reserve Birthday

March 5, 2017 - Seabee Birthday

March 13, 2017 - K 9 Veterans Day: March 13, 1942 is the official birthday of the United States K9 Corps. Remember and celebrate these warriors.

March 29, 2017 - Vietnam Veterans Day:

Signed into law in 2017 by President Trump, our Vietnam Veterans finally get the recognition they deserve. These Vets were often poorly treated by the media and their fellow citizens. Take a moment to celebrate these men and women.

April

Month of the Military Child: The children of our military also shoulder burden that often goes unacknowledged. Help recognize the character, courage, sacrifices of these young people in your life.

April 5, 2017 - Gold Star Wives Day: Gold Star Wives is a private, non-profit organization formed during WW II to help those families who made the ultimate sacrifice of a spouse or child while serving.

April 14, 2017 - Air Force Reserve Birthday

April 23, 2017 - Army Reserve Birthday

May

National Military Appreciation Month

May 1, 2017 - Loyalty Day: First observed in 1921 and recognized by Congress in 1955, made official in 1958. This day is set aside for American citizens to reaffirm their loyalty to the United States and to recognize the heritage of American freedom.

May 1, 2017 - Silver Star Service Banner Day: Honor the sacrifices of the combat wounded, ill and dying service members on Silver Star Service Banner Day by flying a Silver Service Banner.

May 8, 2017 - VE (Victory in Europe) Day: Marks the Allies World War II victory in Europe in 1945.

May 12, 2017 - Military Spouse Appreciation Day: Honor the tremendous burden and sacrifice of our Military Spouses.

May 13, 2017 - Children of Fallen Patriots Day

May 20, 2017 - Armed Forces Day

May 29, 2017 - Memorial Day: Honor the more than One Million brave souls that have fallen while serving the Republic. This data is from the Department of Veterans affairs:
https://www.va.gov/opa/publications/factsheets/fs_americas_wars.pdf

American Revolution (1775-1783)

Total U.S. Service members 217,000 Battle Deaths 4,435 Non-mortal Woundings 6,188

War of 1812 (1812-1815)

Total U.S. Service members 286,730 Battle Deaths 2,260 Non-mortal Woundings 4,505

Indian Wars (approx. 1817-1898)

Total U.S. Service members (VA estimate) 106,000 Battle Deaths (VA estimate) 1,000

Mexican War (1846-1848)

Total U.S. Service members 78,718 Battle Deaths 1,733 Other Deaths (In Theater) 11,550 Non-mortal Woundings 4,152

Civil War (1861-1865)

Total U.S. Service members (Union) 2,213,363 Battle Deaths (Union) 140,414 Other Deaths (In Theater) (Union) 224,097 Non-mortal Woundings (Union) 281,881 Total Servicemembers (Conf.) 1,050,000 Battle Deaths (Confederate) 74,524 Other Deaths (In Theater) (Confederate) 59,297 Non-mortal Woundings (Confederate) Unknown

Spanish-American War (1898-1902)

Total U.S. Service members (Worldwide) 306,760 Battle Deaths 385 Other Deaths in Service (Non-Theater) 2,061 Non-mortal Woundings 1,662

World War I (1917-1918)

Total U.S. Service members (Worldwide) 4,734,991 Battle Deaths 53,402 Other Deaths in Service (Non-Theater) 63,114 Non-mortal Woundings 204,002

World War II (1941 –1945)

Total U.S. Service members (Worldwide) 16,112,566 Battle Deaths 291,557 Other Deaths in Service (Non-Theater) 113,842 Non-mortal Woundings 670,846 Living Veterans 1,711,000

Korean War (1950-1953)

Total U.S. Service members (Worldwide) 5,720,000 Total Serving (In Theater) 1,789,000 Battle Deaths 33,739 Other Deaths (In Theater) 2,835 Other Deaths in Service (Non-Theater) 17,672 Non-mortal Woundings 103,284 Living Veterans 2,275,000

Vietnam War (1964-1975)

Total U.S. Servicemembers (Worldwide) 8,744,000 Deployed to Southeast Asia 3,403,000 Battle Deaths 47,434 Other Deaths (In Theater) 10,786 Other Deaths in Service (Non-Theater) 32,000 Non-mortal Woundings 153,303 Living Veterans 7,391,000

Desert Shield/Desert Storm (1990-1991) Total U.S. Service members (Worldwide) 2,322,000 Deployed to Gulf 694,550 Battle Deaths 148 Other Deaths (In Theater) 235 Other Deaths in Service (Non-Theater) 1,565 Non-mortal Woundings 467 Living Veterans 2,244,583

America's Wars Total (1775 -1991)

U.S. Military Service during Wartime 41,892,128 Battle Deaths 651,031 Other Deaths (In Theater) 308,800 Other Deaths in Service (Non-Theater) 230,254 Non-mortal Woundings 1,430,290 Living War Veterans, 16,962,000 Living Veterans (Periods of War & Peace) 23,234,000

Global War on Terror (Oct 2001 -)

The Global War on Terror (GWOT), including Operation Enduring Freedom (OEF) and Operation Iraqi Freedom (OIF), are ongoing conflicts. For the most current GWOT statistics visit the following Department of Defense Website:

https://www.dmdc.osd.mil/dcas/pages/casualties.xhtml

June

June 6, 2017 – D-Day: Anniversary of the World War II Allied invasion in Normandy, France in 1944

June 14, 2017 - Flag Day

June 14, 2017 - Army Birthday

June 23, 2017 - Coast Guard Auxiliary Birthday

June 25, 2017 - Anniversary of the start of the Korean War (1950)

June 27, 2017 - National PTSD Awareness Day: Our Veterans serve with distinction and sacrifice. Please help raise awareness for PTSD and its impact on our brothers and sisters.

July

July 4, 2017 - Independence Day

July 27, 2017 - Korean War Veterans Armistice Day (1953)

July 29, 2017 - Anniversary of the Army Chaplain Corps

August

August 4, 2017 - Coast Guard Birthday

August 7, 2017 - Purple Heart Day

August 8, 2017 - VJ (Victory over Japan) Day (1945)

August 29, 2017 - Marine Forces Reserve Birthday

September

September 11, 2017 - Patriot Day: Remember those that died during the 9/11 terrorist attacks

September 15, 2017 - POW/MIA Recognition Day

September 18, 2017 - Air Force Birthday

September 24, 2017 - Gold Star Mother's and Family's Day

October

October 26, 2017 - National Day of the Deployed: Deployments are difficult times for the deployed and families they leave behind. Celebrate this day to honor all the brave men and women who have been deployed and are sacrificing, or have sacrificed their lives to fight for our country and acknowledges their families that they are separated from.

November

Military Family Month

November 10, 2017 - Marine Corps Birthday

November 11, 2017 - Armistice Day (France)

November 11, 2017 - Remembrance Day (Britain)

November 11, 2017 - Remembrance Day (Canada)

November 11, 2017 - Veterans Day: On the 11th hour of the 11th day of the 11th month of 1918, an armistice, or temporary cessation of hostilities, was declared between the Allied nations and Germany in the First World War. November 11th became a legal federal holiday in the United States in 1938. After the Korean War, this holiday in the US was renamed to "Veterans Day."

December

December 1, 2017 - Civil Air Patrol (USAF Auxiliary) Birthday

December 7, 2017 - Pearl Harbor Day

December 13, 2017 - National Guard Birthday

December 16, 2017 - National Wreaths Across America: Lay a wreath at your local cemetery for a fallen veteran.

December 28, 2017 - Anniversary of the Army Chaplain Assistant

Military demographics

From the Department of Defense's *Data Manpower Data Center website*, updated regularly.

https://www.dmdc.osd.mil/appj/dwp/dwp_reports.jsp

Department of Defense
Active Duty Military Personnel by Rank/Grade
May 31, 2017

Rank/Grade	Army	Navy	Marine Corps	Air Force	Total Services
GENERAL -ADMIRAL	11	9	4	13	37
LT GENERAL -VICE ADMIRAL	44	38	16	42	140
MAJ GENERAL -REAR ADMIRAL (U)	123	63	30	91	307
BRIG GENERAL -REAR ADMIRAL (L)	126	100	36	144	406
COLONEL -CAPTAIN	4,282	3,037	642	3,449	11,410
LIEUTENANT COL -COMMANDER	8,954	6,462	1,896	10,007	27,319
MAJOR -LT COMMANDER	15,114	10,366	3,856	13,452	42,788
CAPTAIN -LIEUTENANT	29,440	18,273	6,253	20,456	74,422
1st LIEUTENANT -LIEUTENANT (JG)	11,214	6,555	3,554	6,819	28,142
2nd LIEUTENANT -ENSIGN	7,285	8,252	2,808	6,998	25,343
CHIEF WARRANT OFFICER W-5	604	70	105	0	779
CHIEF WARRANT OFFICER W-4	2,037	390	300	0	2,727
CHIEF WARRANT OFFICER W-3	4,186	678	614	0	5,478
CHIEF WARRANT OFFICER W-2	5,536	573	751	0	6,860
WARRANT OFFICER W-1	2,025	0	403	0	2,428
TOTAL OFFICER	90,981	54,866	21,268	61,471	228,586
E-9	3,356	2,518	1,569	2,569	10,012
E-8	10,893	6,408	3,848	5,038	26,187
E-7	34,441	20,943	8,021	25,001	88,406
E-6	53,789	46,413	15,136	39,717	155,055
E-5	64,788	62,853	26,391	61,299	215,331
E-4	110,069	51,852	35,295	55,004	252,220
E-3	44,218	52,201	43,726	49,112	189,257
E-2	30,875	13,069	20,289	8,109	72,342
E-1	18,205	8,312	7,851	10,329	44,697
TOTAL ENLISTED	370,634	264,569	162,126	256,178	1,053,507
CADETS-MIDSHIPMEN	3,460	3,304	0	3,100	9,864
GRAND TOTAL	465,075	322,739	183,394	320,749	1,291,957

Veterans Unemployment Compensation by State

State	Max Weekly	State Unemployment Agency	Max Wks
Alabama	$265	Alabama Unemployment Information	26
Alaska	$370	Alaska Unemployment Insurance State Website	26
Arizona	$240	Arizona Department of Economic Security	26
Arkansas	$451	Arkansas Department of Workforce Services	20
California	$450	CA.gov EDD details	26
Colorado	$568	Colorado Department of Labor and Employment	26
Connecticut	$598	Connecticut Department of Labor	26
Delaware	$330	Delaware Division of Unemployment Insurance	26
District of Columbia	$425	DC Dept. of Employment Services	26
Florida	$275	Florida	12
Georgia	$330	GA Department of Labor	20
Hawaii	$551	Hawaii Unemployment Insurance State Website	26
Idaho	$410	Idaho Dept. of Labor	26
Illinois	$449 to $613	IL Unemployment Insurance State Website	26
Indiana	$390	Indiana Department of Workforce Development	26
Iowa	$447 to $548	Iowa Workforce Development	26
Kansas	$474	Kansas Department of Labor	16
Kentucky	$415	Kentucky Career Center	26
Louisiana	$247	Louisiana Workforce Commission	26
Maine	$410	Maine Department of Labor	26
Maryland	$430	MD Department of Labor (DLLR)	26
Massachusetts	$742	MA Labor and Workforce Development	30
Michigan	$362	Michigan UIA	20
Minnesota	$683	MN Department of Employment and Economic Development	26
Mississippi	$235	MS Department of Employment Security	26
Missouri	$320	MO Department of Labor and Industrial Relations	20

State	Max Weekly	State Unemployment Agency	Max Wks
Montana	$487	MT Department of Labor and Industry	26
Nebraska	$392	NE Department of Labor	26
Nevada	$407	NV Dept. of Employment, Training and Rehab	26
New Hampshire	$427	NH Department of Employment Security	26
New Jersey	$677	NJ Dept. of Labor and Workforce Development	26
New Mexico	$425	NM Department of Workforce Solutions	26
New York	$430	NY Dept. of Labor	26
North Carolina	$350	NC Division of Employment Security	20
North Dakota	$633	ND Job Service	26
Ohio	$435 to $587	Ohio Dept. of Job and Family Services	26
Oklahoma	$505	Oklahoma UI Home Page	26
Oregon	$590	Oregon Employment Department	26
Pennsylvania	$573	PA Office of Unemployment Compensation	26
Puerto Rico	$42 or $133	PR Department of Labor & HR	26
Rhode Island	$566	RI Dept. of Labor and Training	26
South Carolina	$326	SC Dept. of Employment & Workforce	20
South Dakota	$345	SD Department of Labor & Regulation	26
Tennessee	$275	TN Dept. of Labor and Workforce Development	26
Texas	$493	Texas Workforce Commission	26
Utah	$496	Dept. of Workforce Services	26
Vermont	$458	VT Dept. of Labor	26
Virginia	$378	VA Employment Commission	26
Washington	$681	WA Employment Security Department	26
West Virginia	$424	West Virginia Unemployment Insurance Page	26
Wisconsin	$370	WI Dept. of Workforce Development	26
Wyoming	$471	Wyoming Unemployment Insurance Home Page	26

Veteran Preference – Federal Regulations

This information is taken directly from the US Government publishing office. It is formally part of *Title 5, United States Code, Section 2108*

Here are a couple of ways to link to it (buyer beware, all links change over time)

Title 5 → Chapter I → Subchapter B → Part 211 (or)

http://www.ecfr.gov/cgi-bin/retrieveECFR?gp=4&SID=838c203f865b92ec52db34bc00b8fa75&h=L&mc=true&r=PART&n=pt5.1.211

Title 5: Administrative Personnel

PART 211—VETERAN PREFERENCE

AUTHORITY: 5 U.S.C. 1302, 2108, 2108a.

SOURCE: 79 FR 77835, Dec. 29, 2014, unless otherwise noted.

§211.101 Purpose.

The purpose of this part is to define Veterans' preference and the administration of preference in Federal employment. (5 U.S.C. 2108, 2108a)

§211.102 Definitions.

For the purposes of preference in Federal employment, the following definitions apply:

(a) *Veteran* means a person who has been discharged or released from active duty in the armed forces under honorable conditions, or who has a certification as defined in paragraph (h) of this section, if the active duty service was performed:

(1) In a war;

(2) In a campaign or expedition for which a campaign badge has been authorized;

(3) During the period beginning April 28, 1952, and ending July 1, 1955;

(4) For more than 180 consecutive days, other than for training, any part of which occurred during the period beginning February 1, 1955, and ending October 14, 1976;

(5) During the period beginning August 2, 1990, and ending January 2, 1992; or

(6) For more than 180 consecutive days, other than for training, any part of which occurred during the period beginning September 11, 2001, and ending on August 31, 2010, the last day of Operation Iraqi Freedom.

(b) *Disabled Veteran* means a person who has been discharged or released from active duty in the armed forces under honorable conditions performed at any time, or who has a certification as defined in paragraph (h) of this section, and who has established the present existence of a service-connected disability or is receiving compensation, disability retirement benefits, or a pension because of a statute administered by the Department of Veterans Affairs or a military department.

(c) *Sole survivor Veteran* means a person who was discharged or released from a period of active duty after August 29, 2008, by reason of a sole survivorship discharge (as that term is defined in 10 U.S.C. 1174(i)), and who meets the definition of a "Veteran" in paragraph (a) of this section, with the exception that he or she is not required to meet any of the length of service requirements prescribed by paragraph (a).

(d) *Preference eligible* means a Veteran, disabled Veteran, sole survivor Veteran, spouse, widow, widower, or mother who meets the definition of "preference eligible" in 5 U.S.C. 2108.

(1) Preference eligibles other than sole survivor Veterans are entitled to have 5 or 10 points added to their earned score on a civil service examination in accordance with 5 U.S.C. 3309.

(2) Under numerical ranking and selection procedures for competitive service hiring, preference eligibles are entered on registers in the order prescribed by section 332.401 of this chapter.

(3) Under excepted service examining procedures in part 302 of this chapter, preference eligibles are listed ahead of persons with the same ratings who are not preference eligibles, or listed ahead of non-preference eligibles if numerical scores have not been assigned.

(4) Under alternative ranking and selection procedures, *i.e.*, category rating, preference eligibles are listed ahead of individuals who are not preference eligibles in accordance with 5 U.S.C. 3319.

(5) Preference eligibles, other than those who have not yet been discharged or released from active duty, are accorded a higher retention standing than non-preference eligibles in the event of a reduction in force in accordance with 5 U.S.C. 3502.

(6) Veterans' preference does not apply, however, to inservice placement actions such as promotions.

(e) *Armed forces* means the United States Army, Navy, Air Force, Marine Corps, and Coast Guard.

(f) *Active duty* or *active military duty*:

(1) For Veterans defined in paragraphs (a)(1) through (3) and disabled Veterans defined in paragraph (b) of this section, means active duty with military pay and allowances in the armed forces, and includes training, determining physical fitness, and service in the Reserves or National Guard; and

(2) For Veterans defined in paragraphs (a)(4) through (6) of this section, means full-time duty with military pay and allowances in the armed forces, and does not include training, determining physical fitness, or service in the Reserves or National Guard.

(g) *Discharged or released from active duty* means with either an honorable or general discharge from active duty in the armed forces. The Departments of Defense is responsible for administering and defining military discharges.

(h) *Certification* means any written document from the armed forces that certifies the service member is expected to be discharged or released from active duty service in the armed forces under honorable conditions not later than 120 days after the date the certification is submitted for consideration in the hiring process, at the time and in the manner prescribed by the applicable job opportunity announcement. Prior to appointment, the service member's character of service and qualifying discharge or release must be verified through a DD form 214 or equivalent documentation.

§211.103   Administration of preference.

Agencies are responsible for making all preference determinations except for preference based on a common law marriage. Such a claim must be referred to OPM's General Counsel for decision.

Veteran Assistance and/or Benefits Programs by state;

1. Alabama – http://www.military.com/benefits/Veteran-state-benefits/alabama-state-Veterans-benefits.html
2. Alaska - http://www.Veterans.alaska.gov/state_benefits.htm
3. American Samoa - http://www2.va.gov/directory/guide/state.asp?STATE=AS&dnum=ALL
4. Arizona - http://www.military.com/benefits/Veteran-state-benefits/arizona-state-Veterans-benefits.html
5. Arkansas - http://www.Veterans.arkansas.gov/
6. California - http://www.calvet.ca.gov/
7. Colorado - http://www.military.com/benefits/Veteran-state-benefits/colorado-state-Veterans-benefits.html
8. Connecticut - http://www.ct.gov/ctva/site/default.asp
9. Delaware - http://www.military.com/benefits/Veteran-state-benefits/delaware-state-Veterans-benefits.html
10. District of Columbia - http://www.va.gov/
11. Florida - http://floridavets.org/
12. Georgia – http://Veterans.georgia.gov/
13. Guam - http://www2.va.gov/directory/guide/state.asp?STATE=GU&dnum=ALL
14. Hawaii - http://www.military.com/benefits/Veteran-state-benefits/hawaii-state-Veterans-benefits.html
15. Idaho - http://Veterans.idaho.gov/
16. Illinois - http://www2.illinois.gov/Veterans/Pages/default.aspx
17. Indiana - http://www.military.com/benefits/Veteran-state-benefits/indiana-state-Veterans-benefits.html
18. Iowa – https://www.va.iowa.gov/benefits/index.html
19. Kansas - http://kcva.ks.gov/
20. Kentucky – http://www.military.com/benefits/Veteran-state-benefits/kentucky-state-Veterans-benefits.html
21. Louisiana – http://www.military.com/benefits/Veteran-state-benefits/louisiana-state-Veterans-benefits.html
22. Maine – http://www.maine.gov/dvem/bvs/
23. Maryland – http://www.mdva.state.md.us/
24. Massachusetts – http://www.military.com/benefits/Veteran-state-benefits/massachusetts-state-Veterans-benefits.html

25. Michigan – http://www.military.com/benefits/Veteran-state-benefits/michigan-state-Veterans-benefits.html
26. Minnesota - http://mn.gov/mdva/
27. Mississippi - http://www.military.com/benefits/Veteran-state-benefits/mississippi-state-Veterans-benefits.html
28. Missouri - http://www.military.com/benefits/Veteran-state-benefits/missouri-state-Veterans-benefits.html
29. Montana - http://www.military.com/benefits/Veteran-state-benefits/montana-state-Veterans-benefits.html
30. Nebraska - http://www.military.com/benefits/Veteran-state-benefits/nebraska-state-Veterans-benefits.html
31. Nevada - http://www.Veterans.nv.gov/
32. New Hampshire - http://www.military.com/benefits/Veteran-state-benefits/new-hampshire-state-Veterans-benefits.html
33. New Jersey - http://www.state.nj.us/military/
34. New Mexico - http://www.dvs.state.nm.us/
35. New York – http://Veterans.ny.gov/
36. North Carolina - http://www.military.com/benefits/Veteran-state-benefits/north-carolina-state-Veterans-benefits.html
37. North Dakota - http://www.military.com/benefits/Veteran-state-benefits/north-dakota-state-Veterans-benefits.html
38. Northern Marianas Islands - http://www.militaryta.com/benefits/northern-marianas-islands-military-education-benefits.shtml
39. Ohio – http://www.military.com/benefits/Veteran-state-benefits/ohio-state-Veterans-benefits.html
40. Oklahoma - http://www.military.com/benefits/Veteran-state-benefits/oklahoma-state-Veterans-benefits.html
41. Oregon - http://www.military.com/benefits/Veteran-state-benefits/oregon-state-Veterans-benefits.html
42. Pennsylvania - http://www.military.com/benefits/Veteran-state-benefits/pennsylvania-state-Veterans-benefits.html
43. Puerto Rico - http://www.military.com/benefits/Veteran-state-benefits/commonwealth-of-puerto-rico-Veteran-benefits.html
44. Rhode Island - http://www.military.com/benefits/Veteran-state-benefits/rhode-island-state-Veterans-benefits.html
45. South Carolina - http://www.military.com/benefits/Veteran-state-benefits/south-carolina-state-Veterans-benefits.html

46. South Dakota - http://www.military.com/benefits/Veteran-state-benefits/south-dakota-state-Veterans-benefits.html
47. Tennessee - http://www.tn.gov/Veteran/vetdayevents.shtml
48. Texas - http://www.texas.gov/en/Veterans/Pages/assist-benefits.aspx
49. Utah - http://www.military.com/benefits/Veteran-state-benefits/utah-state-Veterans-benefits.html
50. Vermont - http://www.military.com/benefits/Veteran-state-benefits/vermont-state-Veterans-benefits.html
51. Virginia - http://www.military.com/benefits/Veteran-state-benefits/virginia-state-Veterans-benefits.html
52. Virgin Islands - http://www.military.com/benefits/Veteran-state-benefits/virgin-island-vet-benefits.html
53. Washington - http://www.military.com/benefits/Veteran-state-benefits/washington-state-Veterans-benefits.html
54. West Virginia - http://www.military.com/benefits/Veteran-state-benefits/west-virginia-state-Veterans-benefits.html
55. Wisconsin - http://www.military.com/benefits/Veteran-state-benefits/wisconsin-state-Veterans-benefits.html
56. Wyoming - http://www.military.com/benefits/Veteran-state-benefits/wyoming-state-Veterans-benefits.html

List of trusted Veterans organizations that you should be aware of;

Again, there are just too many to list them all, but this is a good starter list:

Air Force Association - http://www.afa.org/home
Air Force Sergeants Association - http://www.hqafsa.org/
American Ex-Prisoners of War - http://www.axpow.org/
American G.I. Forum - http://www.agif-nvop.org/
American Legion - http://www.legion.org/
American Veterans for Equal Rights - http://aver.us/
AMVETS - http://www.amvets.org/
Aztec Club of 1847 - http://www.aztecclub.com/
Blinded Veterans Association - http://bva.org/
Catholic War Veterans - http://www.cwv.org/
Disabled American Veterans - http://www.dav.org/
Fleet Reserve Association - http://www.fra.org/
GI Bill - www.GIBill.va.gov
The Greatest Generations Foundation - http://www.tggf.org/
Healing Heroes Network - http://www.healingheroes.org/
HeroBox - http://www.herobox.org/
Hope for The Warriors - http://www.hopeforthewarriors.org/
Iraq and Afghanistan Veterans of America - http://iava.org/
Jewish War Veterans of the USA - http://www.jwv.org/
Marine Corps League - https://www.mclnational.org/
Medal of Honor - http://www.cmohs.org/
Military Officers Association of America - http://www.moaa.org/
Military Order of the Carabao - http://www.carabao.org/
Military Order of Foreign Wars - http://mofwus.org/
Military Order of the Loyal Legion of the United States - http://suvcw.org/mollus/
Military Order of the Purple Heart - http://www.purpleheart.org/
Navy League of the United States - http://navyleague.org/
National Association for Black Veterans - http://www.nabvetsportland.org/
National Coalition for Homeless Veterans - http://nchv.org/
Operation Sacred Trust - http://411Veterans.pairs.com/
Operation Stand Down - http://osdtn.org/
Paralyzed Veterans of America - http://www.pva.org/site/
Pearl Harbor Survivors Association - www.pearlharborsurvivorsonline.org/
Retired Enlisted Association (TREA) - http://trea.org/

Society of the Cincinnati - http://societyofthecincinnati.org/
Student Veterans of America - http://studentVeterans.org/
United Service Organizations - http://www.uso.org/
United States Submarine Veterans Inc. (USSVI) - http://ussvicb.org/
United States Submarine Veterans of World War II - http://subvetpaul.com/
Veterans Admin by state – http://www.va.gov/statedva.htm
Veterans for America - http://www.Veteransforamerica.us/
Veterans for Peace - http://www.Veteransforpeace.org/
Veterans History Project - http://www.loc.gov/vets/
Veterans of Foreign Wars - http://www.vfw.org/
Veteran Tickets Foundation - http://www.vettix.org/
Vietnamese American Armed Forces Association - http://www.vaafa.org/
Vietnam Veterans of America - http://vva.org/
Wounded Warrior Project - https://support.woundedwarriorproject.org/

US Military Reserve websites
U.S. Air National Guard: www.goang.com
U.S. Air Force Reserves: www.afreserve.com
U.S. Army National Guard: https://www.nationalguard.com/
U.S. Army Reserves: www.army.mil
U.S Coast Guard Reserves: www.uscg.mil
U.S. Marine Corps: www.marforres.marines.mil
U.S. Navy Reserve: www.navyreserve.mil

Miscellaneous Military Discounts
People appreciate your service and your business. Take advantage of it, you've earned it!

The offers are constantly changing and these links may break. If nothing else, you can use the link descriptions as search variables on the internet. Just do a simple search for "military discount" on your favorite search engine. If you are looking for shoes, "military discount shoes" is your search string. On Google that search returned a ridiculous number of hits.

A simple search for "military discount" returned over 91 million hits on Google

A simple search for "military discount" returned over 152 million hits on Bing

Websites when looking for military discounts.

> http://www.rather-be-shopping.com/blog/?s=military+discount
>
> http://www.militarydiscountscentral.com
>
> https://www.veteransadvantage.com

Here are a few lists of some of the discount information that can be found on the internet. Please note that this is NOT a complete list. There are state, city and local market discounts too numerous to list. In just one state, there are over 8,000 businesses with military discounts available!

Discounted dining for Military & Veterans

1. **Bennigan's**: Active military and vets get 10% off your total check at Bennigan's.

2. **Ben & Jerry's:**. Varies by location but is typically 15%.

3. **Bob Evans:** 10% discounts with your Veterans ID.

4. **Burger King:** 10% off military discount, just show proper ID.

5. **Chevy's**: 20% discount for active, retired, or uniformed personnel.

6. **CiCi's Pizza**: A large majority of CiCi's locations offer military discounts.

7. **Dairy Queen:** Get a 10% off your food and ice cream at select Dairy Queen locations. Must have valid military ID.

8. **Denny's:** 10% discount to first responders which includes active military.

9. **Famous Dave's BBQ:** All active and retired military can get a 10% discount. Just ask your server for your discount.

10. **Fuddruckers Burgers:** Show your server your military ID and get a discount of either 10% or 15% off.

11. **Golden Corral:** Flash your military ID and get 10% off your bill.

12. **Hardee's:** Most corporate owned stores will give you a 10% discount if you tell them you're a vet.

13. **Hard Rock Cafe:** Get a 15% off discount when you show your military ID.

14. **Hooter's:** Varies by location but most Hooter's will give a flat 15% off discount to active and retired military personnel.

15. **IHOP:** 10% off your entire meal.

16. **Lone Star Steakhouse:** 15% off discount for military, police, and fire fighters every Monday. The discount is good for the entire table.

17. **Panda Express:** 10% military discount for active personnel.

18. **Papa Murphy's:** They offer $3.00 off each regular priced pizza for Military ID card holders.

19. **Pizza Hut**: Discount amount varies by location but always ask and have your military ID at the ready.

20. **Schlotzsky's Deli:** Schlotzsky's will give a 20% discount with a military ID card.

21. **Texas De Brazil:** Get 15% off your meal total with your military ID.

22. **Texas Roadhouse:** Get up to 20% off your bill total with your active military ID. Discount varies by location.

Fun Discounts for Military & Veterans

1. **AMC Theaters**: After 4 p.m. flash for a discount on movie tickets.

2. **Baseball Hall of Fame:** Free admission year-round for active and retired military.

3. **Busch Gardens (Tampa, FL):** Under the "Waves of Honor" program all active duty military are entitled to a free 1-day admission. Good for up to 3 family members.

4. **Carnival Cruise Line:** All cruise lines owned by Carnival (Carnival, Princess, Cunard, P&O. etc.) offer free onboard credit for military service, current or past.

5. **Camp Jellystone:** Get up to 20% off campsites, cabins, and more across the country. Must show valid military ID.

6. **Disneyland:** Disneyland park hotel discounts are available as well as a 3-day park hopper for only $129.

7. **Dollywood:** They offer a 30% discount on one-day admission tickets for U.S. active or retired military, disabled Veterans, and military reservists, spouses and dependents. Tickets can be purchased exclusively at the front gate of Dollywood.

8. **Knott's Berry Farm:** Free entry on Memorial Day weekend at Knott's Berry Farm and substantial discounts the rest of the year.

9. **Legoland:** 10% military discount at the California Legoland. Military appreciation days at the Florida location gets active and retired vets in the park for free with discounts for family members.

10. **PGA of America:** The PGA of America offers Active Duty, Military Retirees, Active Reserve, National Guard, Department of Defense Civilians, and their accompanying spouse complementary Daily Grounds tickets to PGA tour events.

11. **Regal Cinemas**: Regal Cinema military discounts varies by location. Inquire at your local theater.

12. **San Diego Zoo:** Free 1-day pass to the San Diego Zoo for those who are on active military duty.

13. **SeaWorld**: Via the Waves of Honor program, "any U.S. active duty military, activated or drilling reservist, or National Guardsman gets one complimentary admission per year."

14. **Six Flags:** Their website usually shows a weekend where active duty and three family members can visit for free and retirees get a 50% discount.

15. **Universal Studios:** Offers a discounted 4-day pass.

16. **U.S. National Parks:** Free annual pass to all National Parks in the United States.

Retail Discounts for Military & Veterans

1. **Advance Auto Parts:** According to their website they "offer 10% off regularly priced items for in-store purchases to customers who serve or have served our country's Armed Services."

2. **American Eagle Outfitters**: Show your military ID and get 10% off your in-store purchase at AEO.

3. **Apple Store**: Just ask for a Federal employee discount and show your CAC card.

4. **Auto Accessories Garage.com**: They offer 5-20% off to Veterans and active military members plus their families.

5. **AutoZone**: 10% off your purchase.

6. **Banana Republic Factory Store**: They offer a flat 10% off for Veterans every day of the year.

7. **Bed Bath & Beyond**: Flat 10% off discounts for vets and their families. Varies from store to store.

8. **Bass Pro Shops**: Bass Pro Shops will give you a 10% discount with your military ID starting on the 15th of each month and running for one week.

9. **Best Buy**: Varies from store to store, but many retail locations offer a 10% discount to vets.

10. **Big Lots**: Be sure to shop on Veteran's Day every year to take advantage of their military discount.

11. **Buckle**: The Buckle military discount requires online verification. Once verified, you'll get 10% off all purchases.

12. **Cabela's**: 5% military discount except on firearms at your local Cabela's.

13. **Charlotte Russe**: 10% discount with ID.

14. **Dell Computers**: Dell offers a variety of military discount programs.

15. **Dick's Sporting Goods**: The next time you are shopping at Dick's, ask about their 10% discount for Vets. Varies from store to store.

16. **Finishline**: Offers a 10% discount to vets and active military.

17. **Footaction**: Vets and active military can save an awesome 20% off w/ proper ID. Family members can get the discount as well.

18. **Home Depot:** All year long military personnel, active or retired, can get a 10% discount at the Home Depot for active duty and retirees. For all other Vets, they give a discount on Veteran's Day, 4th of July, and Memorial Day.

19. **Kelly's Auto Parts:** Kelly's offers a 10% discount all the time for all vets and active service members.

20. *BEST discount:* **Lowe's:** They will give a flat military discount of 10% to all active, Veteran and retired military personnel with proper identification (including DD-214). If you register via the MyLowes website, you and your immediate family members are also eligible for the 10% discount. *Thank you Lowes!*

21. **Maurices:** Get a 10% discount on your apparel purchase.

22. **Michaels:** Show your military ID at Michaels and get a flat 15% off. This may vary from store to store so ask a sales associate at Michaels.

23. **New Car:** All major automobile manufacturers offer some type of military discount, cash back or pricing plan.

24. **Nike Store:** Nike offers a 10% in-store discount to Vets, active service, as well as those in the reserves.

25. **Old Navy:** Military Monday's at Old Navy where active and retired military personnel get a 10% discount.

26. **O'Reilly Auto Parts:** According to their website, they offer an "in-store only" discount of 10-15% off with valid ID.

27. **Payless Shoes:** Shop at any of their retail locations and get a 10% military discount.

28. **Pottery Barn:** Most Pottery Barn locations offer a 10% discount for vets.

29. **Walgreens:** Generally offered around Memorial Day, up to 20% off.

30. **Williams-Sonoma:** Flat 10% discount with proper ID or proof of service.

31. **Zales Jewelry:** 10% off discount for active and retired military.

Travel Discounts for Military & Veterans

1. **Alamo Rent a Car**: Discounted rates for military families and free rental insurance and waived fees for military personnel.

2. **Amtrak:** Active military and their families get a 10% discount on train tickets with Amtrak. The Downeaster, which runs between Brunswick, ME, and North Station in Boston, offers on the 11th day of every month $11 one-way fare (normal fare $29). You will need to make reservation three days in advance and show ID.

3. **Best Western:** Discounted room rates for active military. Present ID at check-in or when reserving via the phone.

4. **Choice Hotels:** Discounted room rates for active military and their families. Ask about it when reserving your room.

5. **DoubleTree by Hilton:** Get 15% off Bed & Breakfast rate when booking your room.

6. **Greyhound**: 10% off all walkup fares. Good for active military and vets.

7. **Hampton Inn**: Flat 15% discount on your reservation.

8. **Hertz:** Free car upgrades.

9. **La Quinta Hotels:** La Quinta offers a 12% discount on room reservations.

10. **Marriott Hotels:** When booking your room mention the military discount and you'll get multiple special offers.

11. **Norwegian Cruise Lines:** Save 10% off specific cruises for active military, Veterans, and their families.

12. **U.S. Airways:** From their website, "Special rates to military personnel traveling on an officially excused absence and to discharged personnel within 7 days of discharge."

Banking Discounts for Military & Veterans

1. **American Express:** AMEX waives ALL fees for active duty military, including the annual fees on all of their cards. AMEX Platinum? $0 instead of $450.

2. **Chase Bank:** Show your ID, discharge papers or DD-214 at any Chase branch when opening a checking/savings account and get the Premiere package for free.

3. **U.S. Bank:** US Bank gives all active duty & Veterans free Premiere checking & savings with ID or DD214.

Wireless Discounts for Military & Veterans

1. **AT&T Wireless:** From the AT&T website, Veterans and active military can get 15% off "qualified monthly service charges."

2. **Sprint Wireless:** Get 15% off your monthly bill.

3. **T-Mobile Wireless:** Gives active and retired military 15% off their monthly bill.

4. **Verizon Wireless:** Discounts for active duty, retired and Veterans. You may have to produce your DD-214 if you aren't active duty or retired.

Misc. links

http://plans.collegesavings.org
http://militarybenefits.info/military-discounts/
http://www.mynextmove.org/vets/find/military
https://www.dol.gov/vets/goldcard.html
http://www.benefits.va.gov/vow/
https://www.opm.gov/policy-data-oversight/Veterans-services/
https://fedshirevets.gov/about/index.aspx
https://www.dmdc.osd.mil/tgps/
https://www.usajobs.gov/
https://www.usajobs.gov/Help/working-in-government/unique-hiring-paths/
https://www.careeronestop.org/jobsearch/findjobs/state-job-banks.aspx
http://benefits.va.gov/gibill/
www.sba.gov
http://www.dantes.doded.mil/index.html
https://www.vetcenter.va.gov/
https://www.thebalance.com/becoming-a-citizen-in-the-u-s-military-3356945
https://www.uscis.gov/news/fact-sheets/naturalization-through-military-service-fact-sheet
http://www.military.com/join-armed-forces/eligibility-requirements/the-us-military-helps-naturlize-non-citizens.html
http://www.federaljobs.net/veterans.htm
https://www.dodtap.mil/
https://www.dmdc.osd.mil/appj/dwp/service_members.jsp
https://www.linkedin.com/

Find more useful links at www.olanprentice.com

Made in the USA
Columbia, SC
21 September 2024